IMAGES
of America

PALM COAST

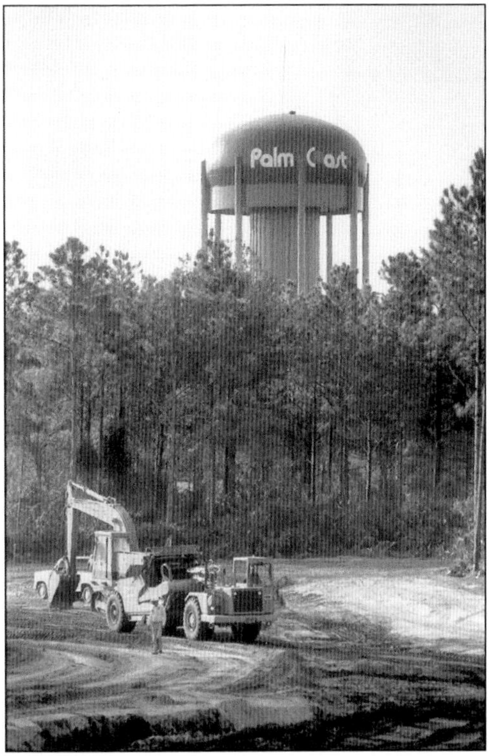

WATER TOWER. In the memories of the many travelers of Route I-95 between Jacksonville and Daytona Beach since the 1970s, the existence of Palm Coast was proclaimed by the name painted on the water tower uniquely visible standing alone along the highway with unbroken miles of trees before and after it. Constructed before there was even an interchange, the tower was painted in ITT's adopted colors of blue and orange and its top was adorned for years with a lighted Christmas tree. Although it is now accompanied by a myriad of signs announcing the complete range of services at exit 289 (formerly 91C), the water tower landmark still prominently verifies motorists' arrival in Palm Coast.

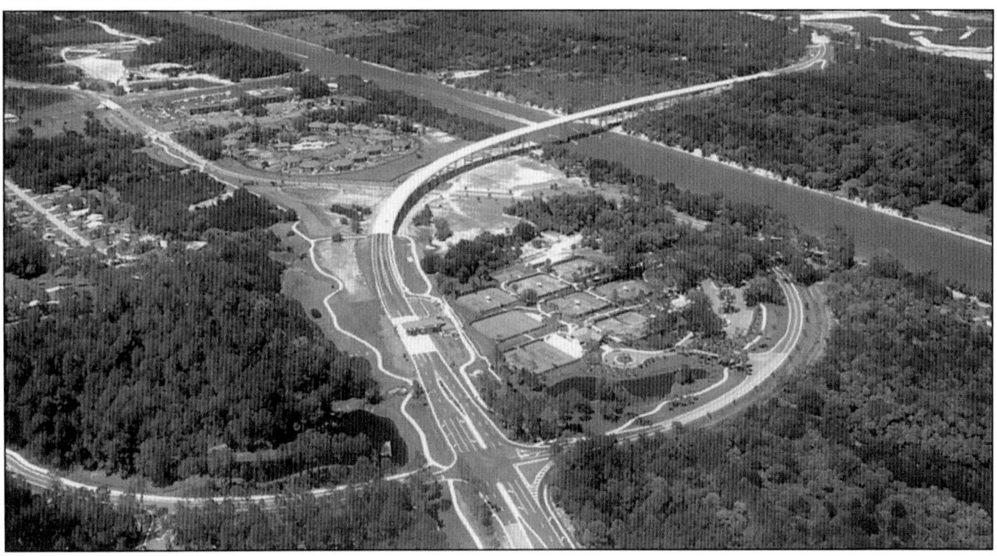

HAMMOCK DUNES BRIDGE, 1989. Originally purchased by ITT in 1969, the area named Palm Coast encompassed six miles of Atlantic Ocean waterfront, ten miles on each side of the Intracoastal Waterway, and interior lands, combining to a total of approximately 68,000 acres in northern Flagler County, Florida. The author treats this entire original area as Palm Coast, recognizing that the boundary of the present-day City of Palm Coast extends only to the western bank of the Intracoastal Waterway. Completed as a toll road in 1988, the Hammock Dunes Bridge connects Palm Coast physically and historically with its Route A1A Corridor on the ocean.

IMAGES
of America

PALM COAST

Arthur E. Dycke

ARCADIA
PUBLISHING

ISBN 978-0-7385-1506-9

Published by Arcadia Publishing
Charleston, South Carolina

Printed in the United States of America

Library of Congress Catalog Card Number: 2002117438

For all general information contact Arcadia Publishing at:
Telephone 843-853-2070
Fax 843-853-0044
E-mail sales@arcadiapublishing.com
For customer service and orders:
Toll-Free 1-888-313-2665

Visit us on the Internet at www.arcadiapublishing.com

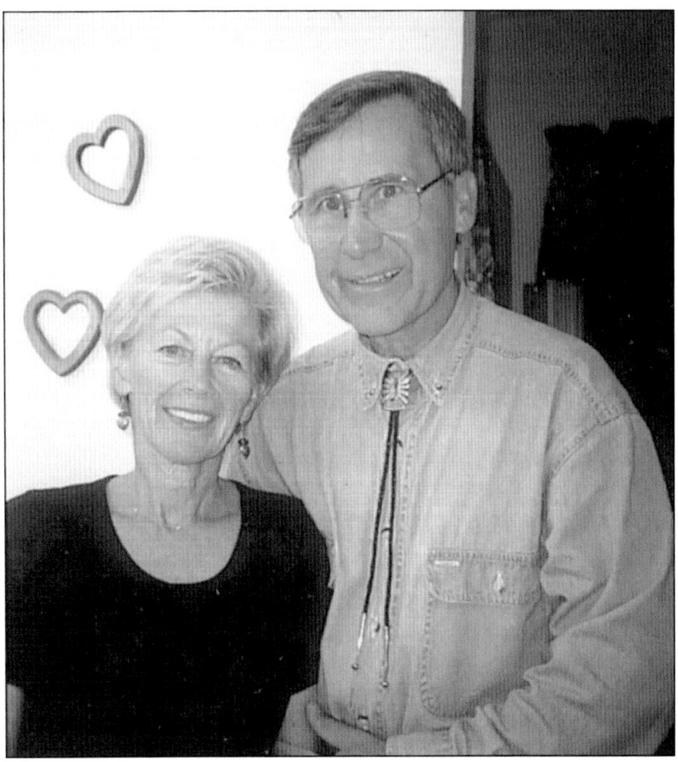

This book is dedicated to my wife, Louise, without whose support, it could not have been written. It is dedicated further to recently deceased James F. Holland as a representative of talented civic volunteers and government leaders who selflessly contribute enormous amounts of time and energy for the enrichment and benefit of the communities in which they serve.

Contents

About the Author

Arthur E. Dycke was born in the Bronx, New York, in 1934. There he attended public school 3, Cardinal Hayes High School, and Hunter College, receiving a bachelor of arts in history and elementary education. Awarded a master of arts in social studies education at UCNY and a professional diploma as teacher of history, Columbia University Teachers College, he taught grades 5–12 for 38 years in the Ardsley, New York school system and social science courses for 28 years at Westchester Community College. Art retired to Palm Coast in 1993 and has been adjunct faculty in history, economics, and government at the Daytona Beach Community College, Flagler Palm Coast Campus since 1994.

After working with Marty McLean, Jim Canfield, and Jim Holland of the Palm Coast Home Rule Coalition in drafting a new city charter proposal, he was appointed city co-historian with Margaret Davie in April 2000. He was co-founder and first vice president of the City of Palm Coast Historical Society and continues to serve as a board director.

Art and his wife Louise have three daughters: Kelley Lau, husband Bob, children Abbey and Jacob, living in Colorado; Chris Stapleton and daughter Lauren in South Carolina; and Jackie Norris, husband John, and twins Hunter and Cole, presently living in Washington D.C.. The family loves get-togethers, skiing, tennis, golf, camping, and fishing in New Hampshire and Palm Coast.

Acknowledgments

The author wishes to express his gratitude and appreciation to the many individuals in the Palm Coast community who contributed the photos and information contained in this book. He must especially recognize Debby Geyer, Jerry Full, Jim Miskelly, Alan Smolen, Jack Clegg, Margaret Davie, Barbara Sue Godkin, Jack Holt, Jim and Claire Sheekey, Don DeVito, Kathleen Bishop, Mary Ann and Jim Canfield, the ITT Corporation whose Jim Gardner contributed a major amount of the material in this book, the city council, administration, and members of the city of Palm Coast Historical Society. Pauline King was the intelligent typist of this entire book.

INTRODUCTION

This book presents Palm Coast's relatively short history from the time of its naming and development by the International Telephone and Telegraph Corporation (ITT) in 1969 until the present. The area's long rich history before that time is briefly outlined in the description listed below.

In the beginning, Palm Coast, like all of Florida, was under water. As the ocean receded, the land was occupied by animals such as mastodons and giant sloths. They were followed by Paleo-Indian hunters, about 15,000 years ago, who were ancestors to the area's Timucuan Indians who occupied the land until the early 1800s. Ponce de Leon sailed past Palm Coast in 1513, claiming the land for Spain. Spaniards defeated the French at Matanzas Inlet but lost the land in 1763 to the English, who later built the Kings Road through the area. In 1783, Florida was returned to the Spaniards, and they occupied Palm Coast until it became a United States Territory in 1819 from military action by Andrew Jackson. The Spanish operated a mission here in the 16th century, and in the early 1800s they deeded huge land areas to Joseph M. Hernandez. He later built Bulow, St. Joseph, and Mala Compra Plantations on the land. James Audubon visited in 1832. The plantations were later destroyed in the Seminole Indian Wars, lasting from 1836 until 1842. Slaves built the St. Joe Canal. It is believed that Salt Road was used to supply the Confederacy until 1865. Thereafter, cattlemen, "crackers," lumbermen, and small farmers shared the land with orange growers—who later went out of business due to a killing frost in 1895. In the 1880s and 1890s, Henry Flagler's railroads and the Intracoastal Waterway's canals were constructed. Flagler County was created in 1917. The area experienced increasing tourism, a land boom, and substantial moonshining in the 1920s. The Great Depression followed, hitting the county hard. During World War II, coastal spy watches occurred in the area. Those here in the 1950s witnessed the widening of U.S. 1, the construction of I-95, a school segregation dispute, and the building and operation of a large, modern Lehigh Cement Plant, in operation from 1952 until 1965.

Most of the aforementioned events affected only the developed lands around an east-west line running along route 100 from Flagler Beach to the county seat in Bunnell. By 1969, the vast, mostly unpopulated area north of that line consisted primarily of endless pine forest, considerable swamp land, and six miles of coquina strewn, sand-barred ocean front. There were some rutted dirt roads, a few farms, a turpentine distillery, scattered beach houses, and businesses along the paved route A1A corridor, along with an empty and unused modern cement factory. Area residents boasted outstanding fishing and hunting that could be shared with rich visitors in a camp for a fee. Then, International Telephone and Telegraph Rayonier, Inc. (ITT) came to the region.

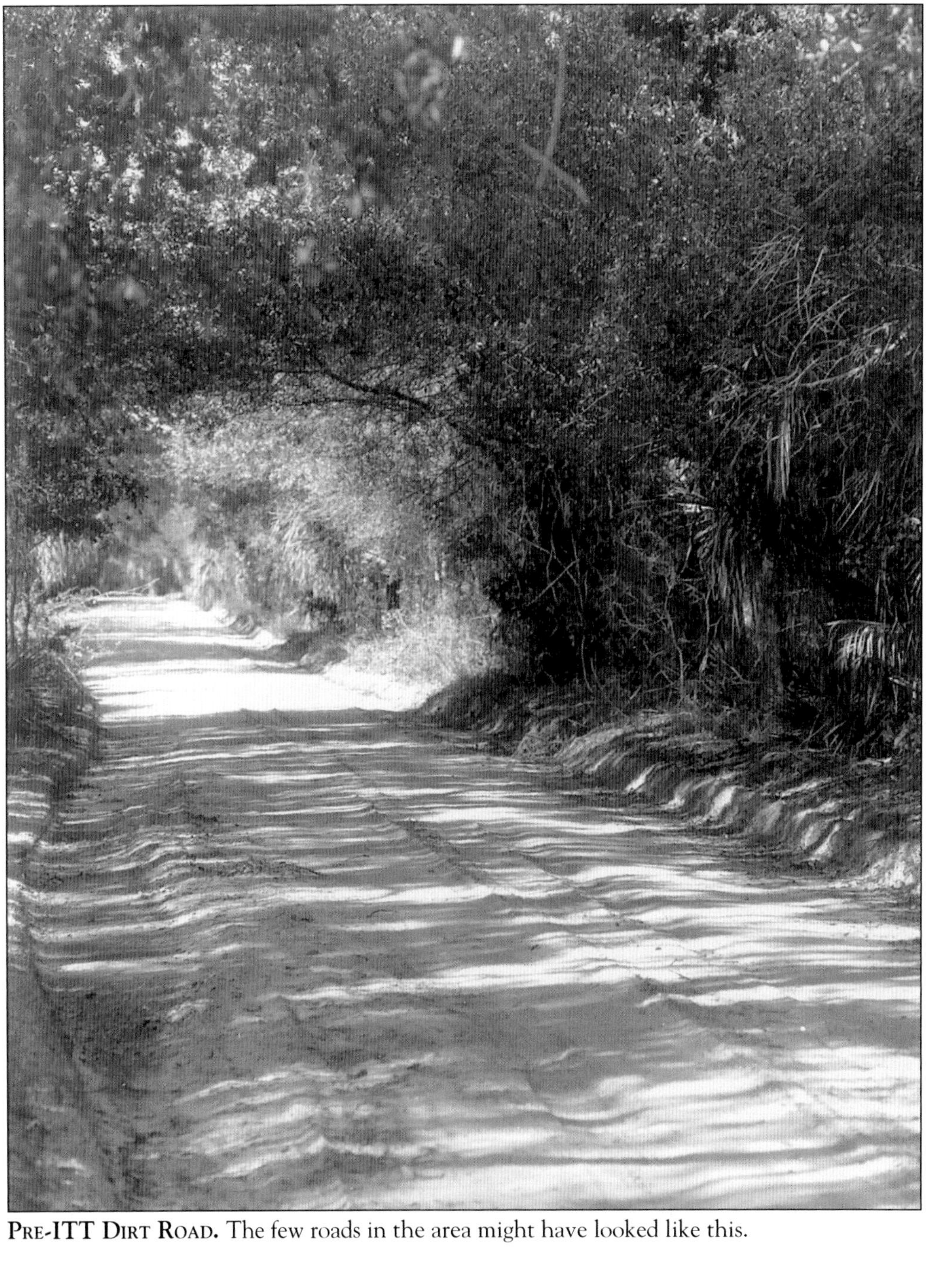

PRE-ITT DIRT ROAD. The few roads in the area might have looked like this.

One

ITT Builds Palm Coast

"An abandoned plantation, a big pine covered swamp which a little corporate imagination turned into thousands of tiny slices of land which were sold as lots . . . for lots of money." Could this strange wild empty land be tamed and made livable?

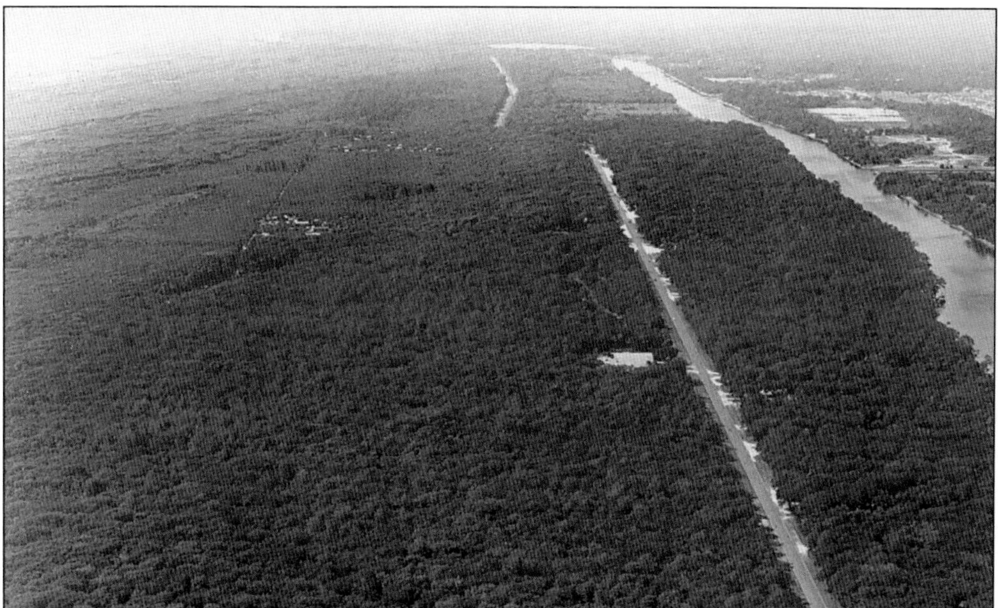

Route A1A Oceanfront, c. 1973. This aerial photo showing part of the coastal A1A corridor acquired by ITT was taken just a few years after the beginning of the Palm Coast development project. It pictures the area from a few miles north of the present Hammock Dunes Bridge facing south toward Flagler Beach. Notice the main canal and marina land clearing just starting on the west side of the Intracoastal Waterway (ICW). The Atlantic Ocean is barely visible in the upper left-hand corner of the picture. The land is almost completely unoccupied. A similar photo taken today would show the bridge and the entire area under full development.

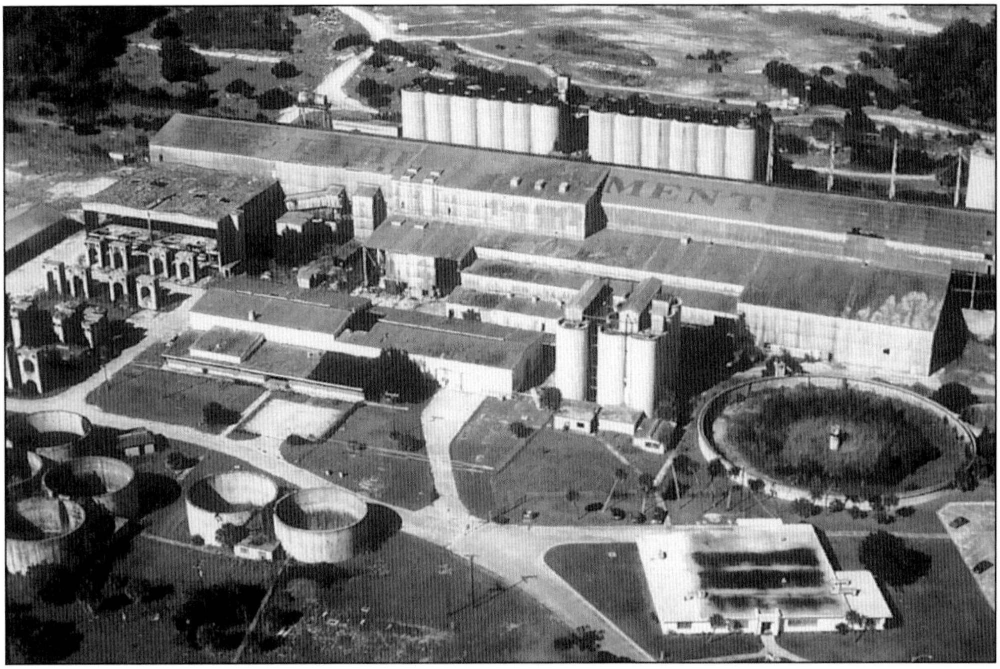

LEHIGH CEMENT PLANT, C. 1965. The first hint that something was going to happen in sparsely populated, rural Flagler County, Florida, came on January 1, 1969, when *The Flagler Tribune* front page announced the headline below.

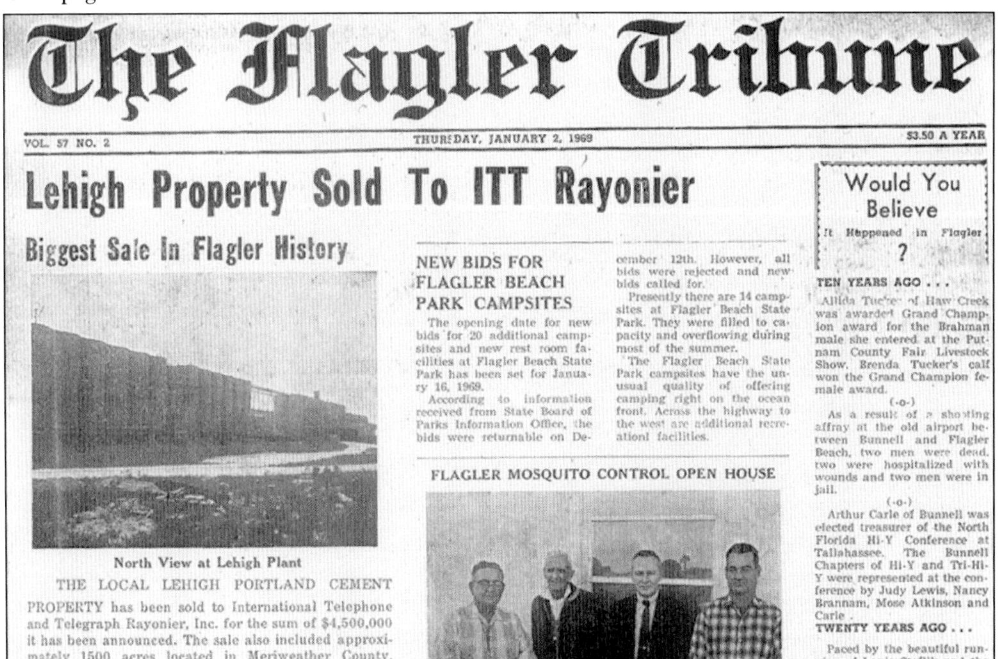

The Flagler Tribune

VOL. 57 NO. 2 | THURSDAY, JANUARY 2, 1969 | $3.50 A YEAR

Lehigh Property Sold To ITT Rayonier

Biggest Sale In Flagler History

North View at Lehigh Plant

THE LOCAL LEHIGH PORTLAND CEMENT PROPERTY has been sold to International Telephone and Telegraph Rayonier, Inc. for the sum of $4,500,000 it has been announced. The sale also included approximately 1500 acres located in Meriwenther County,

NEW BIDS FOR FLAGLER BEACH PARK CAMPSITES

The opening date for new bids for 20 additional campsites and new rest room facilities at Flagler Beach State Park has been set for January 16, 1969.

According to information received from State Board of Parks Information Office, the bids were returnable on December 12th. However, all bids were rejected and new bids called for.

Presently there are 14 campsites at Flagler Beach State Park. They were filled to capacity and overflowing during most of the summer.

The Flagler Beach State Park campsites have the unusual quality of offering camping right on the ocean front. Across the highway to the west are additional recreationl facilities.

FLAGLER MOSQUITO CONTROL OPEN HOUSE

Would You Believe
It Happened in Flagler
?

TEN YEARS AGO . . .

Allida Tucker of Haw Creek was awarded Grand Champion award for the Brahman male she entered at the Putnam County Fair Livestock Show. Brenda Tucker's calf won the Grand Champion female award.

(-o-)

As a result of a shooting affray at the old airport between Bunnell and Flagler Beach, two men were dead, two were hospitalized with wounds and two men were in jail.

(-o-)

Arthur Carle of Bunnell was elected treasurer of the North Florida Hi-Y Conference at Tallahassee. The Bunnell Chapters of Hi-Y and Tri-Hi-Y were represented at the conference by Judy Lewis, Nancy Brannam, Mose Atkinson and Carle .

TWENTY YEARS AGO . . .

Paced by the beautiful running of Louis Steflik and the

"LEHIGH PROPERTY SOLD TO ITT RAYONIER." The story continued, "The local Lehigh Portland Cement property has been sold to International Telephone and Telegraph Rayonier, Inc. for the sum of $4,500,000." The plant had been in operation from 1952 until 1965 and had been the only major industry and non-farm employer in this predominantly agricultural area.

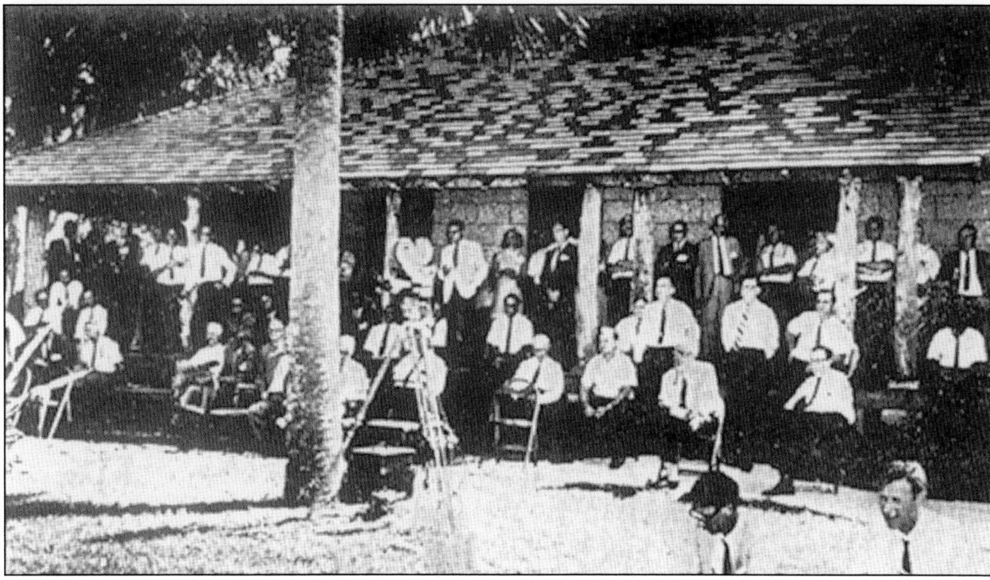

Project Announcement at Princess Place, June 1969. ITT Rayonier purchased 6,000 acres of property from prominent Flagler businessman Lewis E. Wadsworth and others. This was added to their newly acquired 13,000-acre Lehigh tract and combined with approximately 70,000 acres of forest land that the company already owned in Flagler and St. Johns Counties. On June 16, 1969, over 175 invited guests, mostly consisting of state and county legislators, local officials, chamber of commerce members, other business leaders, and a large press and television corps, attended an announcement cocktail party held by ITT officials at Wadsworth's Princess Place estate in northern Flagler County. There ITT Rayonier announced that they would turn over their recently purchased Flagler properties to ITT subsidiary, Levitt and Sons, for a massive land development project.

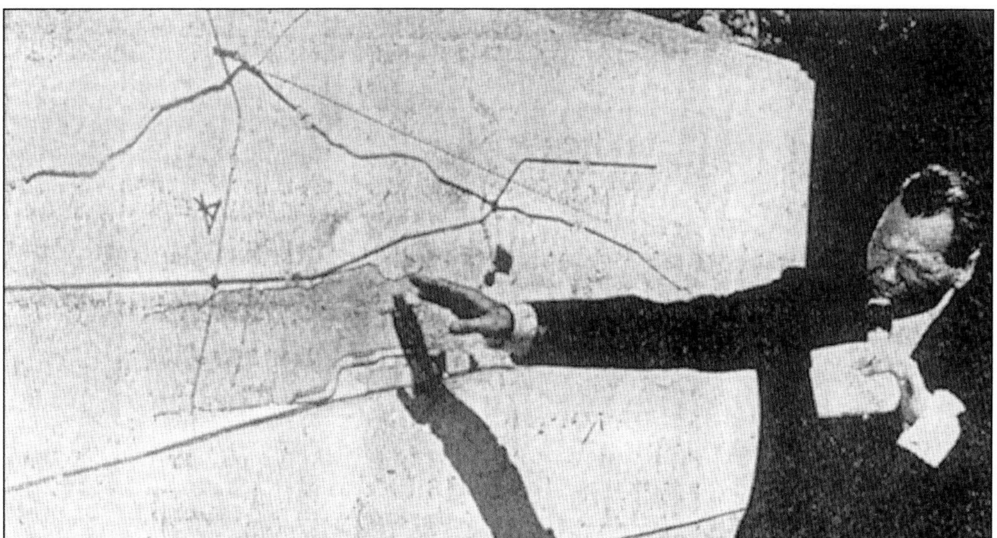

Project Boundaries Shown. Dr. Norman Young pointed out the location of the project, which was to developed by Levitt and Sons, on a large map that had been set up for the announcement party. The company he represented had an outstanding reputation for post-war land and housing developments including the legendary Levittown on Long Island in New York.

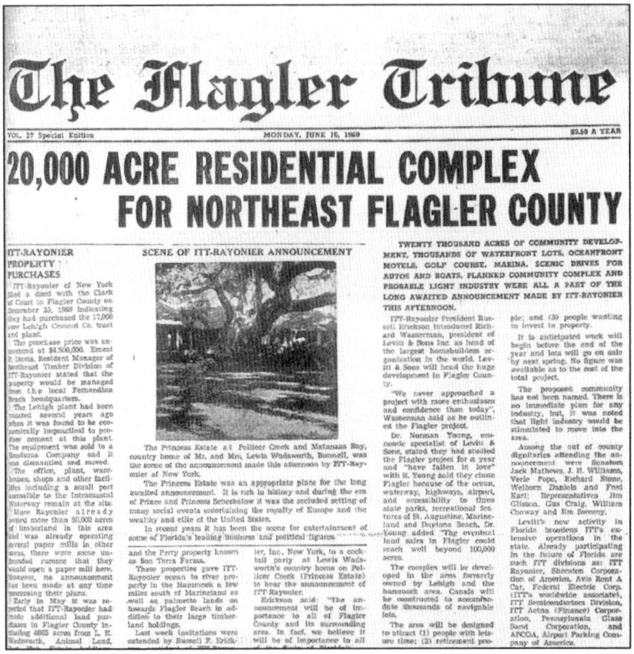

The Flagler Tribune

VOL. 57 Special Edition | MONDAY, JUNE 16, 1969 | $3.50 A YEAR

20,000 ACRE RESIDENTIAL COMPLEX FOR NORTHEAST FLAGLER COUNTY

ITT-RAYONIER PROPERTY PURCHASES

ITT-Rayonier of New York filed a deed with the Clark of Court in Flagler County on December 23, 1968 indicating they had purchased the 17,000 acre Lehigh Cement Co. tract and plant.

The purchase price was announced at $4,500,000. Ernest P. Davis, Resident Manager of Southeast Timber Division of ITT-Rayonier stated that the property would be managed from the local Fernandina Beach headquarters.

The Lehigh plant had been vacated several years ago when it was found to be economically impractical to produce cement at this plant. The equipment was sold to a Honduras Company and it was dismantled and moved.

The office, plant, warehouses, shops and other facilities including a small port accessible to the Intracoastal Waterway remain at the site.

Since Rayonier already owned more than 50,000 acres of timberland in this area and was already operating several paper mills in other areas, there were some unfounded rumors that they would open a paper mill here. However, no announcement has been made at any time concerning their plans.

Early in May it was reported that ITT-Rayonier had made additional land purchases in Flagler County including 4665 acres from L. E. Wadsworth, Animal Land, and the Perry property known as Bon Terra Farms.

These properties gave ITT-Rayonier ocean to river property in the Hammock a few miles south of Marineland as well as palmetto lands on towards Flagler Beach in addition to their large timberland holdings.

Last week invitations were extended by Russell F. Erickson, ... ITT-Rayonier, Inc., New York, to a cocktail party at Lewis Wadsworth's country home on Pellicer Creek (Princess Estate) to hear the announcement of ITT Rayonier.

Erickson said: "The announcement will be of importance to all of Flagler County and its surrounding area. In fact, we believe it will be of importance to all ...

SCENE OF ITT-RAYONIER ANNOUNCEMENT

The Princess Estate at Pellicer Creek and Matanzas Bay, country home of Mr. and Mrs. Lewis Wadsworth, Bunnell, was the scene of the announcement made this afternoon by ITT-Rayonier of New York.

The Princess Estate was an appropriate place for the long awaited announcement. It is rich in history and during the era of Prince and Princess Scherbatow it was the secluded setting of many social events entertaining the royalty of Europe and the wealthy and elite of the United States.

In recent years it has been the scene for entertainment of some of Florida's leading business and political figures.

TWENTY THOUSAND ACRES OF COMMUNITY DEVELOPMENT, THOUSANDS OF WATERFRONT LOTS, OCEANFRONT MOTELS, GOLF COURSE, MARINA, SCENIC DRIVES FOR AUTOS AND BOATS, PLANNED COMMUNITY COMPLEX AND PROBABLE LIGHT INDUSTRY WERE ALL A PART OF THE LONG AWAITED ANNOUNCEMENT MADE BY ITT-RAYONIER THIS AFTERNOON.

ITT-Rayonier President Russell Erickson introduced Richard Wasserman, president of Levitt & Sons Inc. as head of the largest homebuilders organization in the world. Levitt & Sons will head the huge development in Flagler County.

"We never approached a project with more enthusiasm and confidence than today", Wasserman said as he outlined the Flagler project.

Dr. Norman Young, economic specialist of Levitt & Sons, stated they had studied the Flagler project for a year and "have fallen in love" with it. Young said they chose Flagler because of the ocean, waterway, highways, airport, and accessibility to three state parks, recreational features of St. Augustine, Marineland and Daytona Beach. Dr. Young added "The eventual land sales in Flagler could reach well beyond 100,000 acres.

The complex will be developed in the area formerly owned by Lehigh and the hammock area. Canals will be constructed to accommodate thousands of navigable lots.

The area will be designed to attract (1) people with leisure time; (2) retirement people; and (3) people wanting to invest in property.

It is anticipated work will begin before the end of the year and lots will go on sale by next spring. No figure was available as to the cost of the total project.

The proposed community has not been named. There is no immediate plan for any industry, but, it was noted that light industry would be stimulated to move into the area.

Among the out of county dignitaries attending the announcement were Senators Jack Mathews, J. H. Williams, Verle Pope, Richard Stone, Welborn Daniels and Fred Karl; Representatives Jim Glisson, Gus Craig, William Conway and Jim Sweeny.

Levitt's new activity in Florida broadens ITT's extensive operations in the state. Already participating in the future of Florida are such ITT divisions as: ITT Rayonier, Sheraton Corporation of America, Avis Rent A Car, Federal Electric Corp. (ITT's worldwide associate), ITT Semiconductors Division, ITT Aetna (Finance) Corporation, Pennsylvania Glass Sand Corporation, and APCOA, Airport Parking Company of America.

PROJECT ANNOUNCEMENT HEADLINE, JUNE 16, 1969. The headline subtitle states "20,000 acres of community development, thousands of waterfront lots, ocean front hotel, golf course, marina, scenic drives for autos and boats, planned community complex, and probable light industry were all a part of the long awaited announcement made by ITT Rayonier." According to Dr. Norman Young, the initial offering was designed to attract people with leisure time, those in retirement, and investors.

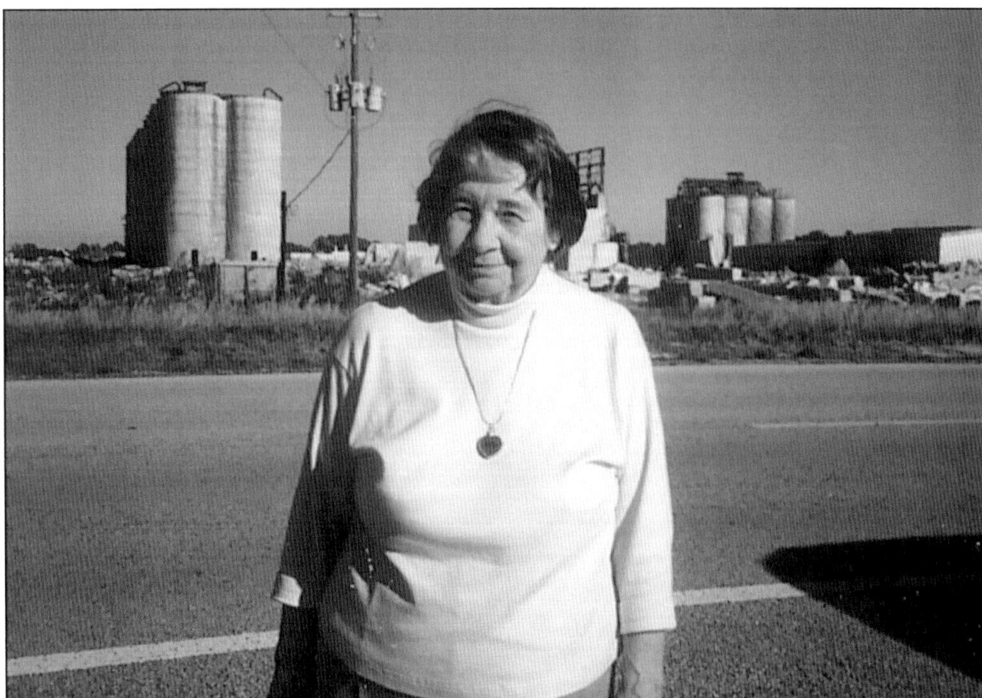

PROJECT CONSTRUCTION OFFICE, 1970. Surveying, lot platting, engineering design, and land clearing began immediately. The construction of roads, canals, and utility infrastructure for the first 20,000 acres to be developed followed soon thereafter. Palm Coast resident Connie Horvath stands beside Colbert Lane in front of the Lehigh plant, which is now being demolished. Connie was secretary/assistant to ITT Levitt's first project manager, Dan Cooper. The construction office was established in the old cement factory.

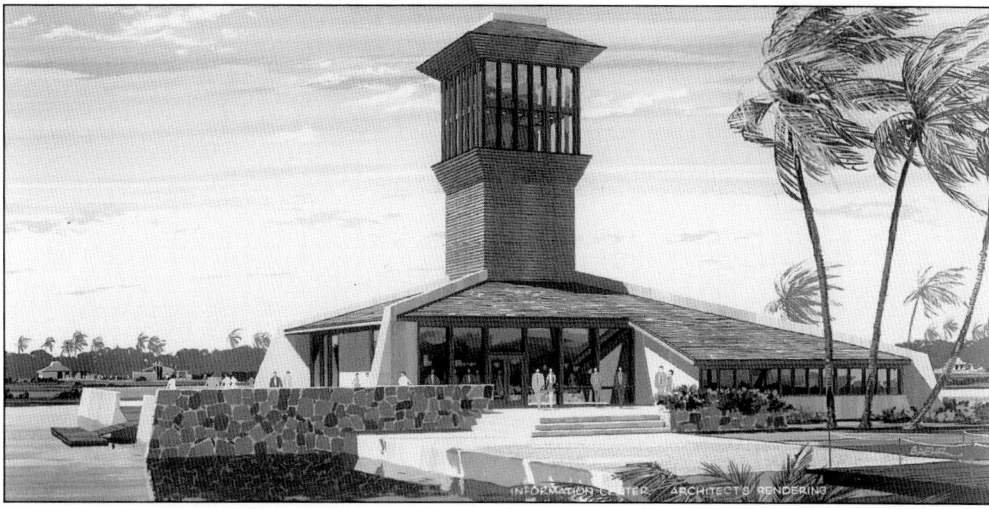

Proposed Information Center. In February 1970, Dr. Norman Young, president of ITT Levitt Development Corporation, made a progress report to the Flagler Chamber of Commerce. He envisioned an observation tower overlooking the planned residential area, a tri-winged motel to be constructed on the oceanfront, lighted highways including Kings Road and St. Joe Grade, a high span bridge over the Intracoastal Waterway, and a central interchange at Interstate 95. The tower, golf course, and model homes were to be completed by the end of the year. Levitt marketers in New York had by now given the project the name of Palm Coast.

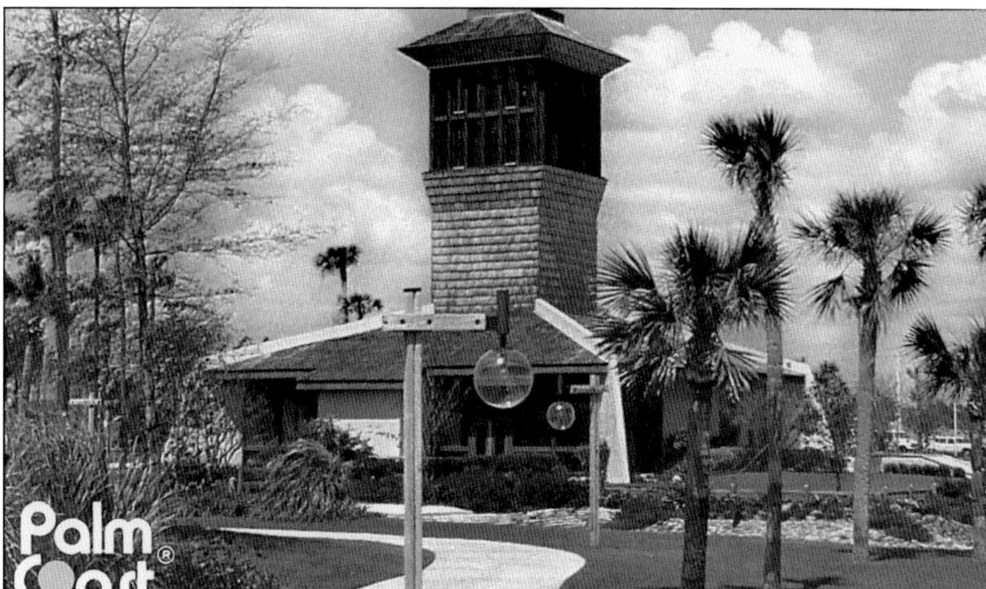

First Building Constructed in Palm Coast, October 1970. The words on the back of this ITT Postcard proclaim, "The Welcome Center at Palm Coast, Florida." The 64 foot tower provides a panoramic view of surrounding woods, lakes and streams." The building was at the center of the first model area and was to serve as the hub of all sales activities. It was a dramatic building with a variety of graphics and audio visual sales materials inside. The main feature was an elevator-accessed, 64-foot-high observation tower affording visitors unobstructed views of their surroundings including the golf course, the model houses, and the inland waterway.

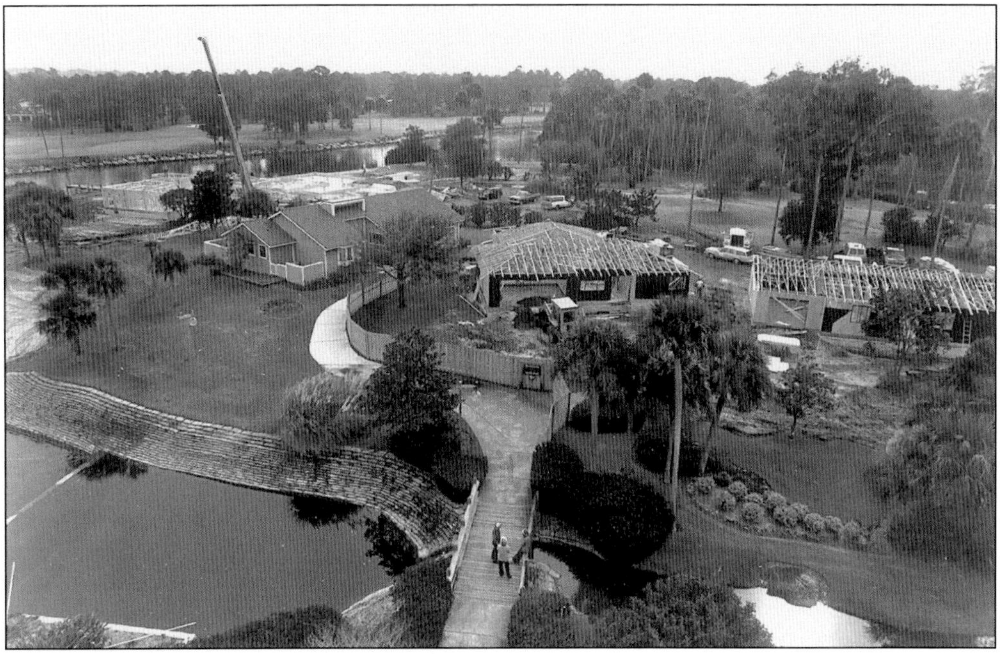

Model Center Construction, October 1970. This picture was taken from the top of the observation tower and shows the construction of the adjacent model center. In June, ITT had opened a land sales office on route A1A north of the present bridge in a building formerly occupied by Animal Land and now used as an Adult Education Center. Prospective buyers were driven to a small dock on the east side of the Intracoastal Waterway across from the present Palm Coast Golf Resort and taken by boat to the emerging welcome center. There land and preconstruction homes were marketed starting at $13,000. Even before Palm Coast opened officially, sales were brisk.

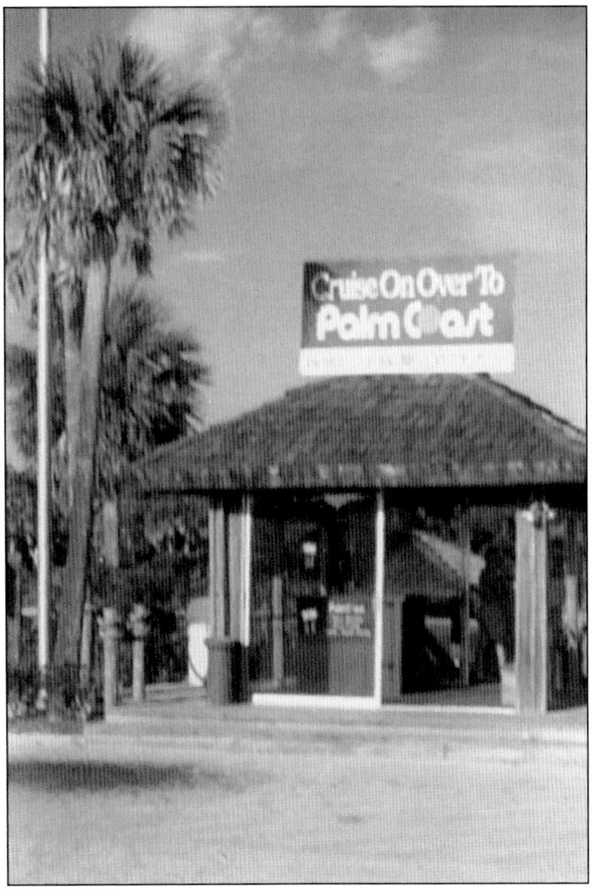

First Boat Dock. Visitors were taken by boat to the tower sales center. The boat dock was located on the east side of the Intracoastal Waterway.

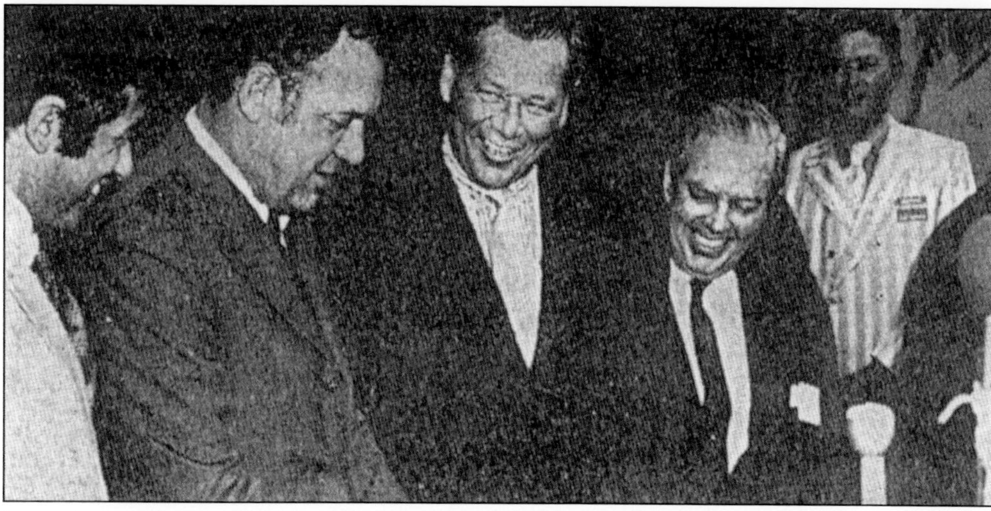

Palm Coast Grand Opening. The official grand opening of the "Unique Total Environmental Community" of Palm Coast took place on October 29, 1970. Florida governor Claude Kirk, Congressman Bill Chappell, ITT and Levitt top level management, community businessmen, golf stars, and TV and press reporters were "wined and dined" under a huge tent erected near the new information center. Boats took visitors on the Intracoastal Waterway and into the canals. An "air view armada" of private planes was provided for those wishing to take a flight over the property. Dr. Young had reported preconstruction sales of over $5 million even before the grand opening ceremonies and now the standard format of early land sales began in earnest.

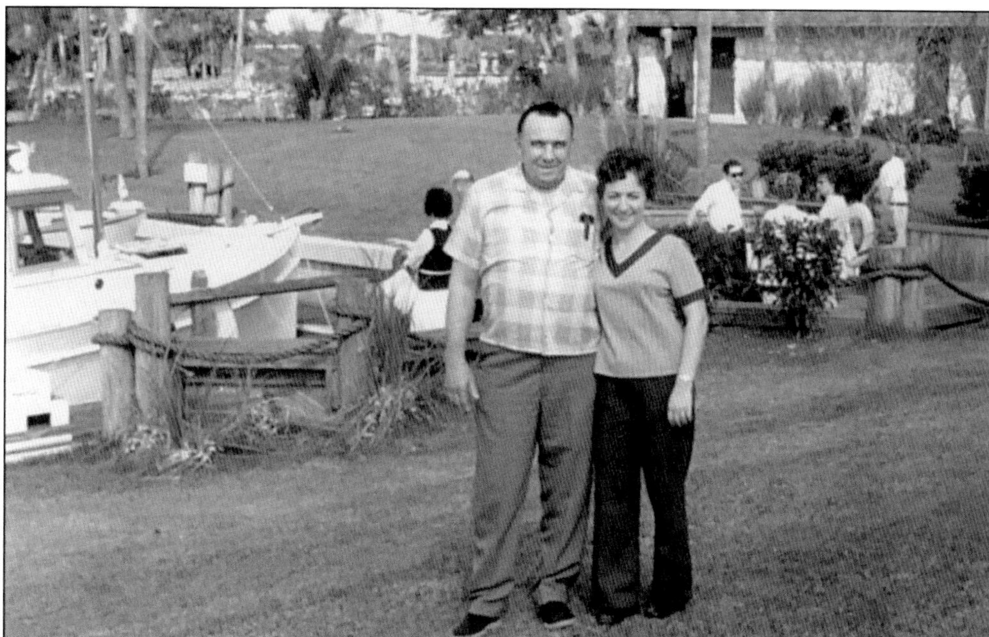

Information Center Visit, 1974. John and Terry Neveras are shown here on the west side of the Intracoastal Waterway after crossing on an ITT tour boat from the original sales building, located on A1A. Active members of the Palm Coast community today, they spent the day viewing the models and the land.

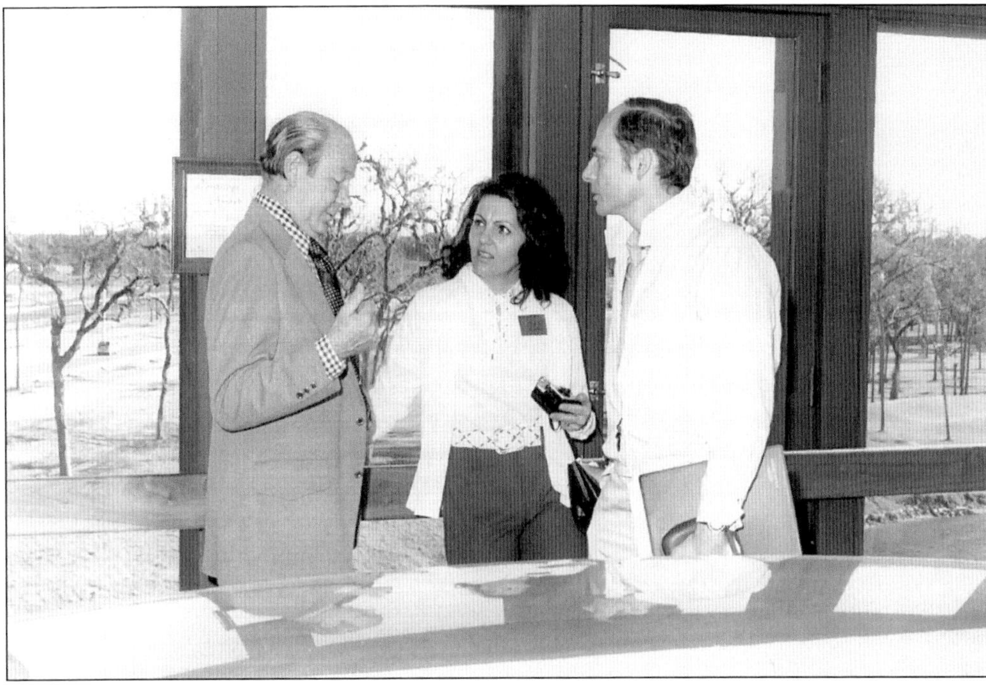

View From the Top, 1970–1975. When prospective buyers arrived by boat at the new welcome center, they were taken to the top of the 64-foot-high tower to view the area. Palm Coast residents Jack and Ann-Marie Pitman are shown here purchasing property from an unidentified salesman in 1972. The cleared land within immediate view of the tower must have looked barren, even desolate, and beyond that stretched a seemingly endless pine forest. Much of the land was sold, sight unseen, from a platted numbered map and the sales person was likely to locate one's property by pointing in some direction from the tower and saying, "It's out there somewhere."

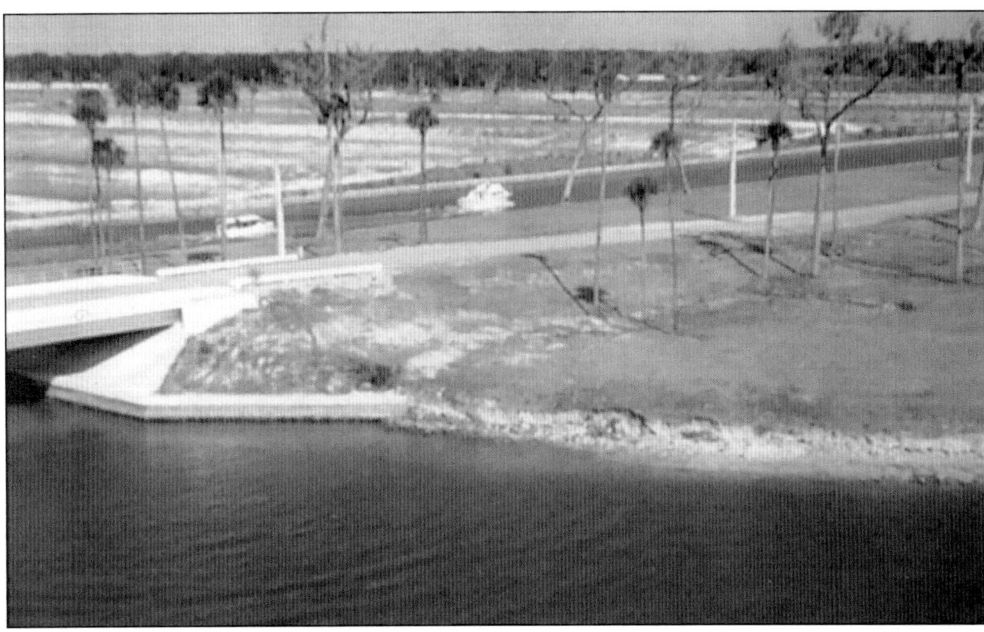

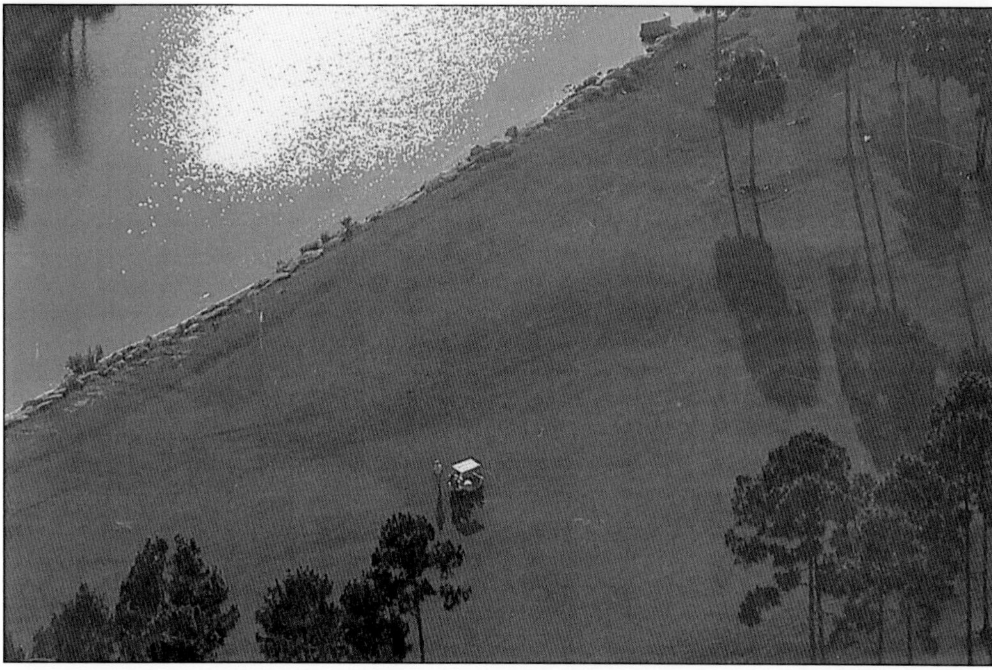

First Nine Holes, September 4, 1971. A postcard picture shows the sixth fairway of the Palm Coast Golf Club, later given its present name Palm Harbor. The course, adjacent to the first residential homes built in Palm Coast, was completed a year later and featured a 19th hole for refreshments that looked like a paddle wheel river boat. Bill Amick was the course designer; Bubba Williams was the first pro; and the popular Jim McGloin was the golf club manager.

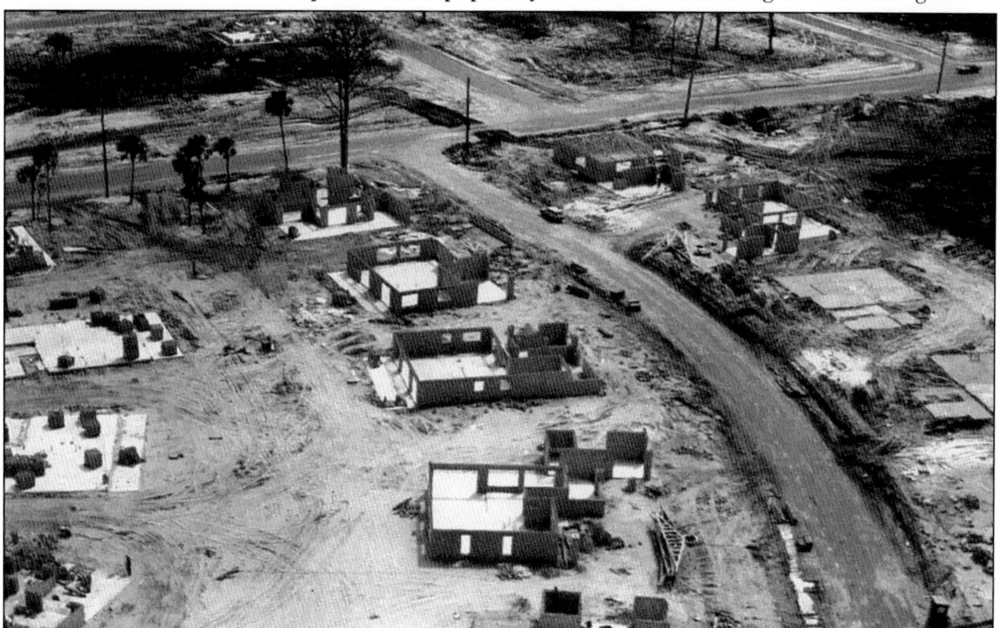

Home Construction Begins August 2, 1971. The first houses in Palm Coast were located off Club House Drive in the area surrounding the present-day Palm Harbor Golf Club. They were ready for their pioneer occupants by January 21, 1972.

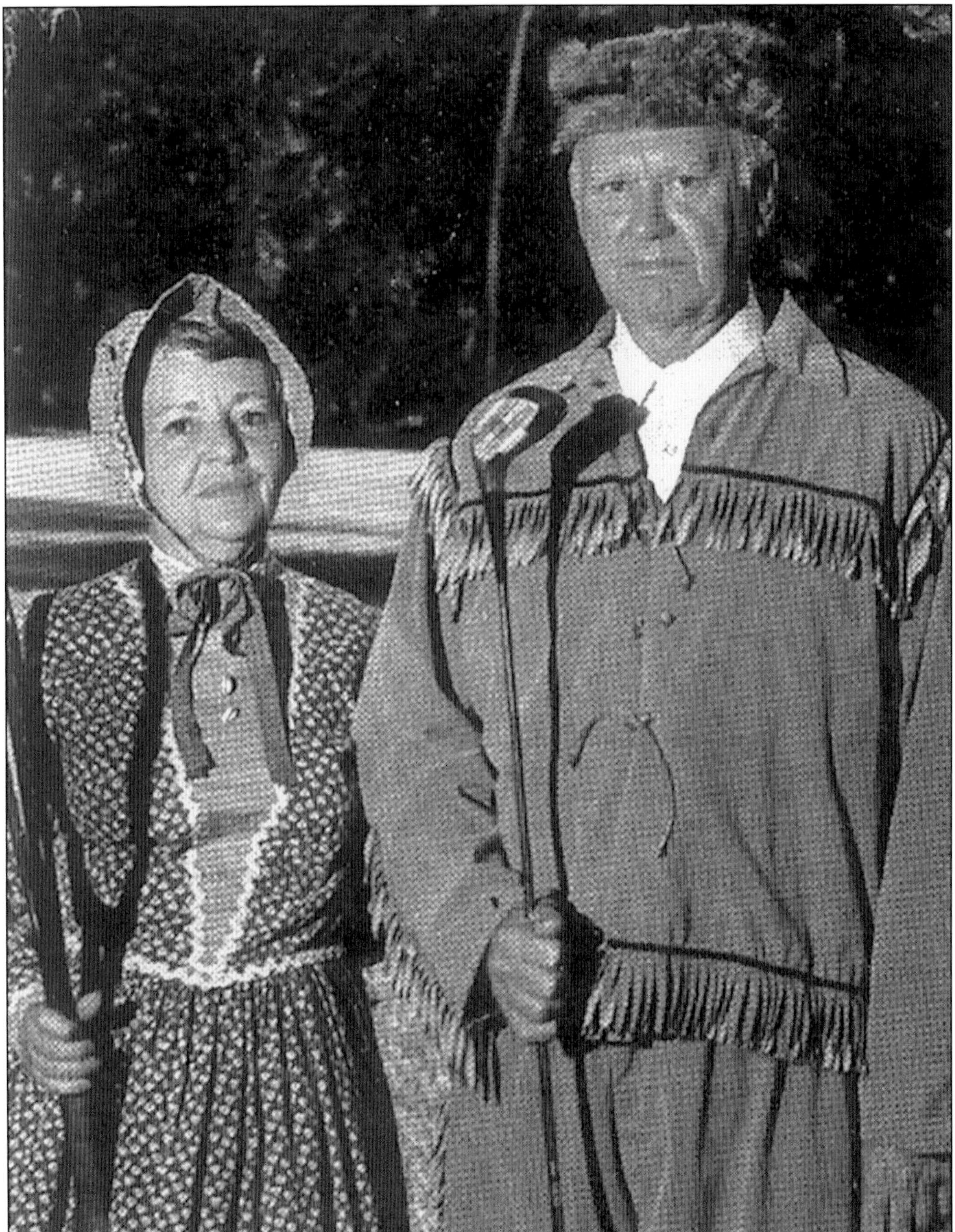

TRUE PIONEERS. Properly dressed with the exception of the golf club and tennis racquets in their hands, early residents Martha and Bob Orf stood prepared to face the perils of being pioneers in a new land. They were the first to come to a newly cleared frontier in an environment far different than the area in which they had been living. There were few neighbors and no stores or other amenities. They either had to drive 12 miles, partly over dirt roads, to get basics such as milk or hope that the ITT-provided "stagecoach" would arrive and bring the necessities they had requested. However, cooperation among the early settlers and their pioneer spirit helped ITT to tame this desolate land and build a prosperous and thriving community.

Two

Pioneers Come to the Frontier

"Pioneer: one who first enters or settles a region, thus opening it for occupation and development by others."

Most of the pioneers had come from organized communities, leaving comfortable homes, family, and friends to go to a strange new land in a sometimes hostile environment. At first, none of the basic community amenities and services that they were used to existed. Could they meet the challenge?

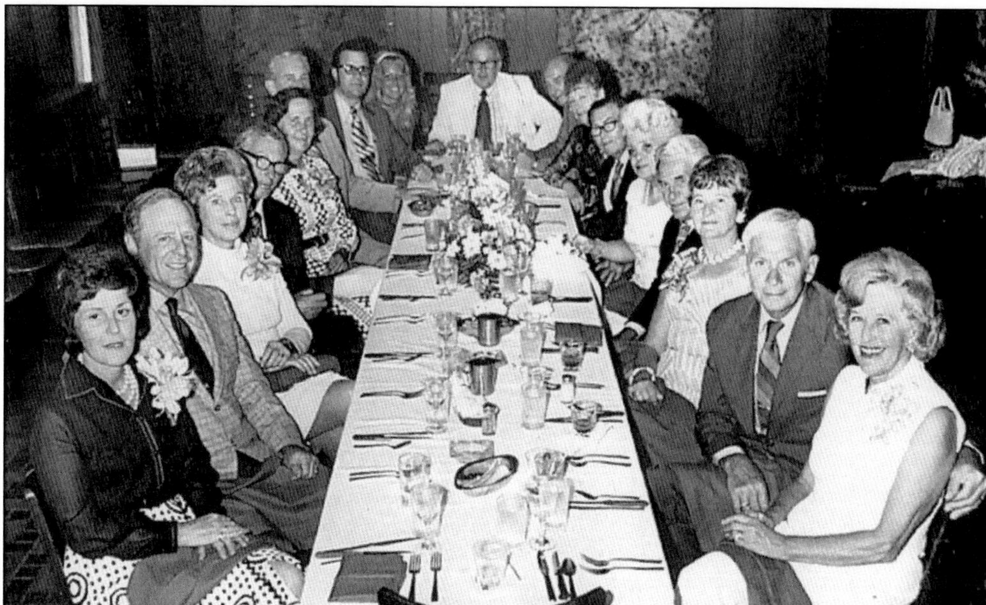

Pioneers of Palm Coast, 1972. On April 18, ICDC hosted a gala dinner party for the first families to move into Palm Coast. Pictured here are the guests of honor and the Palm Coast staff at the start of the festive event. From front to back, are (left side) Mr. and Mrs. William H. Loeb, Mr. and Mrs. Charles Konopasek, Mr. and Mrs. Thomas Simmons (Mr. Simmons was a Palm Coast salesman), Byron Maharrey, Jean Roy, and Ken Hath (at the head of the table); (right side) Mrs. Douglas Guiler, Mr. and Mrs. Winnie (Vincent) Moore, Mr. Guiler, Mr. and Mrs. Matthew Sheehan, and. Mr. and Mrs. Edward White.

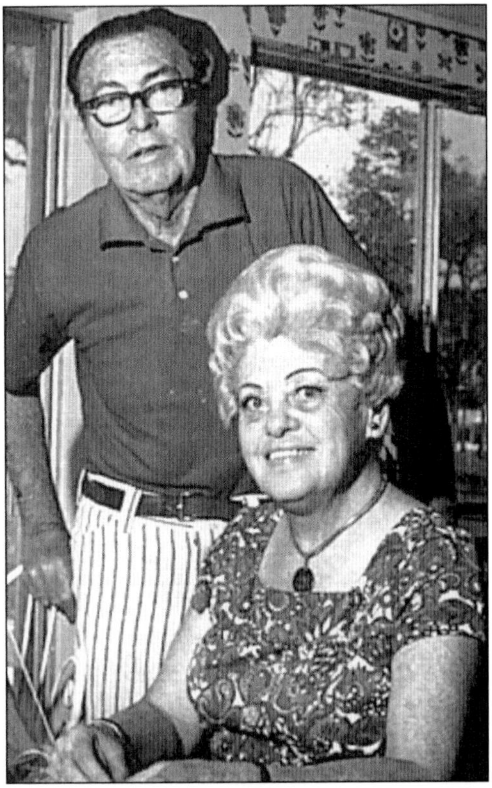

The Pioneers Arrive, 1972. One of the most exciting days in Palm Coast's short history took place on January 21, 1972, when the moving van rolled into Casper Drive and Mr. and Mrs. Matthew Sheehan proceeded to move into their new home as Palm Coast's first residents.

Below left: Mr. and Mrs. Vincent Moore were the second family to move into the area. Moore, a former New York fireman, later became Chief of the Palm Coast Volunteers. *Below right:* Mr. and Mrs. Charles Konopasek, the third family to arrive, received the champagne and roses with which ITT greeted its earliest residents.

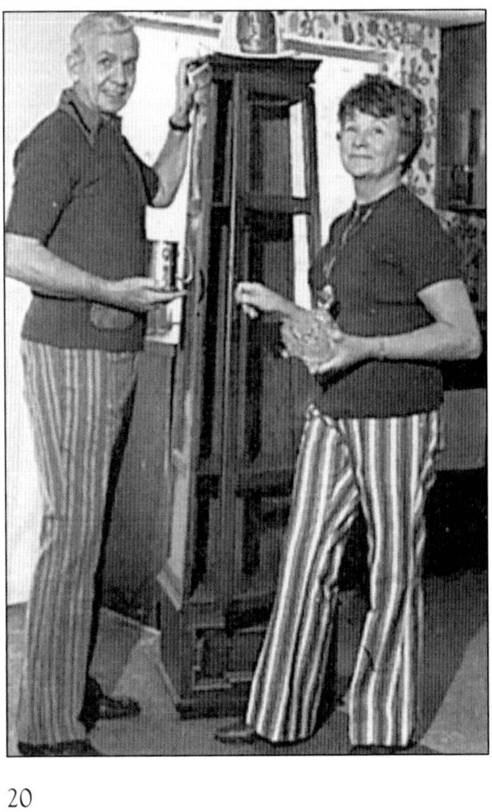

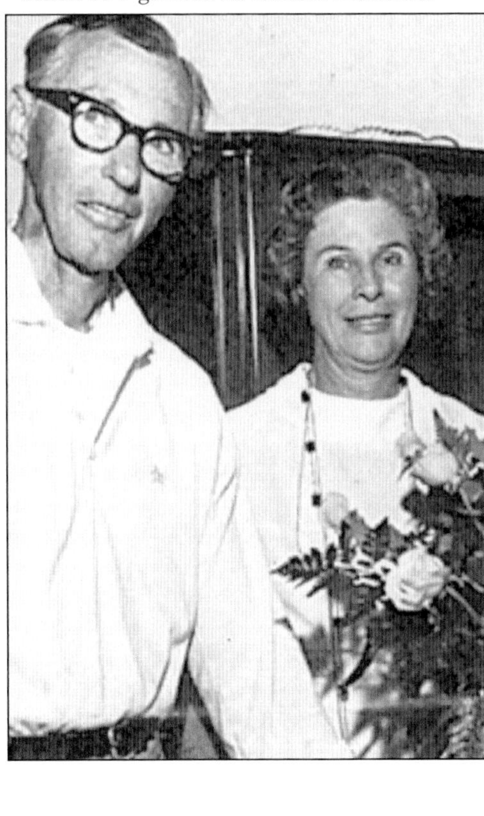

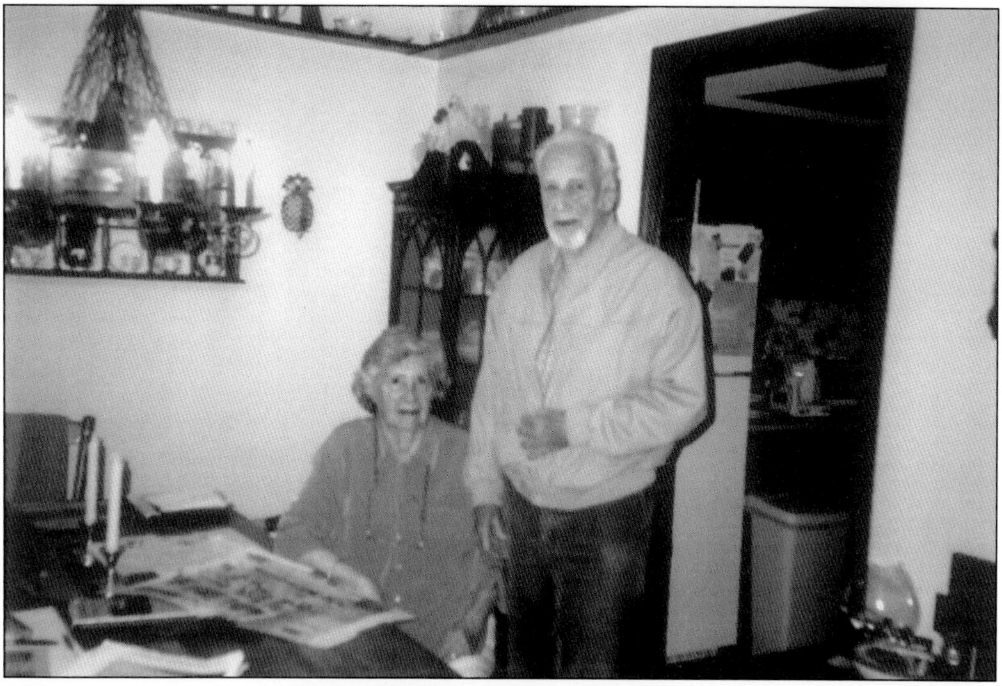

Pioneers in 2003. Betty and Tom Simmons are the only surviving people in the "Pioneers of Palm Coast" who are still living residents of Palm Coast today.

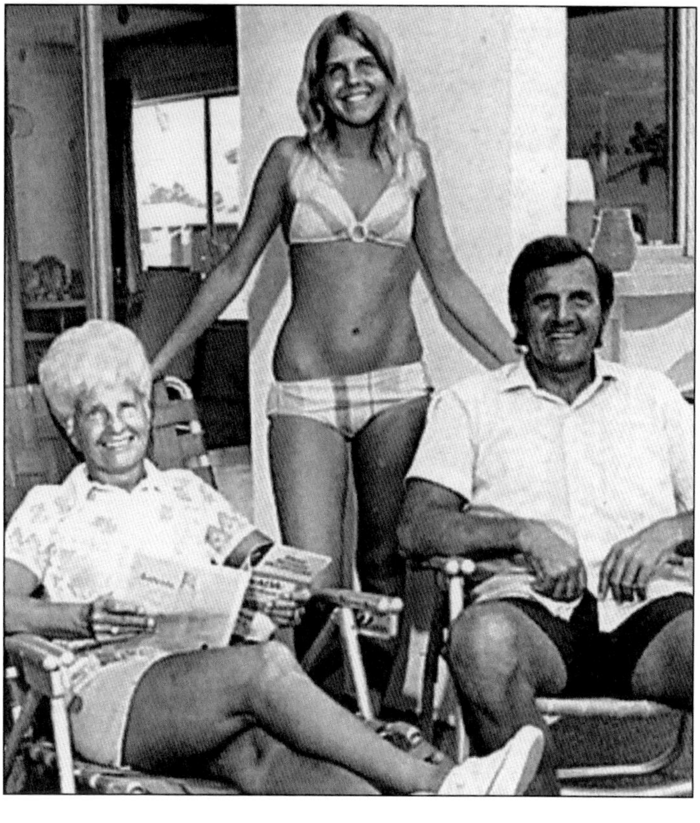

Pioneer Romance. Early settlers William and Bernadette Collier and their lovely daughter Sally are shown enjoying the sun of their new home. Sally met Robert Dunn, son of Dr. Jack Dunn, Palm Coast's first doctor. They were later married in Palm Coast.

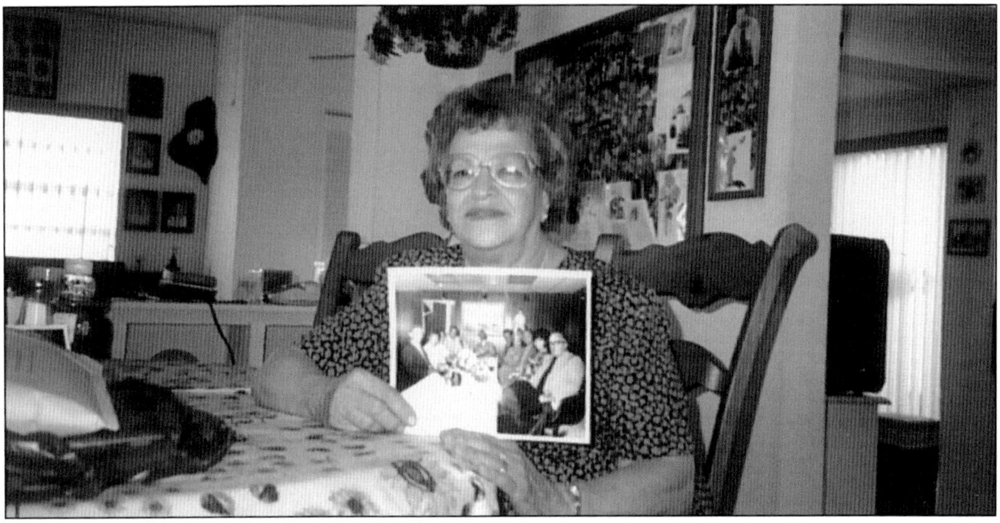

Pioneers Meet and Contribute to Their Community. Ann Tillard still lives in one of the first homes built around the Palm Harbor golf course. She is shown here holding a photo of another ITT dinner to honor newcomers to the community, also shown below. Identified in the picture are Gordon Kipp, Ann and Bill Tillard, and Liz and Ron Deak. Ann and other pioneers described the early settlers and their contributions to the community. Some of the people described were Wilma Weed, who formed the Palm Coast Chapter of the American Heart Association; Dr. Jack Dunn and his wife Augusta, a registered nurse, who, after they came here to retire, opened a medical office because they felt that it was needed; Bill Loeb, who was a prime mover and first president of the civic association; Helen Rutan, who started as a correspondent for the local paper and helped bring everyone together with her Chit Chat columns; "Spud" Clay who specialized in neighborhood protection; and Charles Konopasek, who got the first hole in one on the first golf course.

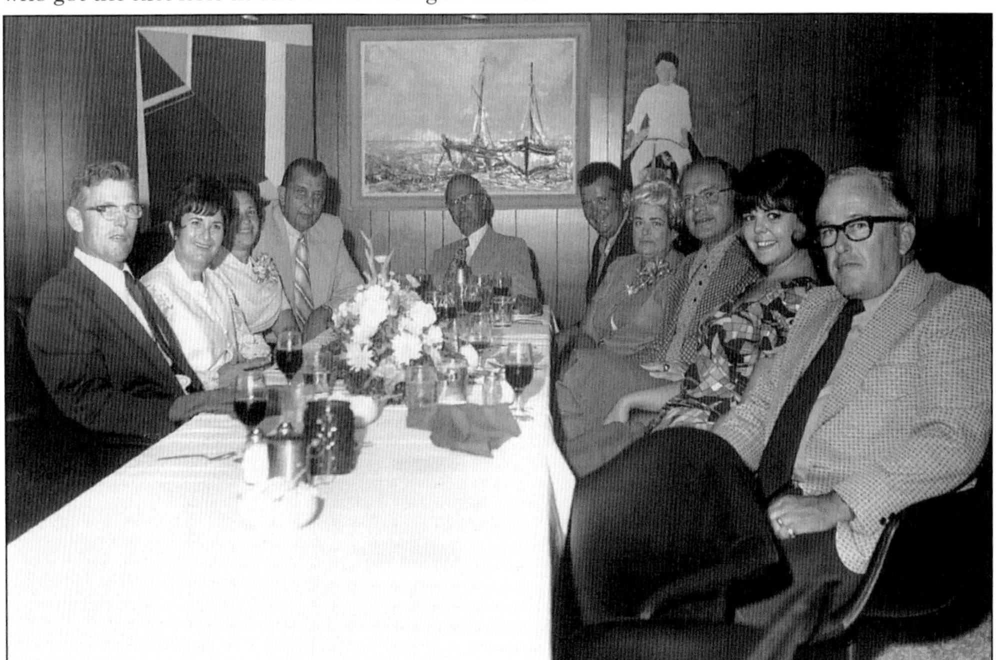

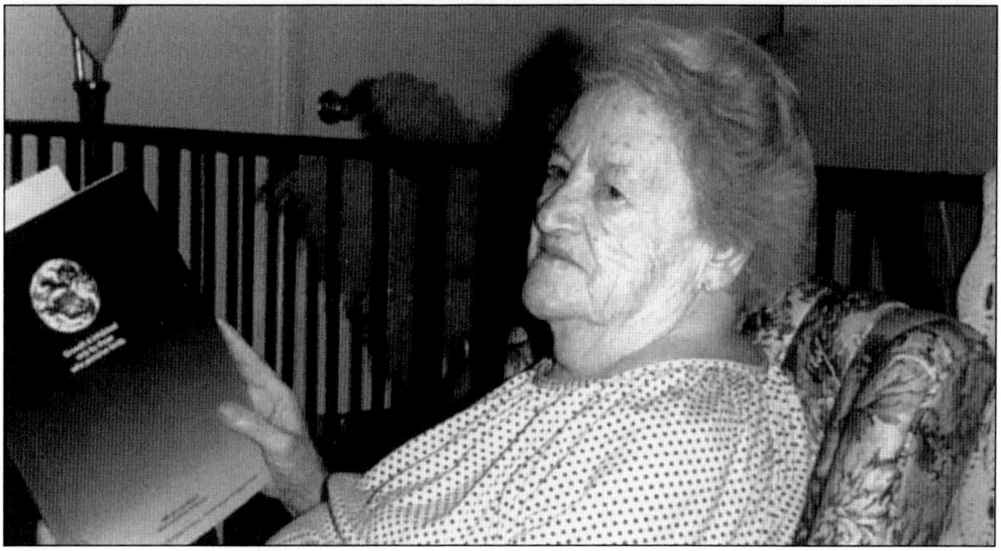

LOOKING FOR A ROOM, BUYS A HOUSE, 1972. A poet and painter in Mexico, Alicia Newton came to Florida in her later years looking for a place to live. She reached Daytona Beach in the middle of motorcycle week. Finding it impossible to get a motel room, she began making her way to St. Augustine, traveling along A1A. She noticed an ICDC advertisement about a boat trip with lunch and stopped for the sandwiches provided. She said that at that time, practically the whole area was desolate and full of snakes, but she took the boat trip to the model home. On July 4, 1972, she became one of the first residents of Palm Coast. "It was no paradise in those days," she said, "just mountains of sand and unsodded yards." There were only 12 families occupying homes when she got there.

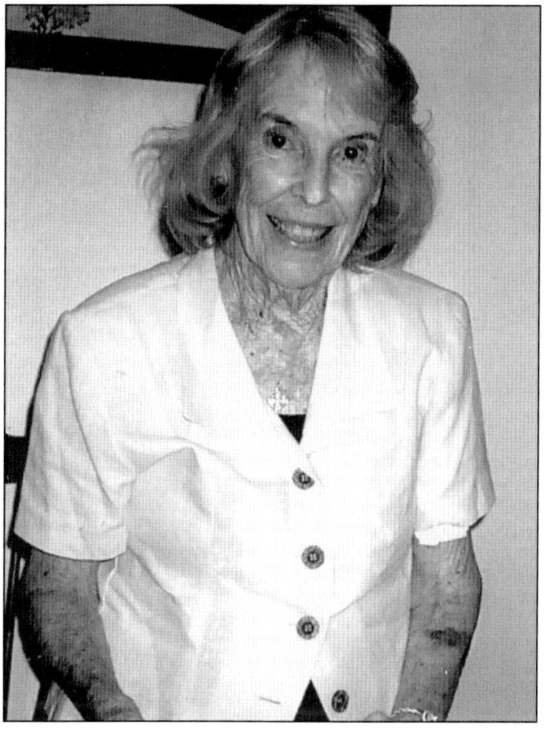

FIRST RELIGIOUS GATHERING RECALLED. Pioneer Dorothea Griffin remembered organizing the first Catholic mass in the only building larger than a home existing in Palm Coast. ITT lent their towered information center to be used as a place of worship to all religious organizations requesting it. For a while, Temple Beth Shalom held services at a house in the model center. Eventually, all denominations used the meeting room at the Palm Coast Yacht Club before constructing their own facilities.

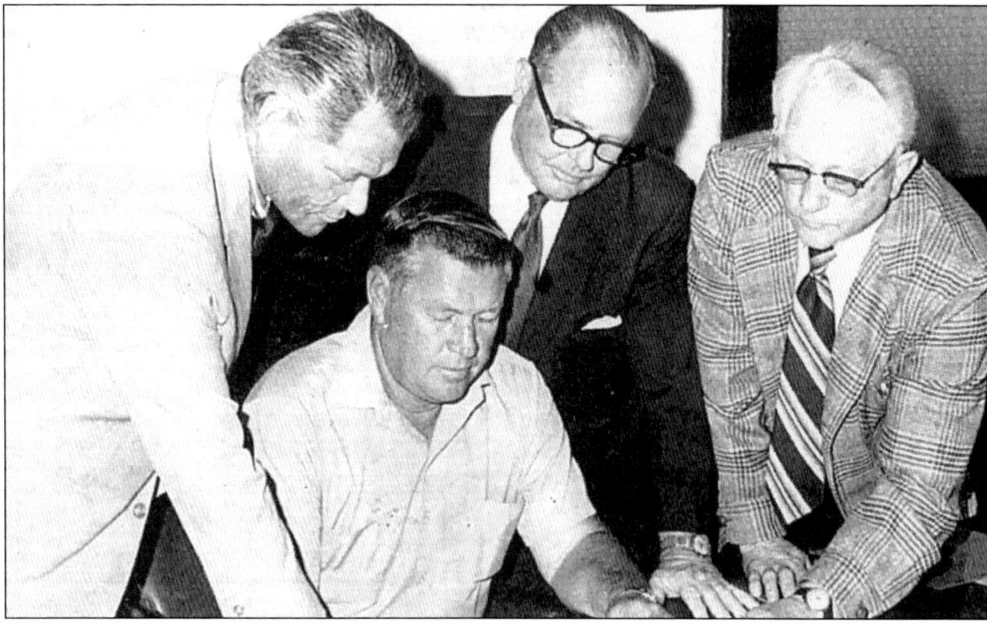

School Site Donation, December 1, 1971. By 1971, the management name for Palm Coast had been changed to International Telephone and Telegraph Rayonier Community Development Corporation (ICDC), and the relationship with the Levitt subsidiary had come to an end. The corporation contributed 40 acres of Palm Coast property to the school board in a ceremony at the Flagler County Courthouse. Pictured from left to right are Dr. Norman Young, ICDC president; Herschel King, vice chairman of the school site selection committee; and J.D. Perritt and Earnest Williams, both school board members. The donation was eventually used to establish the present site of Flagler/Palm Coast High School. This was the first of a number of ICDC donations to religious and civic organizations for the benefit of the community.

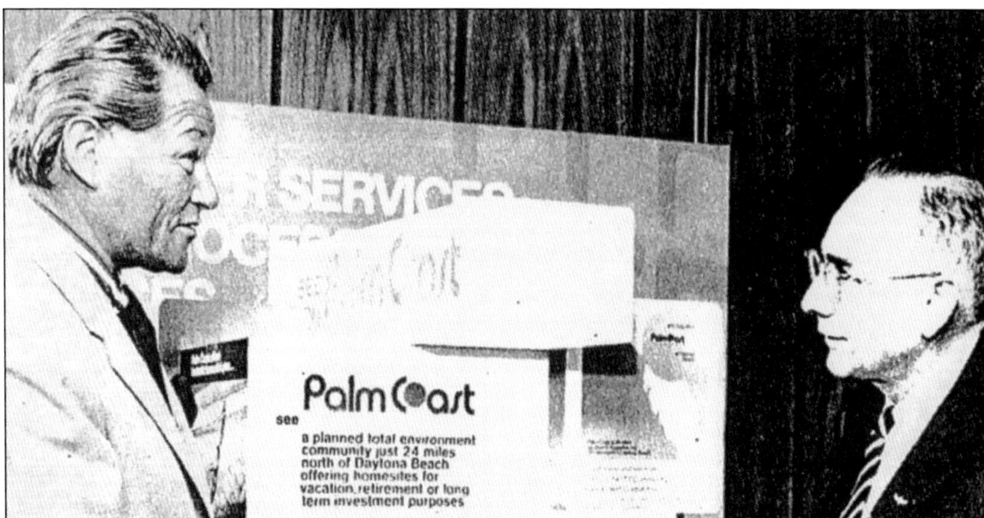

Corporate Pride in Palm Coast, 1972. Dr. Norman Young, president and chairman of ICDC, shows his boss Harold S. Geneen, both chairman and president of ITT, some of the beautiful facilities projected for Palm Coast at the senior corporations annual meeting.

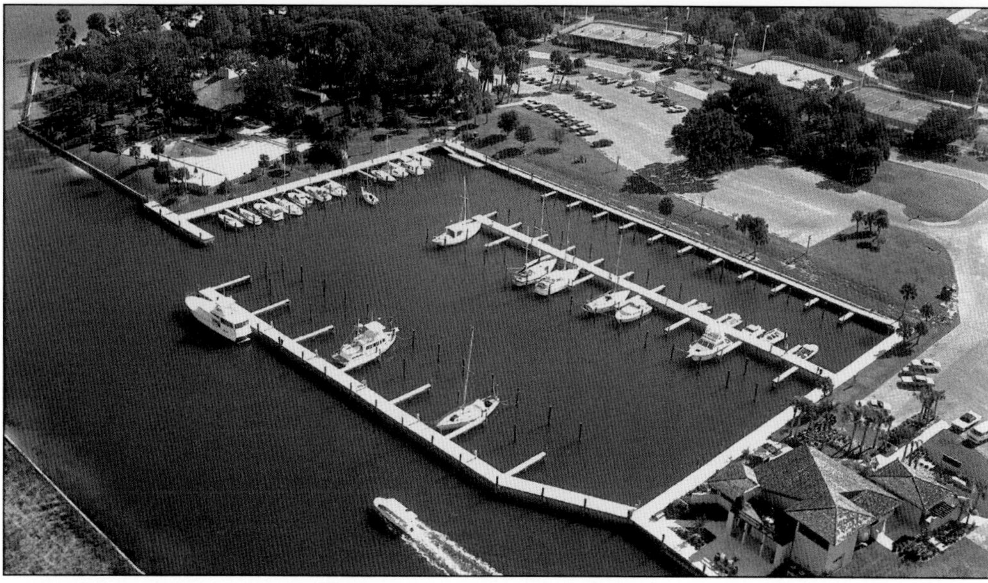

Palm Coast Yacht Club Opens, December 15, 1972. An exclusive party for residents marked the opening of the community's new hub. The marina launching ramp, outdoor pool, and tennis courts are visible in this aerial view, but the main building, which was to become the center of Palm Coast activity, is barely visible among the trees at the junction of the Intracoastal Waterway and the main canal. The club became the religious, political, and social center of the community, with civic associations and religious denominations holding services there. It was the site of parties, dances, social gatherings, art shows, and other entertainment. An early event was a fashion show attended by 200 Palm Coast ladies. By far, the most popular activity at the club was the sumptuous free Friday night buffet, open to all residents of the Palm Coast community, that ITT held as part of their continuing sales promotions to attract new buyers.

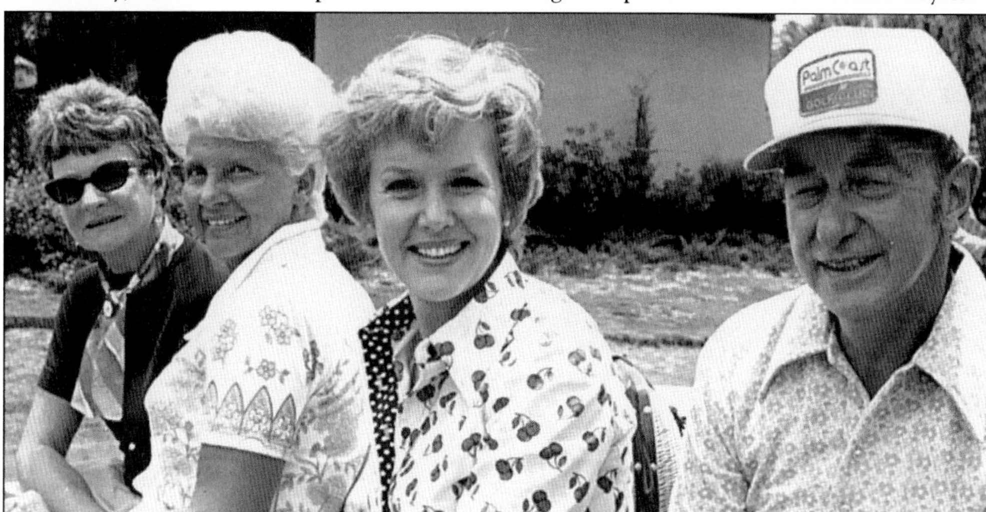

Celebrities Visit, 1972–1973. From the start, ICDC president Norman Young brought television, film, sports, and academic stars to Palm Coast to promote the area. Here Barbara Britton (second from right) takes a break during television filming to relax with residents Mrs. Vincent Moore, Mrs. William Collier, and Mr. Edward White. Other early visitors included John Forsythe, Merv Griffin, James Garner, and Duke Snyder.

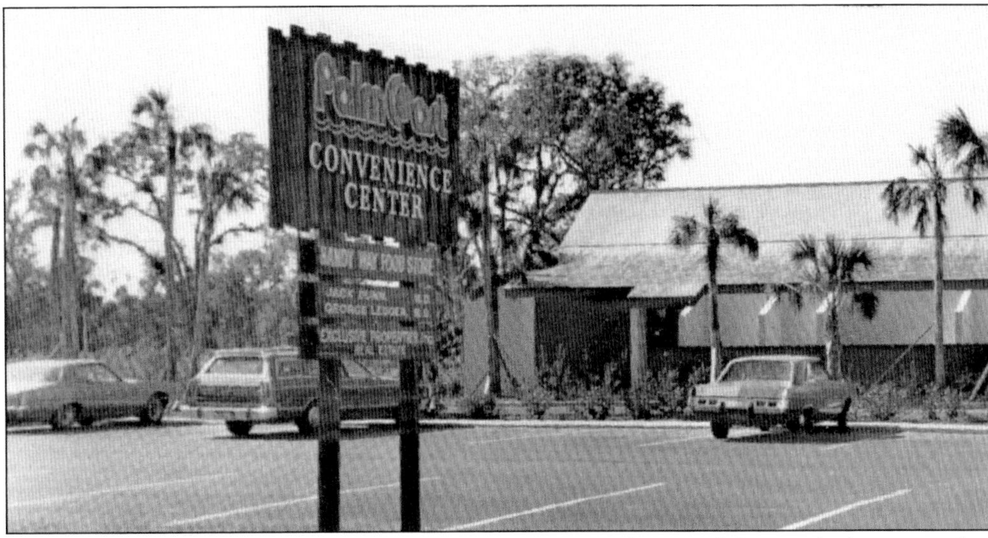

CONVENIENCE COMES TO THE FRONTIER, SEPTEMBER 1973. Pioneer life got a little easier when the Handy-Way Convenience store opened in the one-story building on Club House Drive near Palm Coast Parkway, just minutes from the core residential area. Now basic necessities, even frozen foods, and a place to pick up the mail were close at hand, eliminating the 12-mile drive previously required to serve daily needs. The store soon became the informal local meeting place for friends in the small but rapidly growing community. We are not sure of the identities of the ladies pictured below, but we know that Lee McGowan, our first post-mistress, was located there.

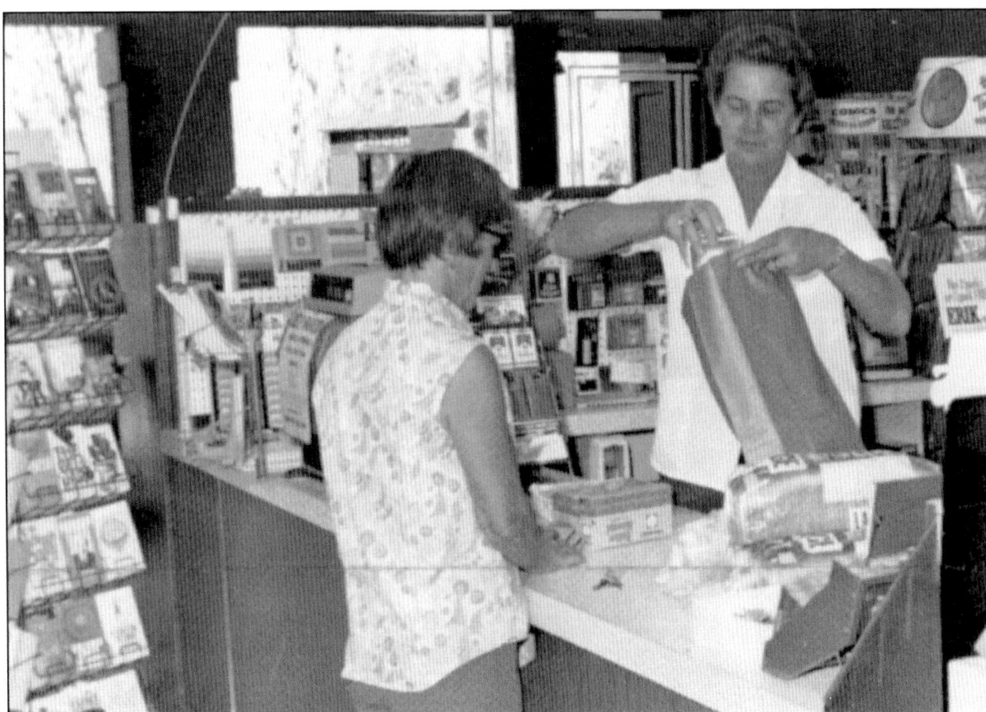

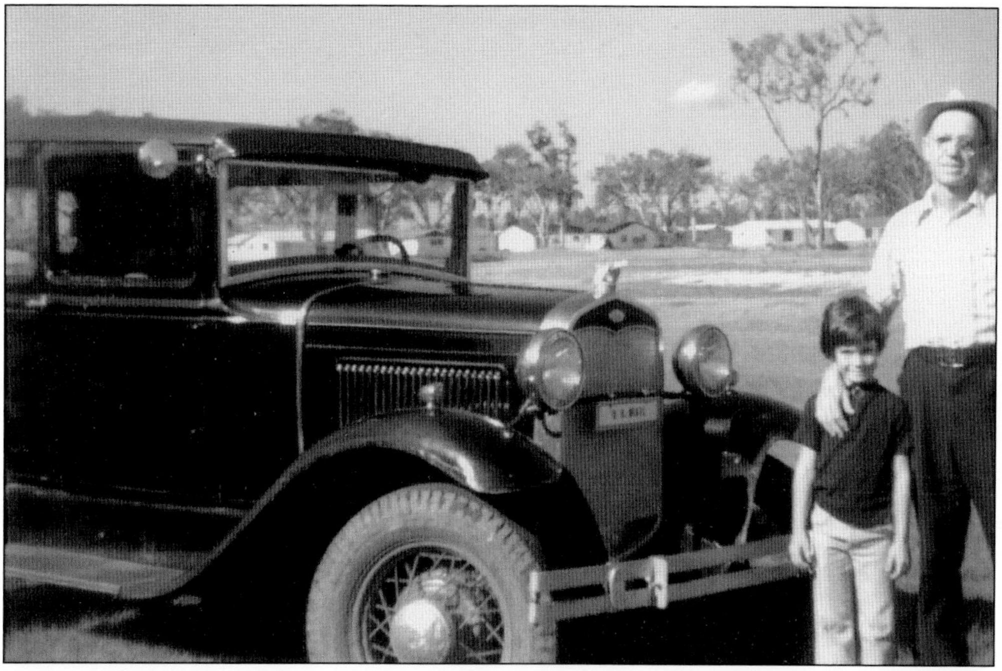

RAIN OR SHINE IN A MODEL A FORD. The postal pick up located in the Handy-Way was serviced for years by H.C. Cobb and his trusty mail coach, shown here with young Eddie Brown. The newly created drop off was part of a 34-mile, 6-days-a-week route for Palm Coast's first mailman.

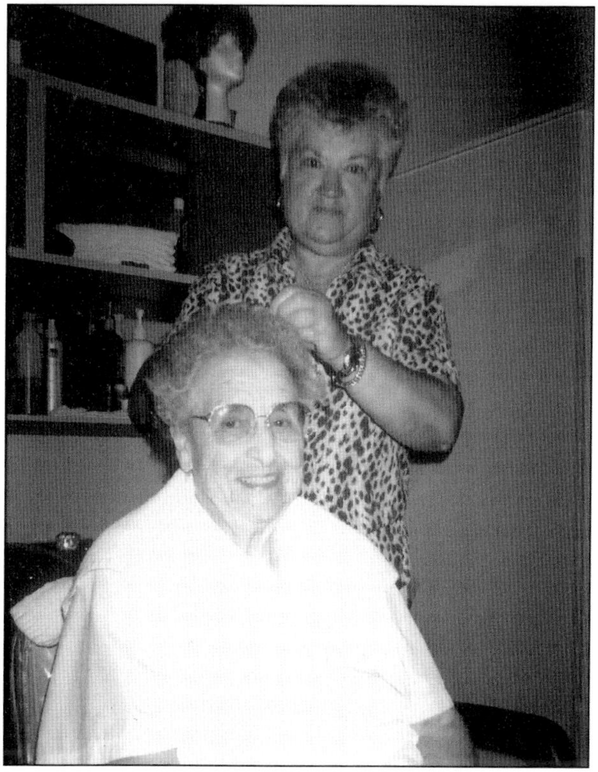

MORE FRONTIER CONVENIENCES, 1973. Sonya Toscano Sapp, shown with steady customer Carolyn Miskelly, opened her hair dressing business in one of the four offices located in the new convenience center. The other two were occupied by Jack Dunn, Palm Coast's first doctor, and by Exclusive Properties, the first non-ITT realtors. Sonya's Beauty Salon has been in continuous operation in Palm Coast ever since. Her salon is now located on Florida Park Drive.

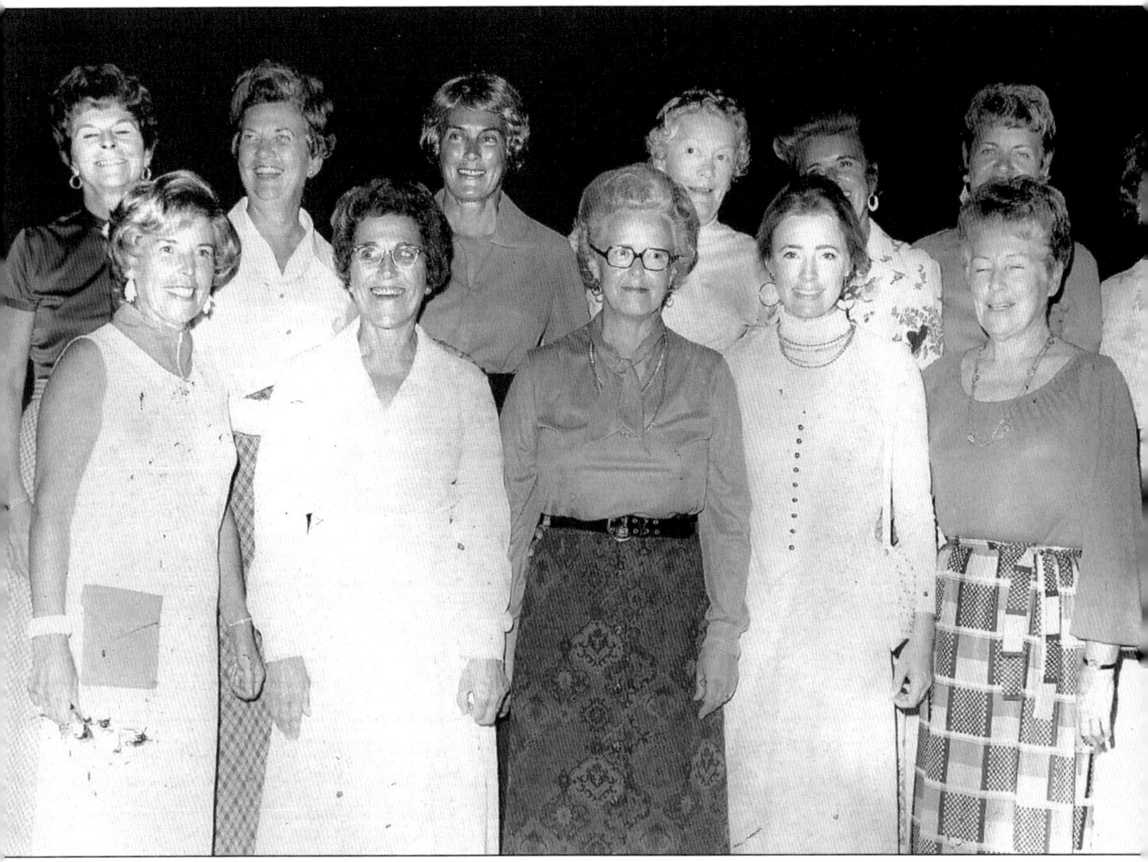

HEART ASSOCIATION WINE TASTING AT YACHT CLUB, 1974. On January 17, more than 300 people attended a gala wine tasting. It was an enormously successful fund-raiser for the American Heart Association. Pictured above are the original members of the association's Palm Coast Committee. Members pictured here from left to right are (front row) Dorothea Griffin, Edith Goldman or Olive Harkins, Wilma Weed, Gladys Mills, and Ruth Palmer; (back row) Lorraine Strandberg, Retia Arndt Sasso, Rae Ledger, Fran White, Marcie Lowe, Anita Rusche, and Naomi Otterbein.

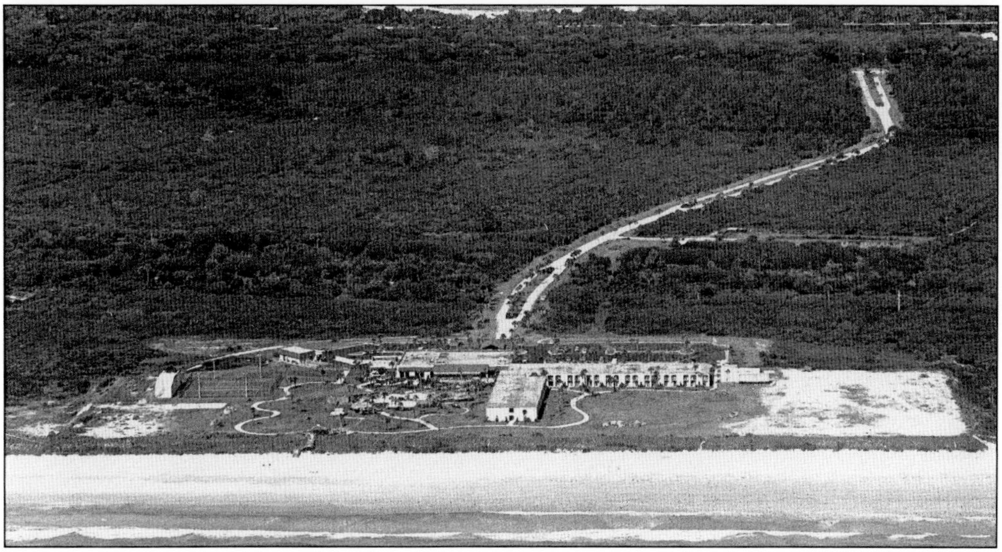

Sheraton Palm Coast Inn, February 1973. With the opening of a 132-room luxury motel on eight beautifully landscaped acres in a tropical paradise right on the Atlantic Ocean, another jewel was added to the crown of promises made by ITT regarding the Palm Coast community. The inn was located at the end of a scenic drive to the ocean from a gated entrance on route A1A and stood at the present location of the Hammock Dunes Club House.

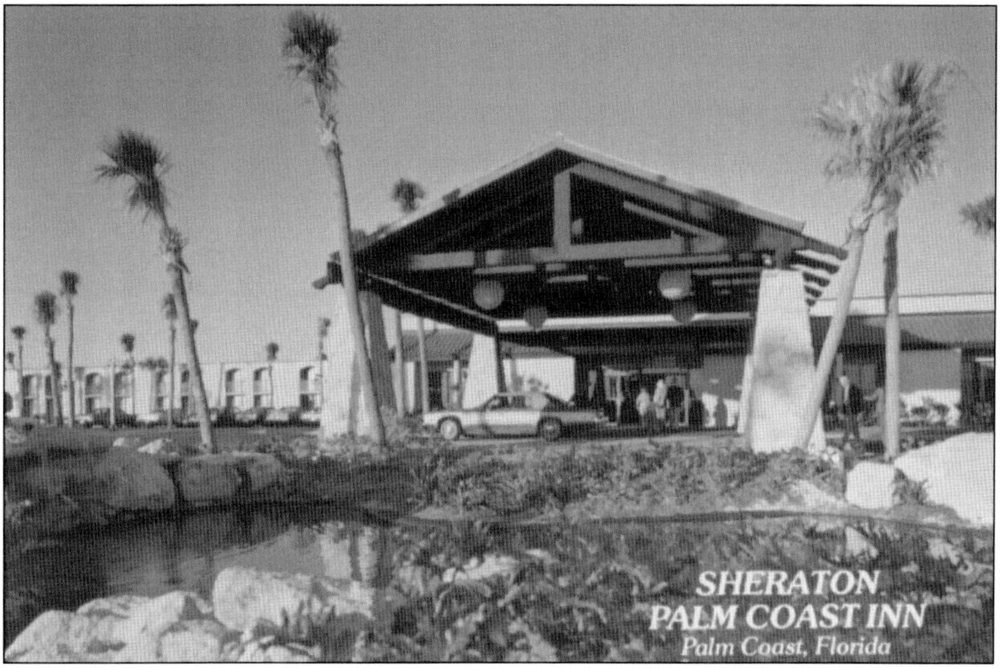

Front Entrance. The Sheraton by the Ocean was built in a Spanish Mission architectural style with a canopied entrance and liberal use of coquina rock. The inn also had a fine dining room that seated approximately 120 people and overlooked the reflecting pools, waterfalls, dunes, beach, and ocean. A banquet room, lounge, bar, and gift shop rounded out the well-planned design for easy living to show off the Florida lifestyle to impress prospective Northern buyers with the desirability of settling in Palm Coast.

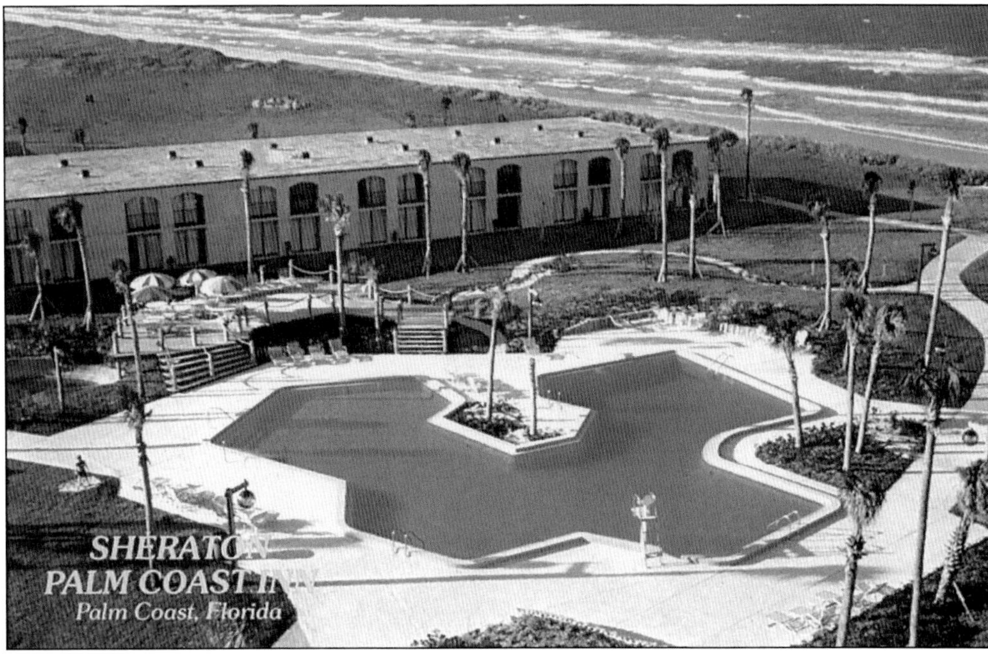

POOL AND SURROUNDINGS. Outside the inn was a free-form swimming pool with a Cyprus wood sundeck. There were overhanging Japanese water gardens and exquisitely sculptured coquina rock gardens that added a peaceful look to the entire scene. Nearby, a series of reflecting pools were spanned by picturesque bridges and three water falls.

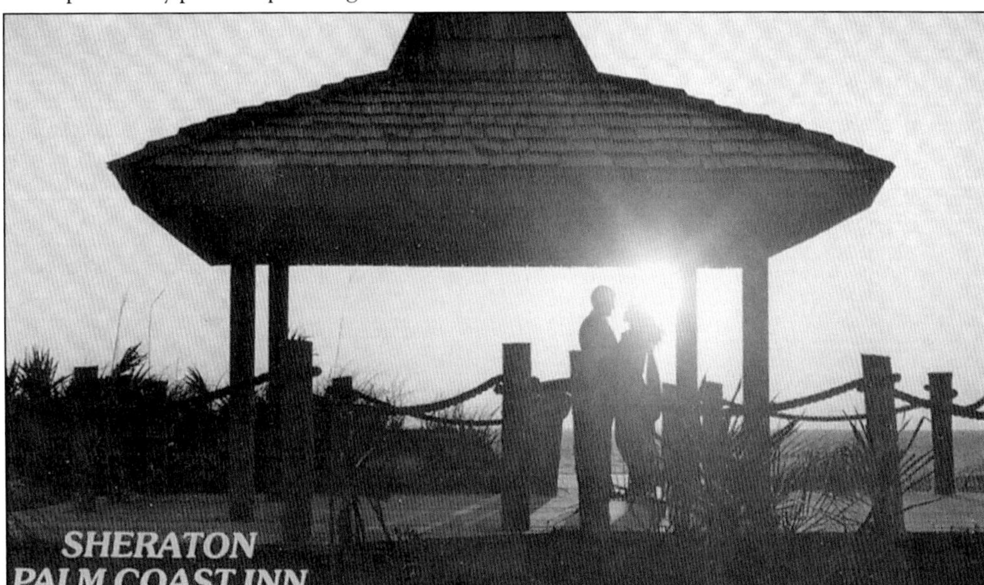

GAZEBO TO OCEAN. There was a large gazebo overlooking the ocean for enjoying the sea air, relaxing in the shade, and crossing the sand dune to the ocean. For those who like to get close to nature, there are still miles and miles of beach in either direction inhabited by egrets, pelicans, and sandpipers. The original gazebo ocean access is the only structure of the original Sheraton Inn that is still standing. Everything else, including the pool, was completely demolished to make way for the Hammock Dunes development.

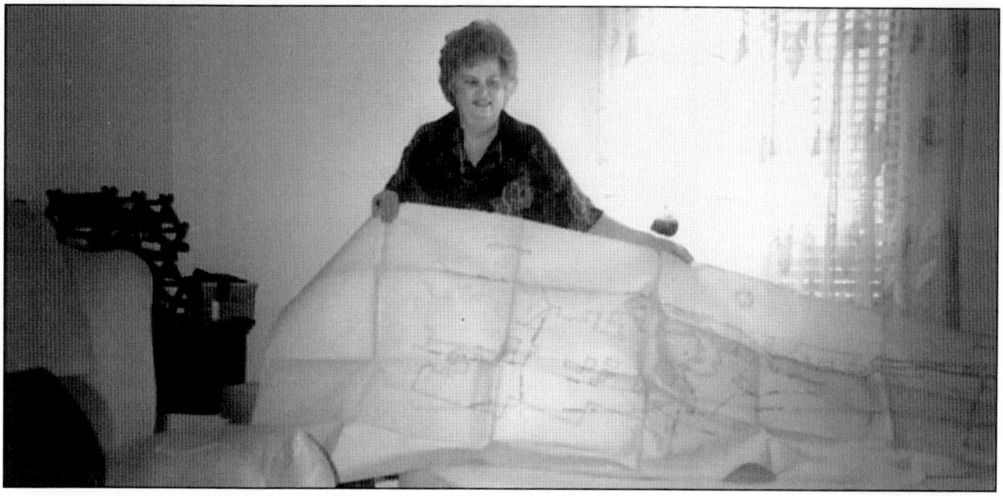

Four Palm Coast Residents Remember the Old Sheraton. Janice Brink. ITT's primary use for the luxury motel by the ocean was to accommodate and impress prospective buyers of home sites in Palm Coast. Most early purchasers came to the area in the following manner: They saw an advertisement in northern, urban, area media markets to call a local ITT "outside representative" to arrange a presentation showing the Palm Coast offering. Janice Brink is shown here holding a well-worn map of property available for sale. She and husband Spencer sold real estate in Fairfax, Virginia, in 1986. Reasons given to consider purchase were listed as lowest interest rates in years (1986), excellent growth and development in the community, no state income tax, outstanding rental market, and the finest amenities, including golf, tennis, boating, and fishing. At the presentation they offered their clients a weekend with a fully guided tour including round trip air transportation, two nights at the Sheraton, two breakfasts, and two dinners for $129 per person.

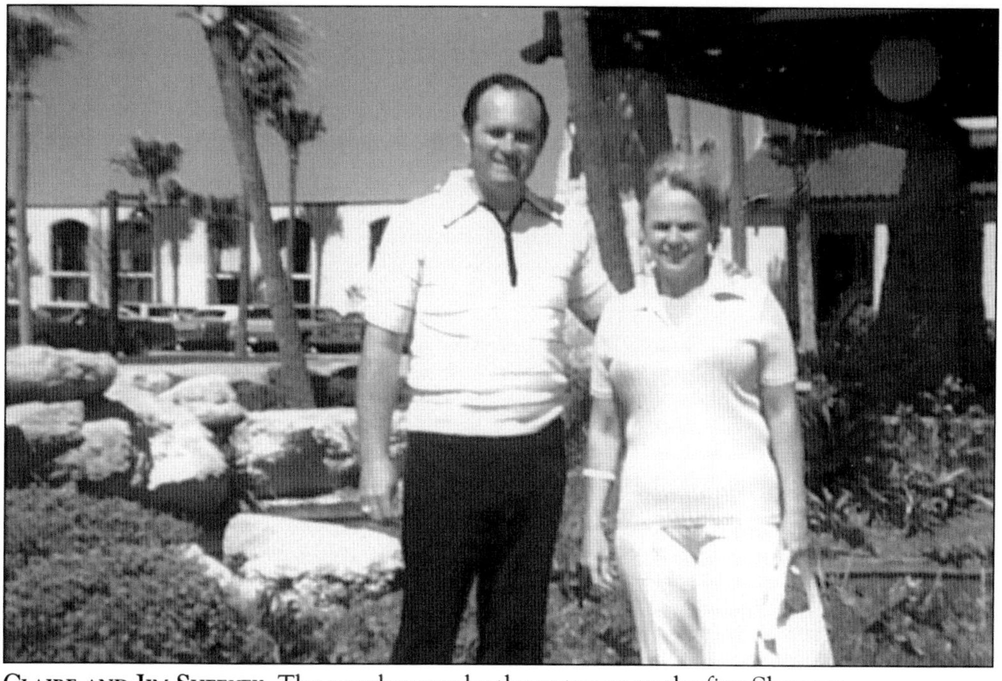

Claire and Jim Sheekey. The couple poses by the entrance to the first Sheraton.

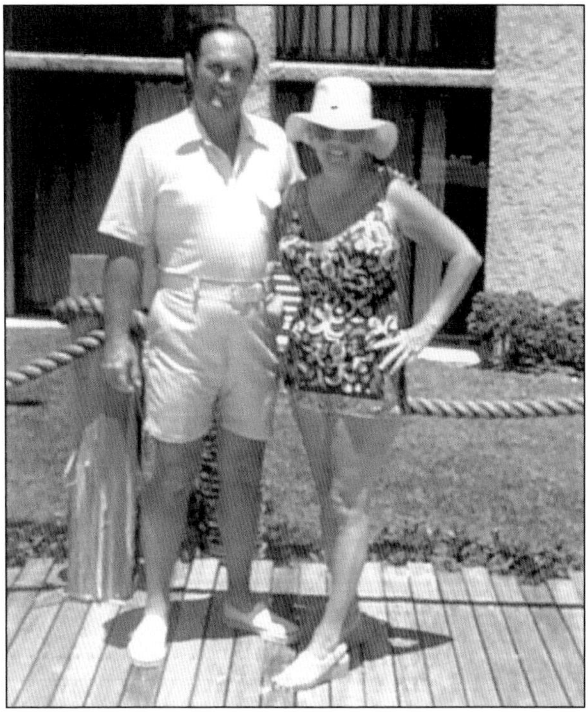

Claire and Jim Sheekey. Shown here outside their Sheraton room are these early Palm Coast residents. The hotel interior was designed to give visitors the Florida "feel" with three six-foot sea shell chandeliers in the lobby, rattan furniture throughout, and white stucco walls with sky blue ceilings in the rooms. Claire and Jim are active members of the City of Palm Coast Historical Society.

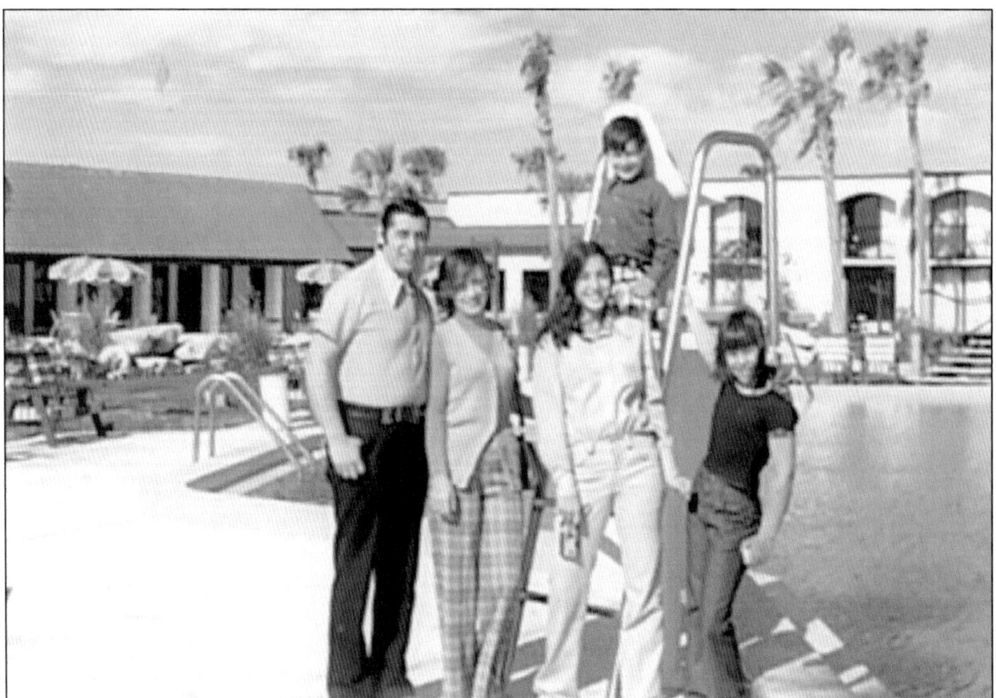

The Lo Monaco Family. Al and Vinnie and their children Linda, Gerard, and Donna are pictured enjoying the pool and the outside environment. In the evening, extensive outdoor lighting helped create another Florida magic atmosphere. They presently enjoy living and swimming in the Grand Haven Community.

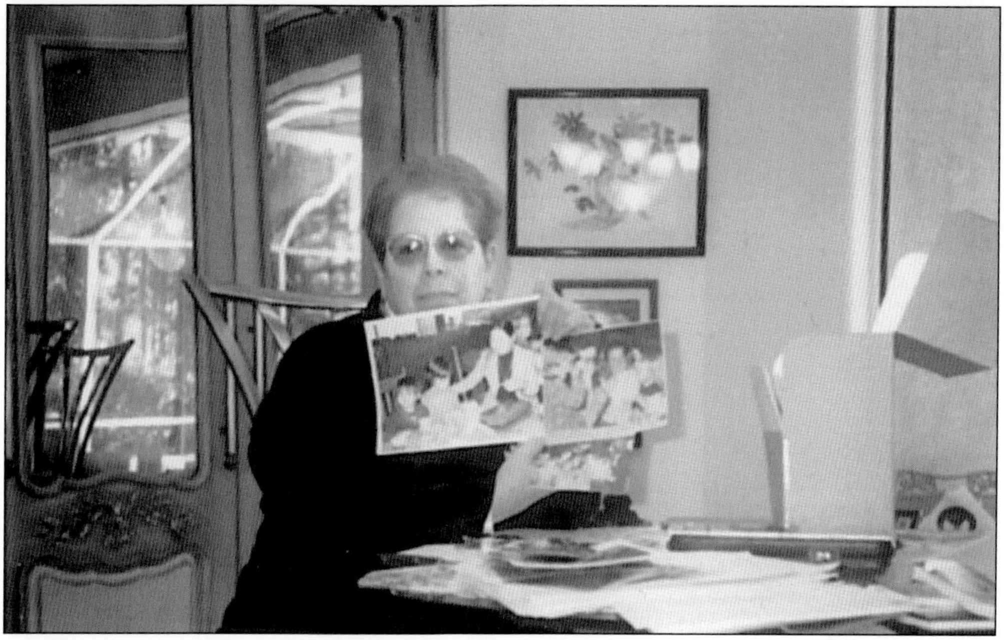

BARBARA SUE GODKIN. Her son Mason, one of the first babies born in Palm Coast, was conceived at the Sheraton by the Ocean. In the photograph she holds an early picture of Naomi Otterbein, which she contributed along with a wealth of historical knowledge and other material regarding Palm Coast's history. Barbara still teaches in the Flagler Public Schools. Five couples stayed at the Sheraton and all five are still active participants in the Palm Coast community today.

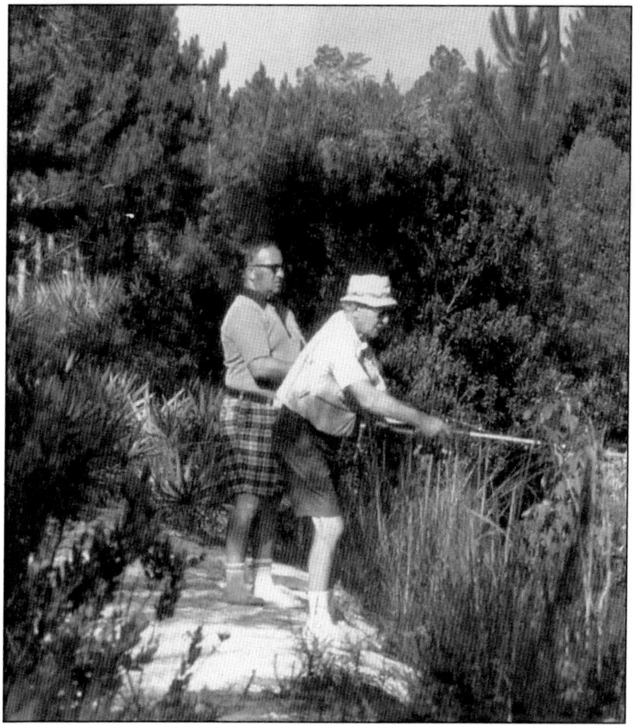

FIRST CONDOMINIUMS, 1974. ITT contracted with independent builders V.J. Medney and Bert Goldstein to privately build a 124 unit, two story garden complex named Shangri-La buffered by trees and landscaping from the Palm Coast Parkway. In the photo, Bert is shown with his friend, Nat Levinson fishing in the lake at the center of the site.

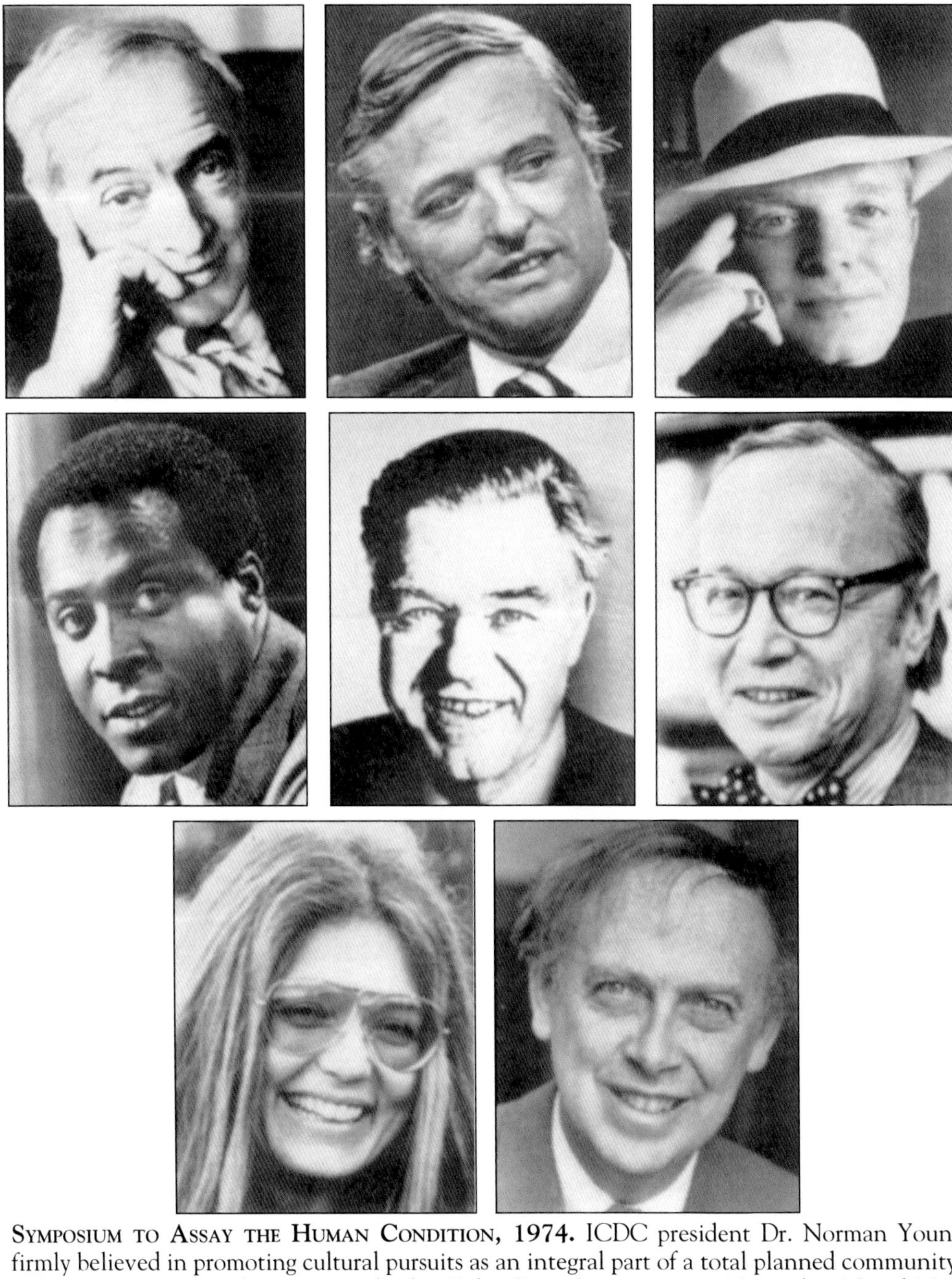

Symposium to Assay the Human Condition, 1974. ICDC president Dr. Norman Young firmly believed in promoting cultural pursuits as an integral part of a total planned community. In his announcement about staging the first Palm Coast Symposium on November 15 and 16 at the Sheraton, he cited, "fulfillment of our social and cultural commitment to the community" and that "a new town needs new ideas" as a rationale for holding it. With a spectacular array of panelists and strong television coverage by Merv Griffen, the symposium focused international attention on Palm Coast. Among the outstanding participants were Saul Bellow, William F. Buckley Jr., Truman Capote, Vernon E. Jordan Jr., Dr. Gunnar Myrdal, Arthur M. Schlesinger Jr., Gloria Steinem, and Dr. James Watson.

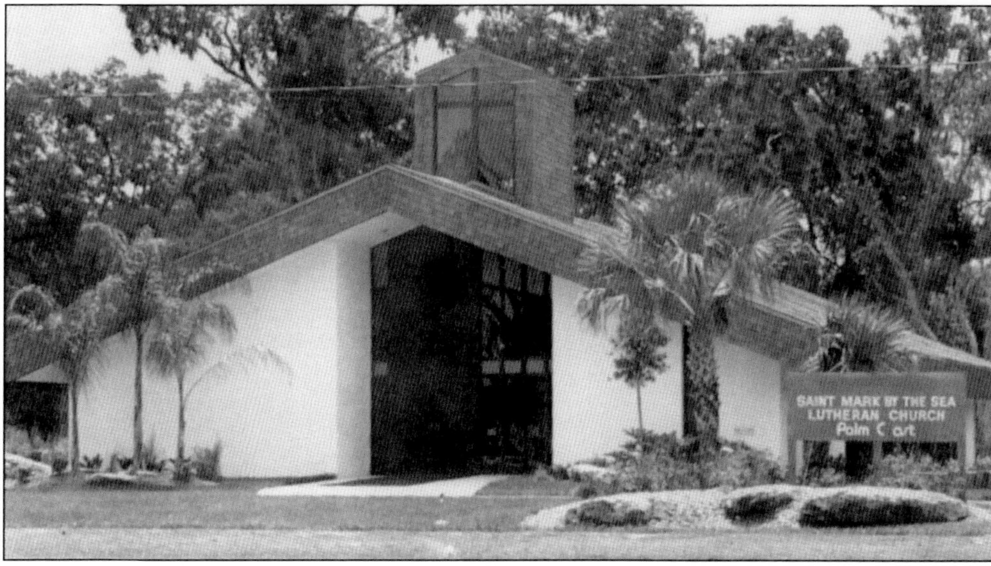

PALM COAST'S FIRST CHURCH, JULY 4, 1976. St. Mark by the Sea Lutheran Church was completed on July 3 and its first service was held on the morning of the Bicentennial 4th of July. Approximately 425 people attended the inaugural service, which was conducted by Rev. Marcus F. Otterbein. "Pastor Marc," as he was affectionately called by Palm Coasters of many religious affiliations, had been conducting interdenominational services at the Yacht Club since Easter 1973. His wife, Naomi, authored an informative and thoroughly charming illustrated *History of Flagler County* for use by students in the elementary schools.

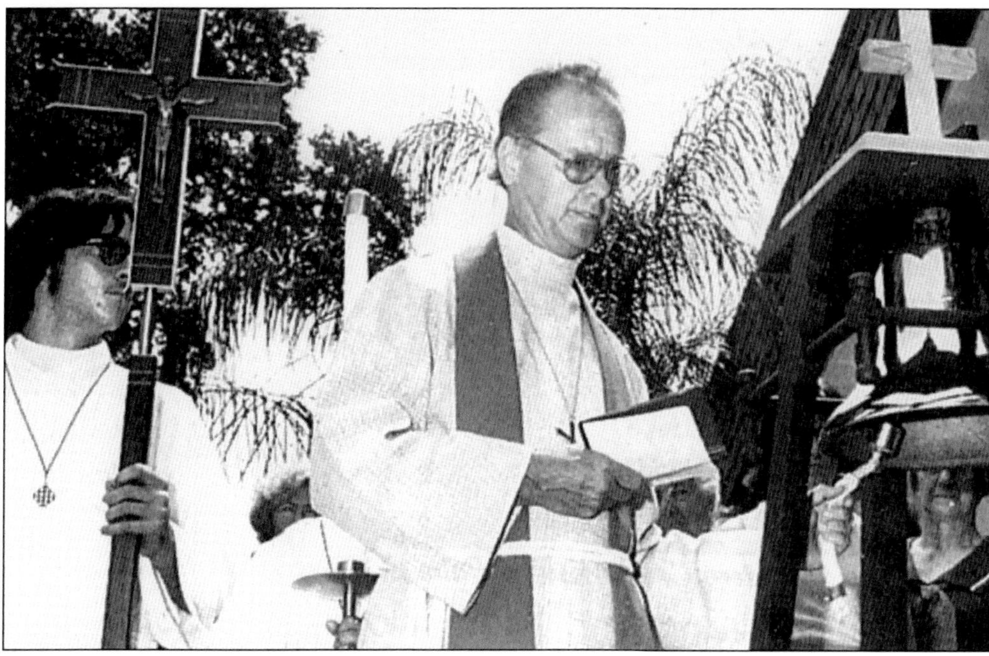

PASTOR MARC. Reverend Otterbein continued to keep his church's doors open to Baptist, Catholic, Jewish, and those of other denominations while they constructed their own buildings. His death from a heart attack in March of 1979 brought grief and a deep sense of loss to the entire community.

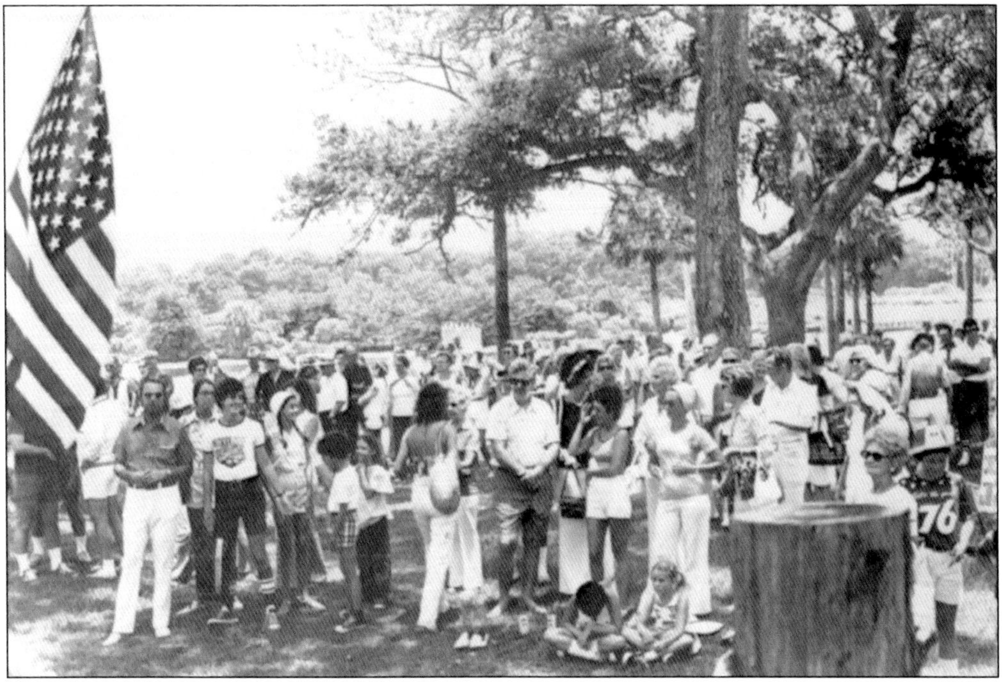

Bicentennial Celebration. More than 500 Palm Coasters celebrated our nation's 200th birthday with a day-long 4th of July picnic sponsored by the civic association and held on the grounds of the Yacht Club. Young and old enjoyed games and contests and food and soft drinks arranged by the Lions Club. In the evening, many of them drove 13 miles to Flagler Beach to enjoy the 23rd year of fireworks display at the pier.

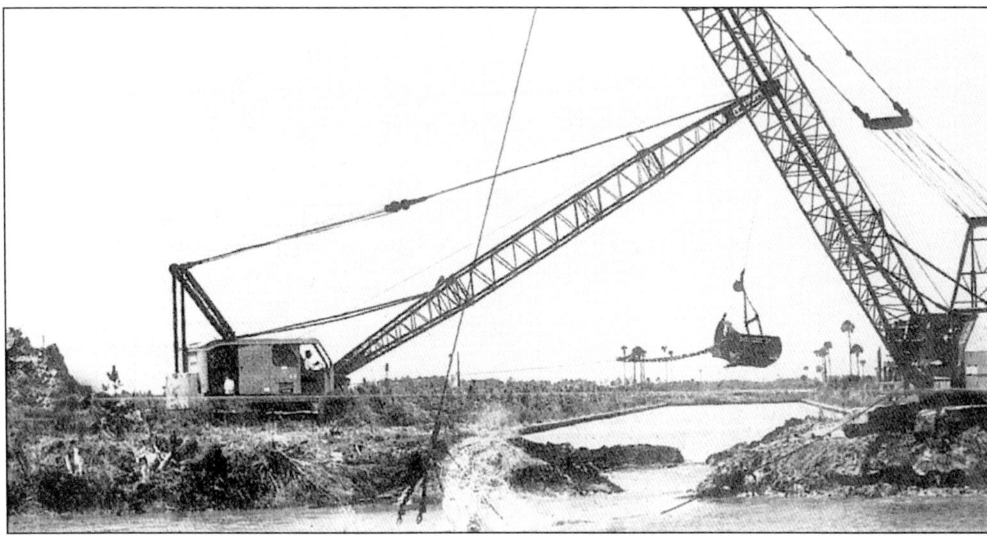

Pulling the Plug, 1976. The Army Corps of Engineers gave ICDC authority to remove the earthen dams on the eight 80-foot-wide finger canals branching from the 125-foot-wide club house waterway. That main canal runs from the Intracoastal Waterway leading past what was then the Palm Coast Yacht Club, the Welcome Center, and the newly built Club House Condominiums connecting to a 15-mile system of canals, with a minimum 8-foot center depth, including the Cochese and Cimmaron systems.

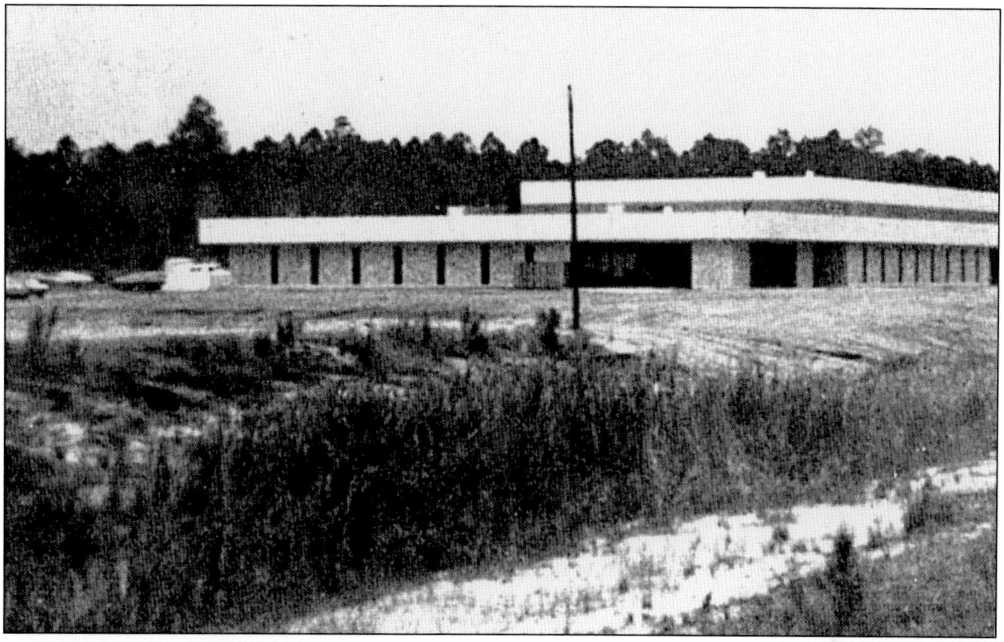

First Industry, 1977. The Palm Coast West Industrial Park got its first tenant when ITT Decca Marine, the U.S. distributor of world-famed radar and other marine electronic equipment, located there on July 25. The opening of the 35,000-square-foot headquarters, office, and warehouse was expected to create some jobs for area residents seeking employment.

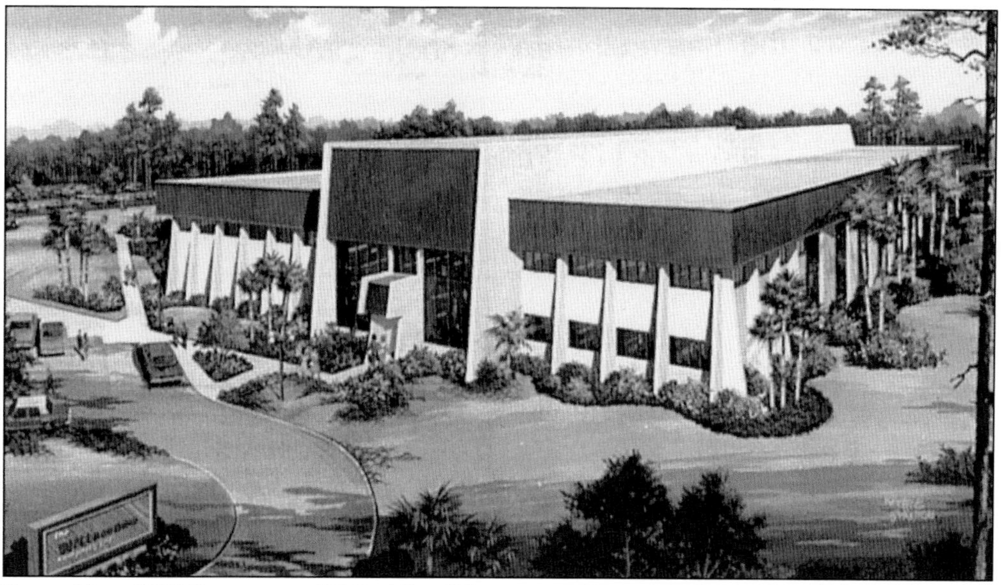

First Non-ITT Industry, 1979. The Wittemann Company, Inc. of Buffalo, New York, manufacturers of carbon dioxide processing equipment for the beer and beverage industry, announced that it would construct a new office and plant facility in the Palm Coast Industrial Park in Palm Coast. ICDC president Alan Smolen, Wittemann Company president Joseph Gruber, and ICDC vice president of marketing Lee Shur signed the contract. Architect Lynn Ten Eycks designed the strikingly beautiful building, which was completed and occupied the following year.

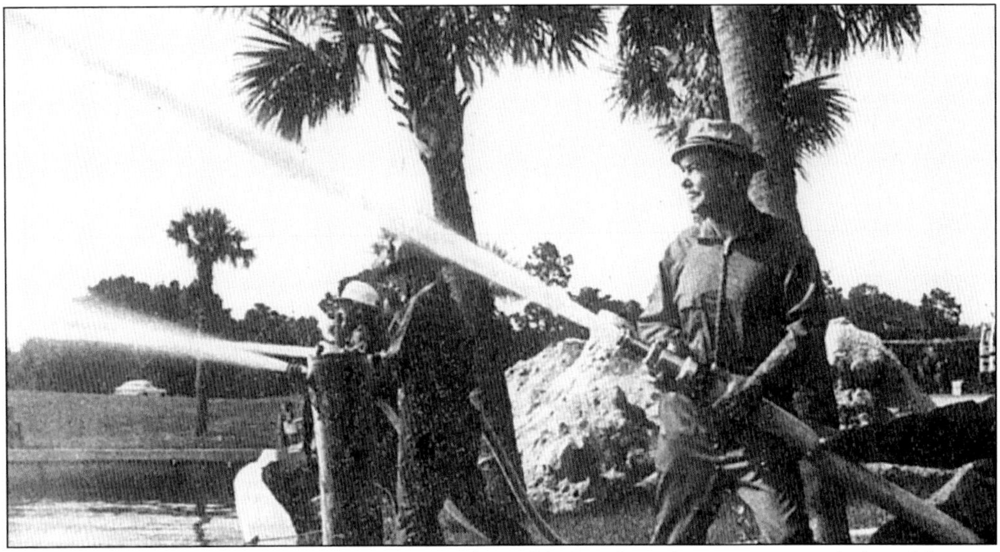

Volunteer Firemen, 1973–1977. A number of Palm Coast's pioneers, including Vincent Moore and Charles Konopasek, were experienced retired fire fighters. They organized and administered a volunteer fire department (VFD) to work closely with the Flagler County Sheriff's Department, ambulance service, and the U.S. Forestry Service to provide emergency protection to the community. From the beginning, ICDC had provided a pumper, five rescue vehicles, emergency equipment, and training for VFD personnel. In 1976 Palm Coast voters agreed overwhelmingly to establish a fire district, and ICDC donated the land and money to build the Palm Coast Emergency Services Building located on an acre of land at the intersection of Palm Coast Parkway and Club House Drive. It was completed in 1977. The spirit and fellowship of the VFD is evident in the hours spent at the fire house in cleaning and continuous training. An auxiliary group called the Fire-Belles aided with community service to make Palm Coast a safer place for everyone.

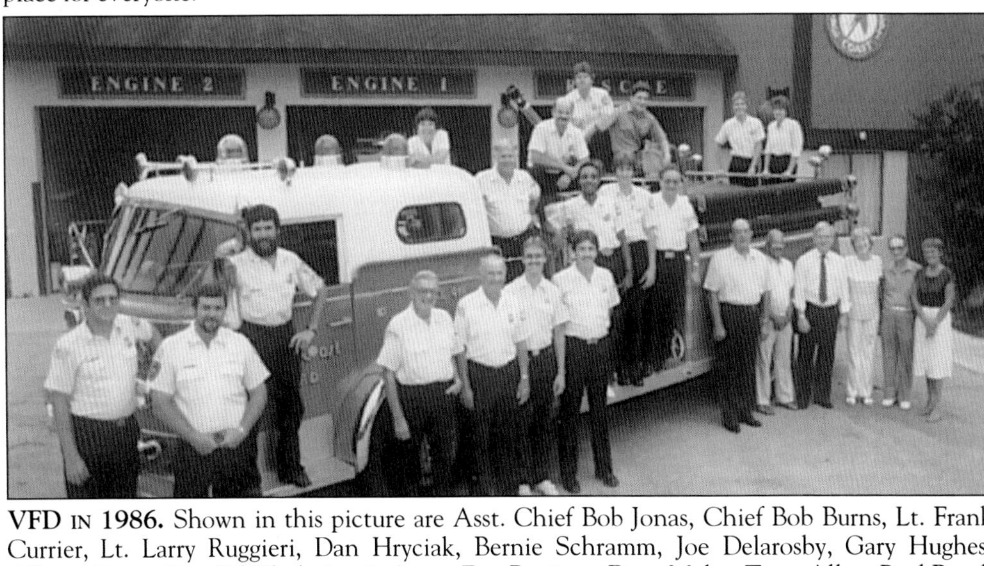

VFD in 1986. Shown in this picture are Asst. Chief Bob Jonas, Chief Bob Burns, Lt. Frank Currier, Lt. Larry Ruggieri, Dan Hryciak, Bernie Schramm, Joe Delarosby, Gary Hughes, Allyson Zampolino, Ed Clark, Lewis Ames, Eric Register, Dave Malta, Tony Allen, Paul Bond, Mike Ricci, Bob Delarosby, Donna King, Dan Nutzul, Ed Reeks, Ken Hansen, Jane Mikido, S.G. Gallo, and Joan Goess.

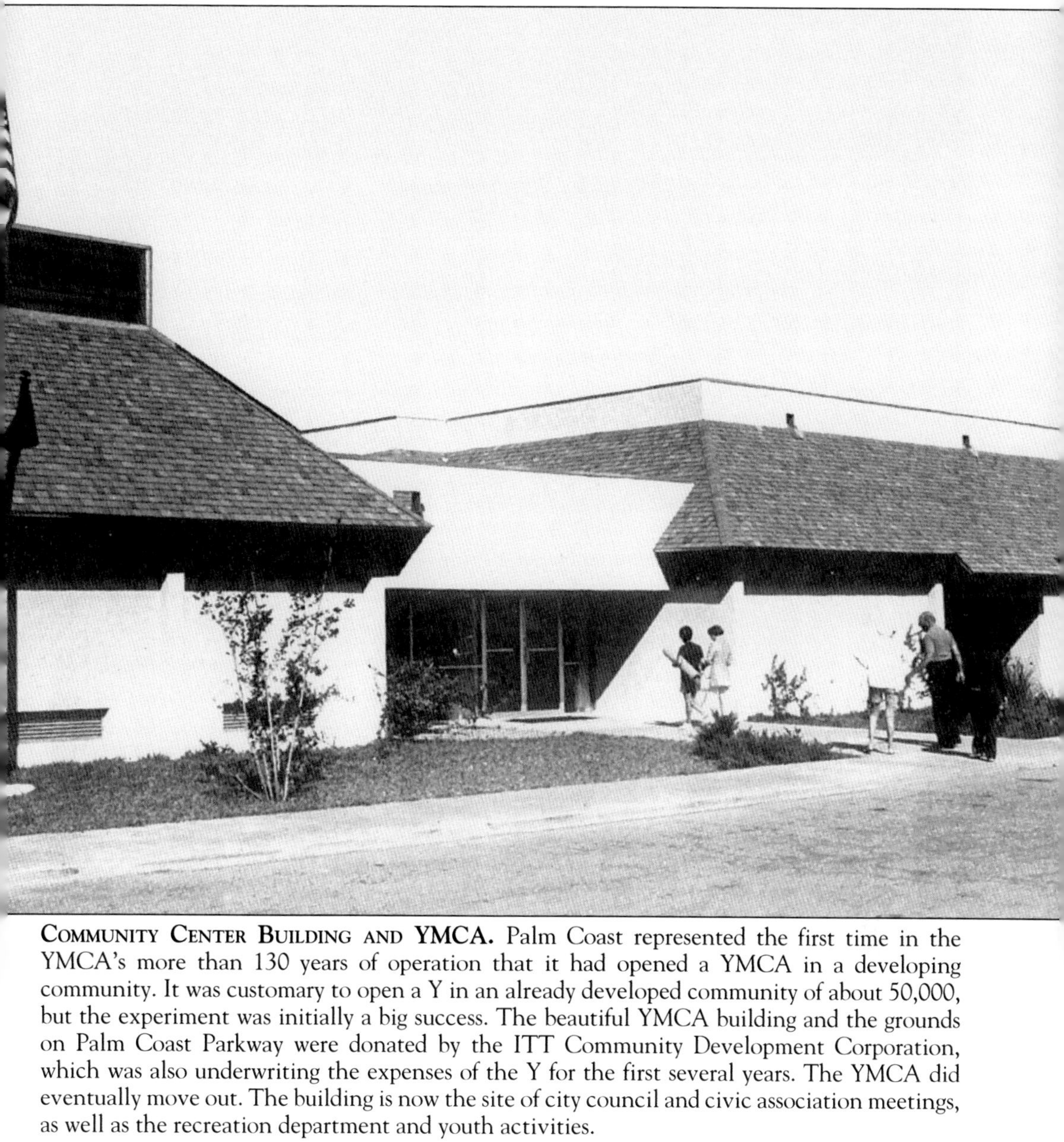

COMMUNITY CENTER BUILDING AND YMCA. Palm Coast represented the first time in the YMCA's more than 130 years of operation that it had opened a YMCA in a developing community. It was customary to open a Y in an already developed community of about 50,000, but the experiment was initially a big success. The beautiful YMCA building and the grounds on Palm Coast Parkway were donated by the ITT Community Development Corporation, which was also underwriting the expenses of the Y for the first several years. The YMCA did eventually move out. The building is now the site of city council and civic association meetings, as well as the recreation department and youth activities.

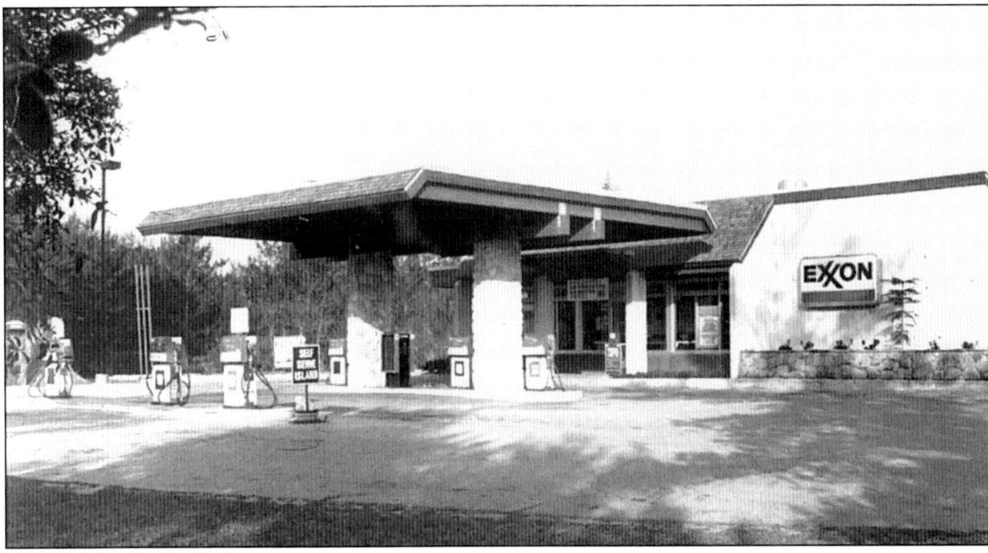

First Service Station, 1978. John Mandarano, a resident since 1975, purchased an out parcel from ICDC and opened one of the community's first private commercial establishments at the Palm Coast Parkway entrance of what would become the Publix/Eckerd's Shopping Complex in the following year. Parkway Exxon opened in February, sporting a unique stucco/coquina exterior that was visually attractive and designed to blend in with the area.

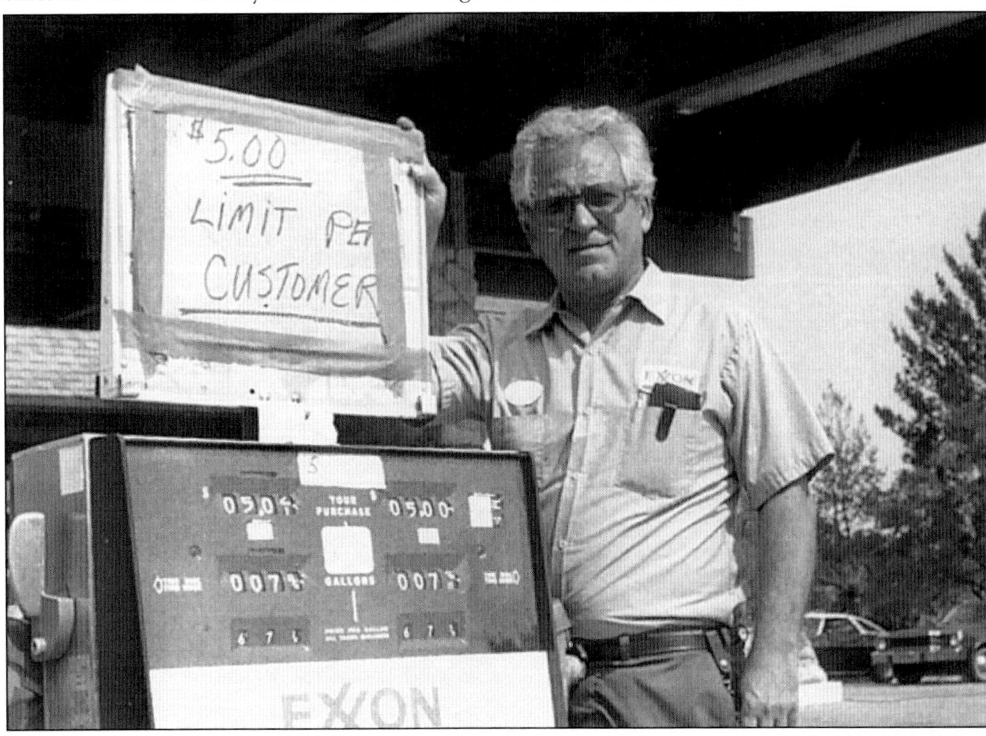

John Mandarano. John, pictured here during the March 1979 gas rationing, offered full auto servicing including providing an expert mechanic. Later he pioneered the first convenience market, gas station, and car wash combination at his Shell station on Old Kings Road and built and owned Coquina Lanes, as well as other businesses in Palm Coast.

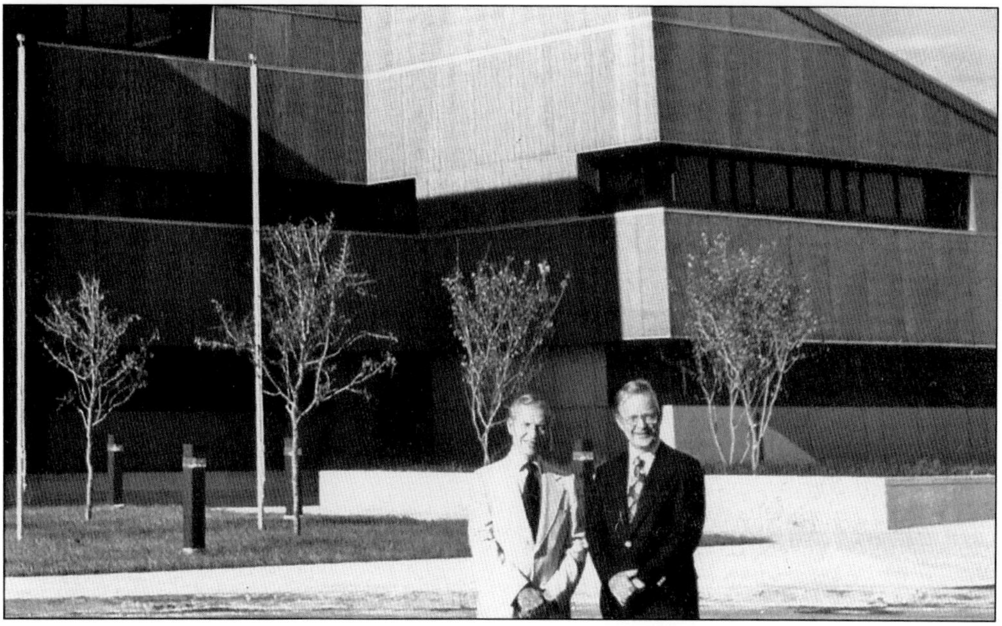

ICDC Locates in Palm Coast, 1979. On August 25 more than 1,500 guests, including Florida lieutenant governor Jim Williams, attended the Grand Opening of ITT Community Development Corporations Headquarters Building at 1 Corporate Drive off St. Joe Road. The ceremony is pictured here with President Alan Smolen and Vice President Gordon Murtough in front. The move fulfilled a promise of full commitment to the community that had been made by President Smolen upon his arrival in 1975. The building currently houses adult eduction, businesses, and a chamber of commerce branch office.

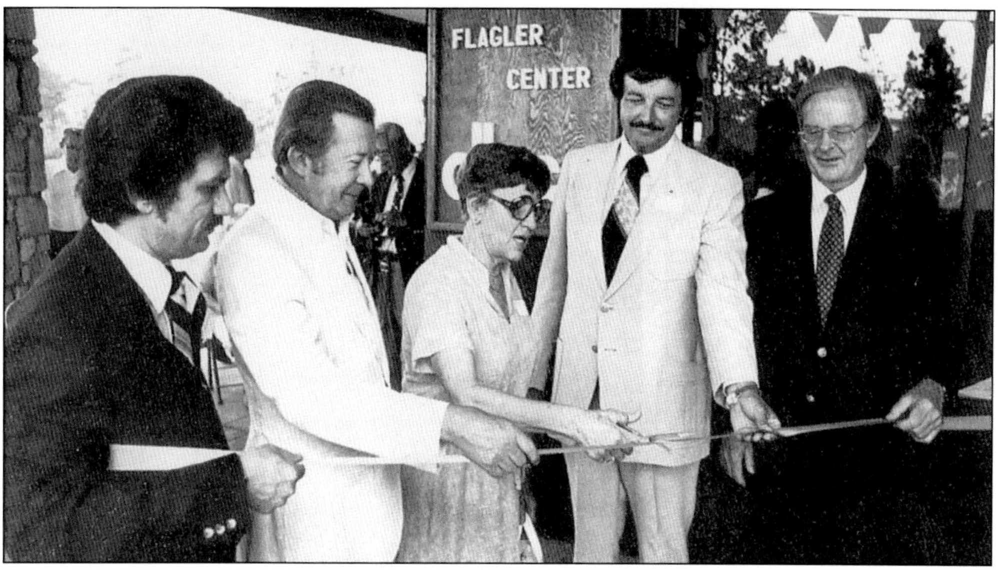

Higher Education, 1979. Daytona Beach Community College opened its Palm Coast Campus in the shopping center on August 14. The open house drew a large attendance. Student enrollment at the time was 365. Joining the ribbon cutting were Charles Polk, DBCC president; Merhl Shoemaker, trustee; Jeanne Goddard, chairman; John McKenney, trustee; and Gordon Murtaugh, senior vice president and director of business development at ICDC.

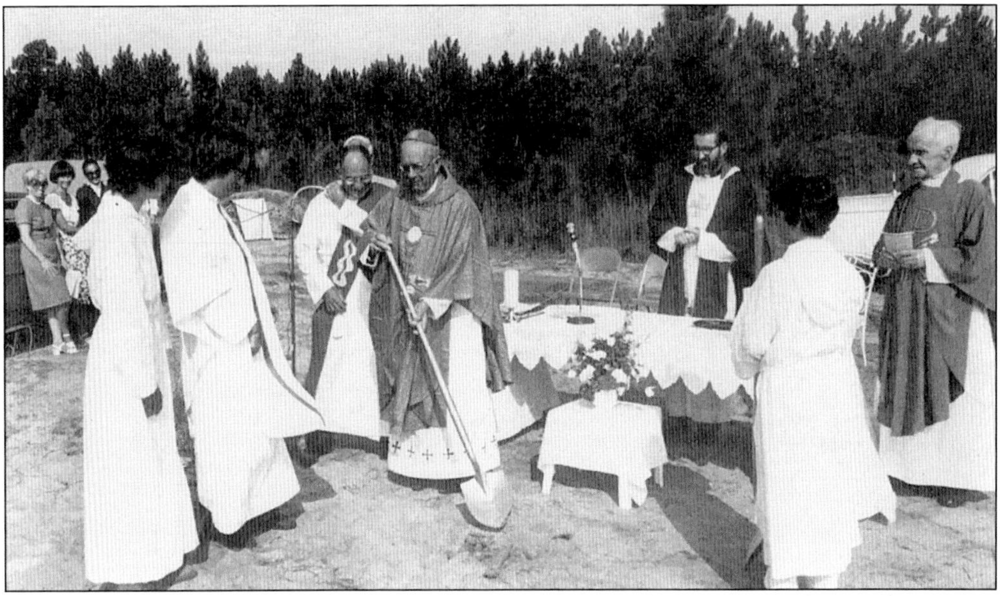

CATHOLIC CHURCH. Groundbreaking was held on September 3, 1978, for Mother Seton Catholic Church to be constructed on a 100-acre site on the east side of Belle Terre Parkway. Pictured in the Celebration Mass are First Pastor Thomas Cody, Deacon Charles Karr, Bishop Paul F. Tanner, Fr. Roland Julien, Monsignor Leo Gildea, and two unidentified altar servers. The first mass in the 600 seat multipurpose church and social hall was on Mother's Day, May 13, 1979. The old church became part of an education complex and the present Saint Elizabeth Ann Seton Church was dedicated on January 22, 1994.

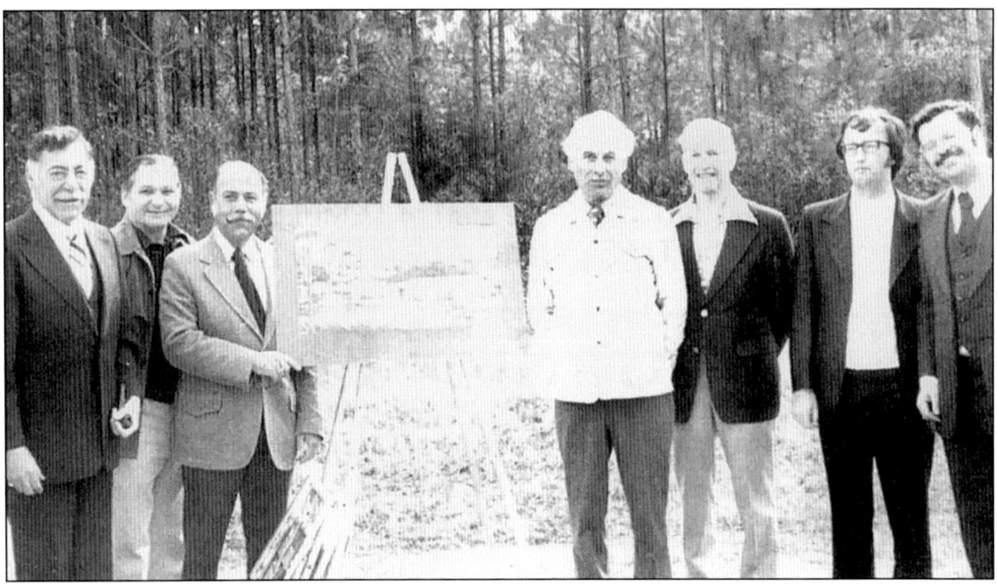

TEMPLE. It was a red-letter day on March 12, 1979, when approximately 60 families gathered at 40 Wellington Drive. President Manny Zuckerman turned over the first shovel of dirt to break ground for the start of Temple Beth Shalom. Ceremony participants pictured above are Joe Bolton, Tim Legakis, Manny Zuckerman, David Siegel, Alan Smolen, Father Cody, and Rabbi Genn.

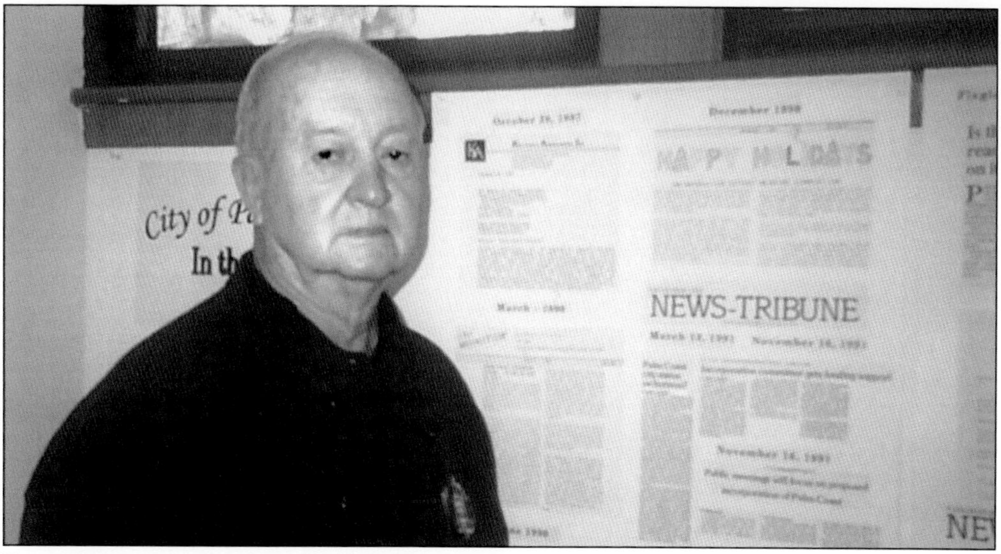

FIRST STEP TOWARDS SELF GOVERNMENT, 1979. In April, the first meeting of the newly appointed advisory board for the East Flagler Service District took place. Attending members were William Donnelly, chair; Raymond Cobb, vice-chair; Morey Englander; Robert Engle; Gary Walters; and George Weeks. The advisory board was to make recommendations regarding the governance of Palm Coast to the Flagler County Commission. Chairman Bill Donnelly is pictured at an open house at City Hall of the newly incorporated city of Palm Coast in the year 2000.

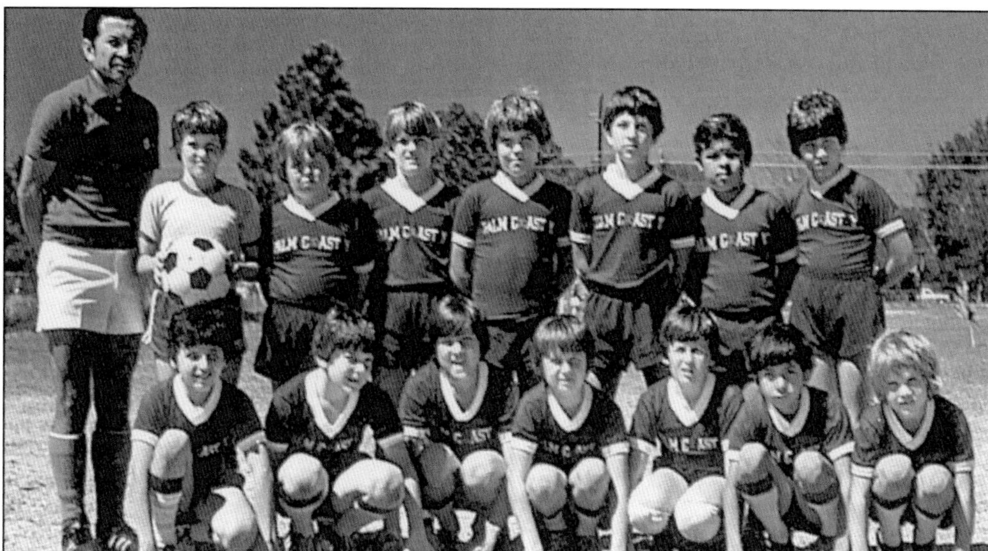

STATE CHAMPS. In 1979, The Palm Coast Pee Wee Soccer Team went undefeated and won the Florida State Youth Soccer Association championship. The team (age 10 and under) won a total of seven games—scoring 23 points to their opponents 2. The team members pictured, from left to right, are (front row) Rafael Barrera, Kelly Alexander, Joe King, Mark Smith, Garett Lamb, Freddie Toro, and Jason Grace; (back row) Coach Edward Herrera, Patrick Fitzgerald, Joe Rhein, Scott Small, Mike Chiumento, (second highest scorer) Bob DeVore, Eddie Herrera (highest scorer), and Mike Milonas.

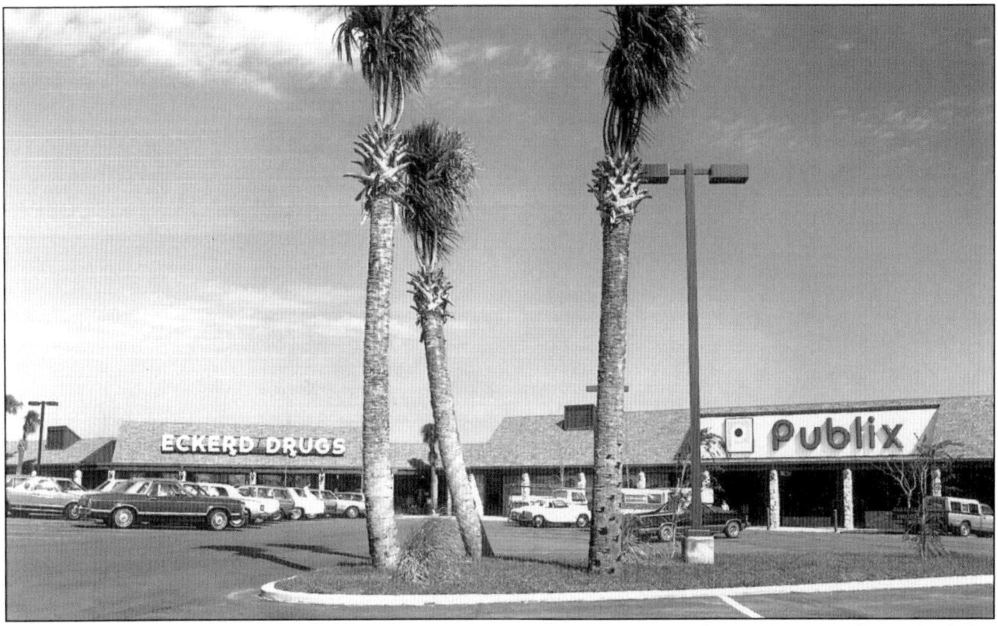

CIVILIZATION COMES TO PALM COAST, SPRING, 1979. ICDC president Alan Smolen asked the crowd awaiting the ribbon cutting outside Publix if this was the most popular of the many grand openings they had attended? "Right" roared the crowd, applauding loudly. With Publix food store, Eckerd's drug store, dry cleaners, hair stylists, travel agents, realtors, banks, gift shops, apparel, sporting goods, plants, a real post office, and a restaurant open now, the time for having to drive 13 miles for shopping was over. Full service shopping had finally come to Palm Coast in the form of a beautiful new $2.5 million shopping center. ICDC Construction project manager Bob DeVore had built coquina stone colored walkways, textured sidewalks, and imaginative landscaping to provide a beautiful setting for parking and shopping.

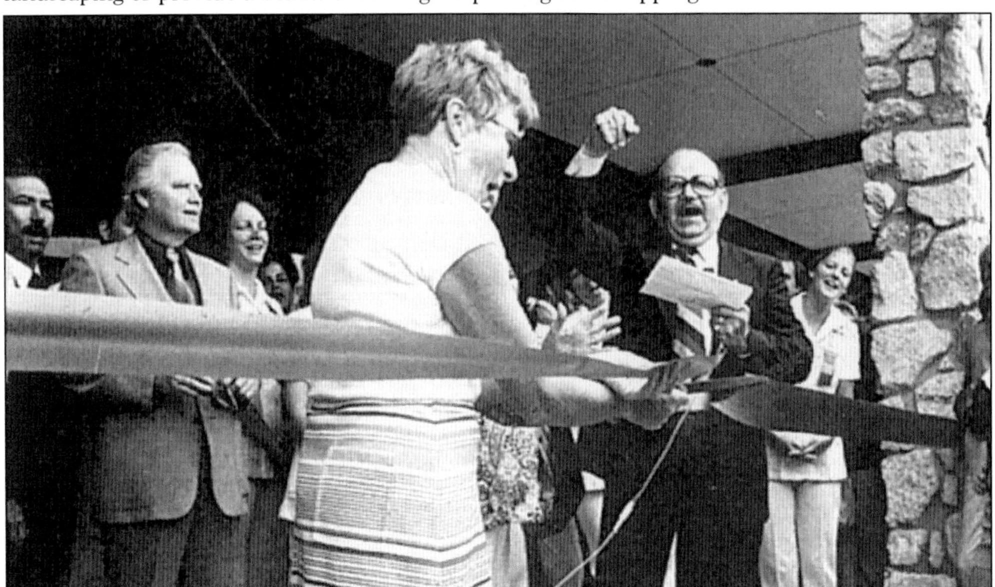

OPENING. Publix manager Tom Links watches the ribbon cutting and immediately all 200 shopping carts were in use by residents exploring the contents of the 36,364-square-foot supermarket.

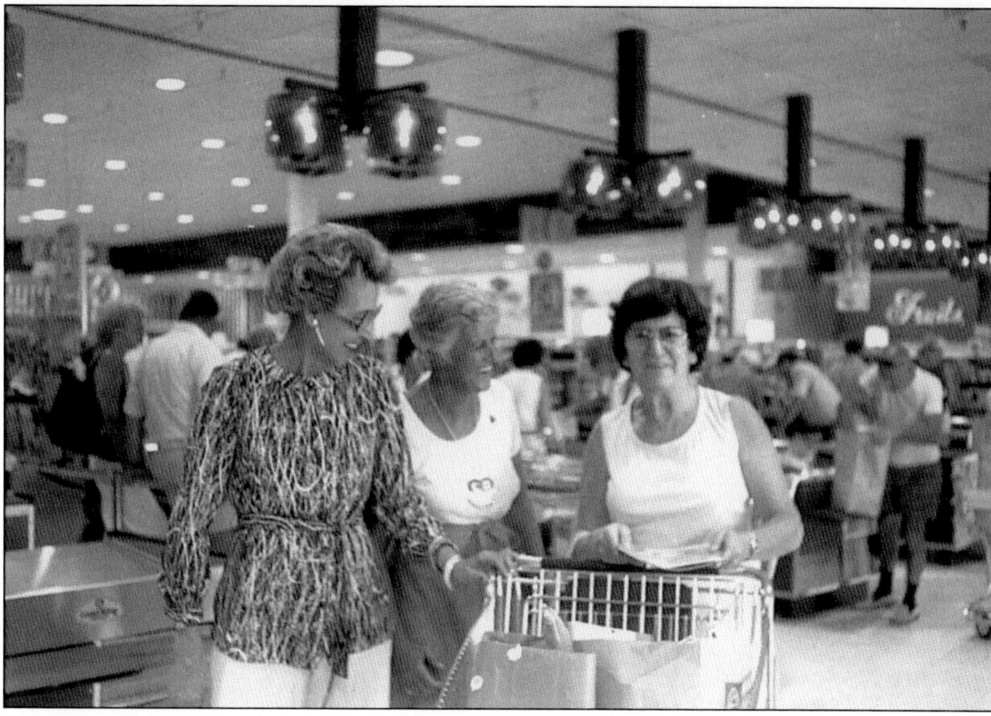

SHOPPING. Fran McLamb and Gentra Vico are photographed with an unidentified customer at a Publix meat department survey soon after the opening.

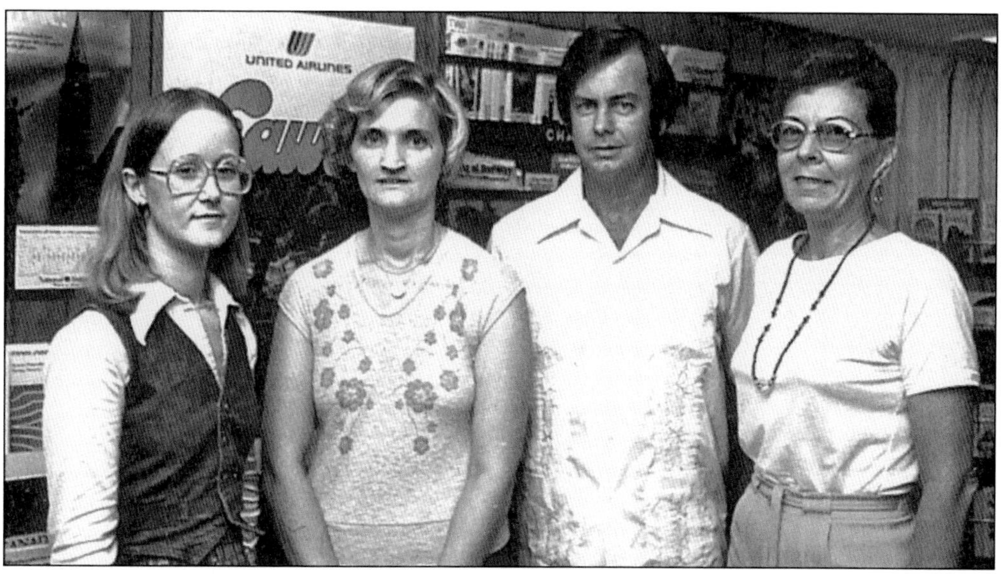

EARLY BUSINESS. Wendy Parrish, owners Marlene and John Seale, and June Scheibel of Flagler Palm Coast Travel opened for business in 1979 and remain in the same location today.

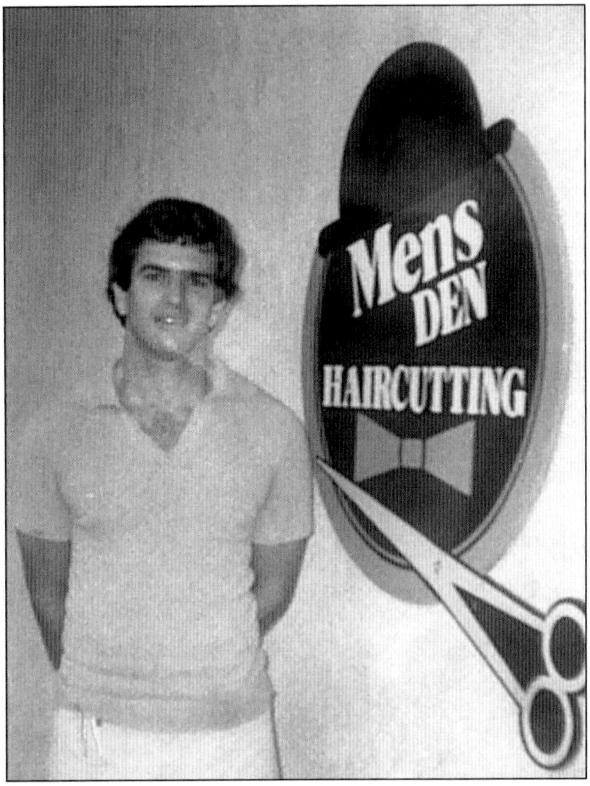

MEN'S DEN, THEN. Terry Conley, owner of the Men's Den in the Palm Coast Shopping Center, opened his shop for business on January 2, 1979.

NOW. You can still drop in to Terry's for a short cut, to talk sports, or to learn more about Palm Coast's rich history. Allen Gatewood gets a haircut from Terry in May 2003 just around the corner from his original 1979 location.

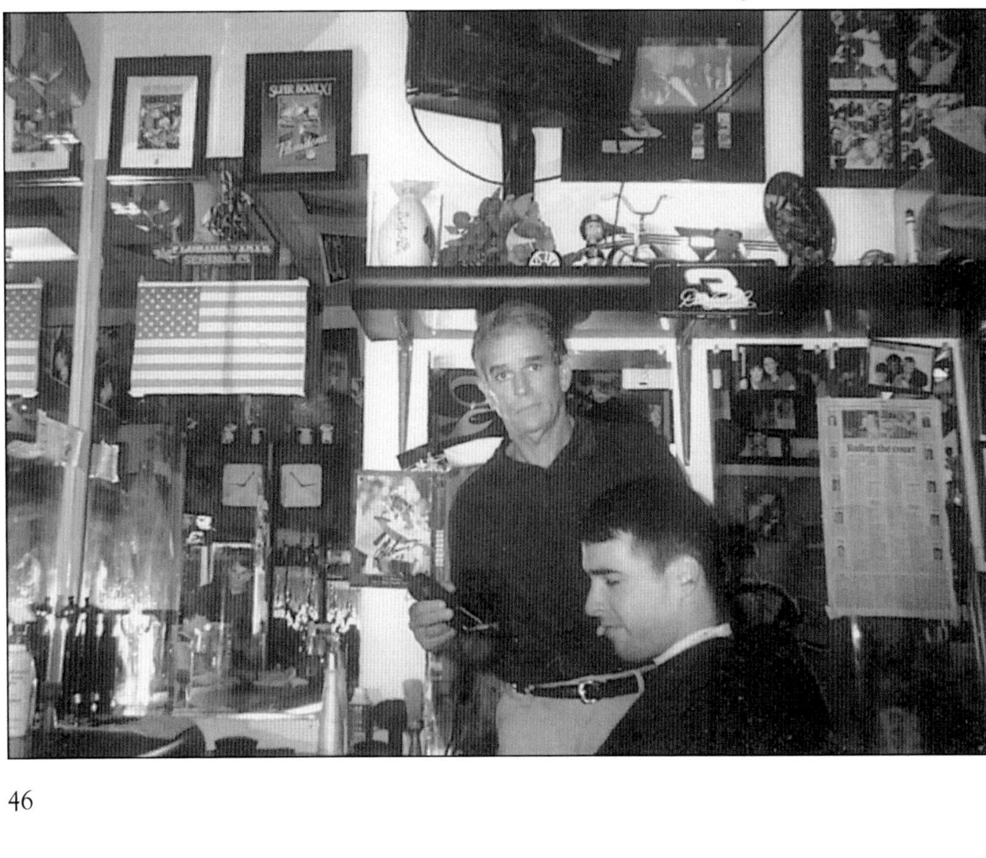

NANCY LOPEZ. LPGA golf champion Nancy Lopez chose Palm Coast as her official place of residence in 1978. The next year she teamed with Lee Trevino to win the Colgate/Palm Coast Mixed Team World Championship on her home course. A dedicated spokesperson for Palm Coast, Nancy was guest of honor at a 1983 baby shower in the community given by the Women's Golf Association.

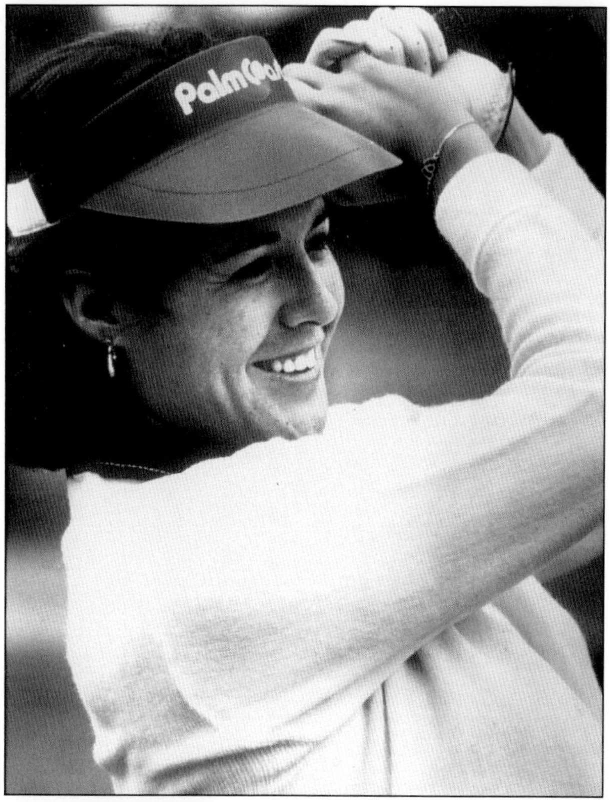

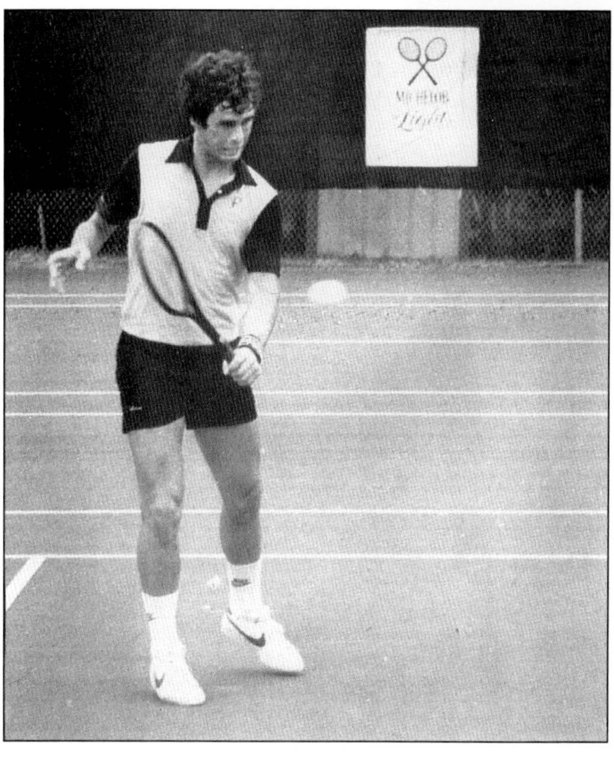

TOM GULIKSON. Tom became Palm Coast's tennis touring pro in 1979. He later became the pro at the Players Club for an illustrious career capped by his serving as coach to America's Davis Cup teams.

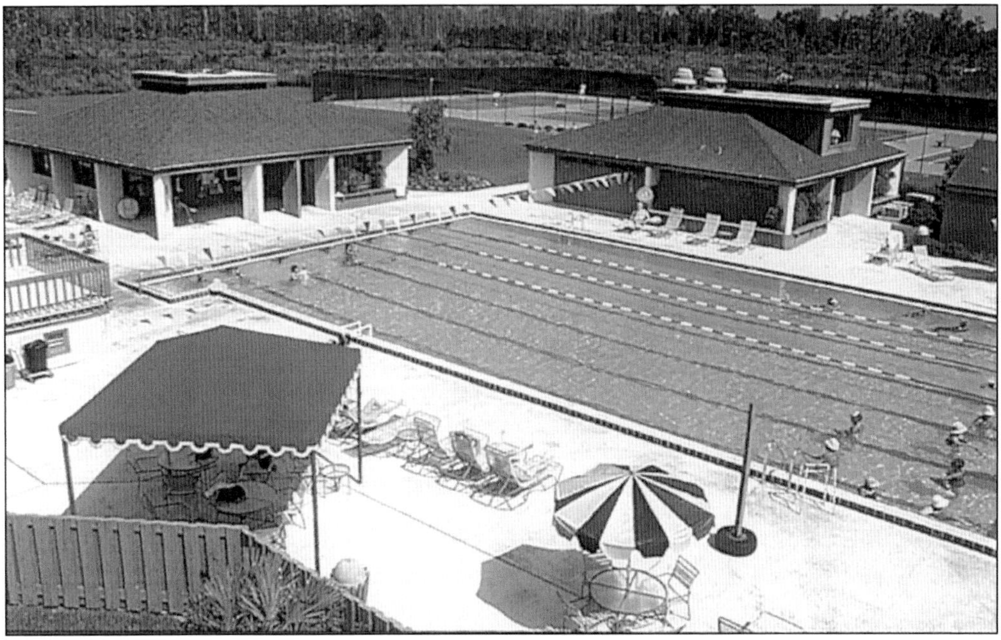

Palm Coast Swim and Racquet Court, 1979. In use since December 1979 and officially opened in April 1980, the club's offerings include a junior Olympic pool, tennis courts, fitness trail, nautilus exercise equipment, sauna, volleyball, shuffleboard courts, lounge, and kiddy pool. It is located east of Belle Terre Parkway south.

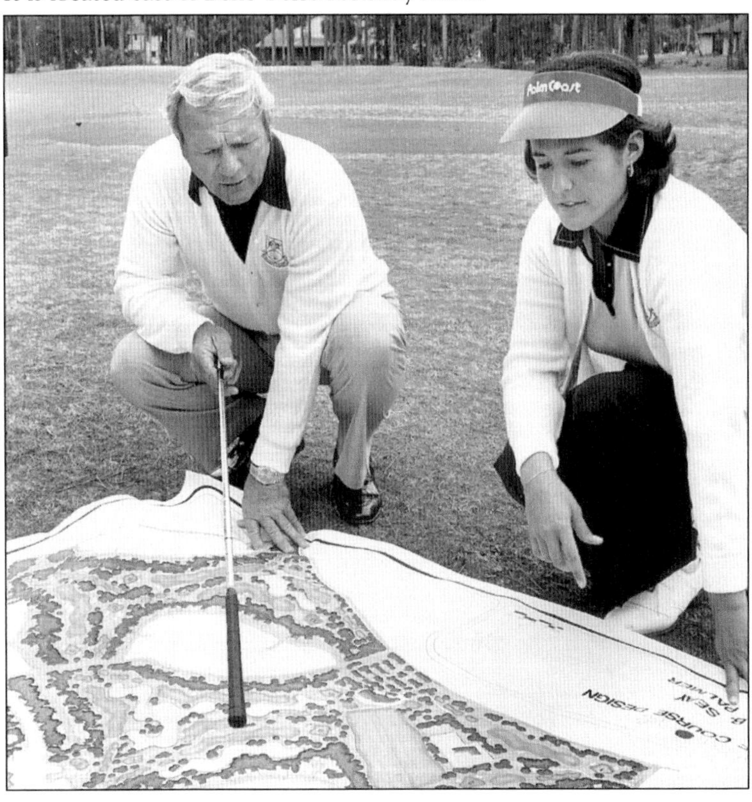

Arnold Palmer's Visit, Pine Lakes Golf Course, 1979. Palmer, co-designer of the planned Pine Lakes Golf Course with architect Ed Seay, looks over the course layout with Nancy Lopez-Melton. The 18-hole PGA course was open for play by January, 1981.

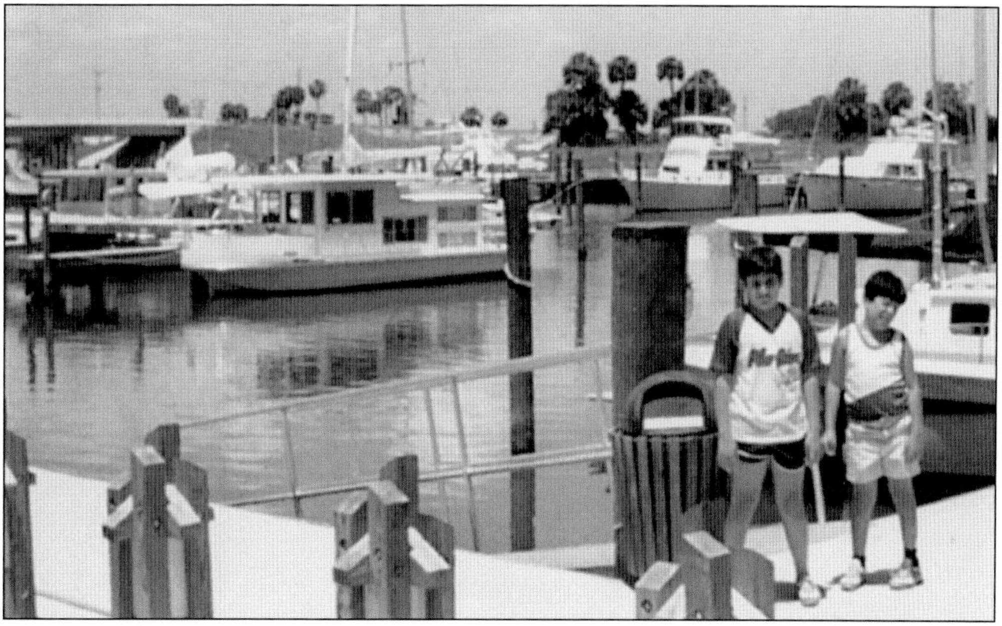

MARINA ADDITION. An 80-slip marina was under construction in 1979 by the Yacht Club. Pictured here are Anthony and Donald, sons of Lora and Donald DeVito, looking at the boats in 1982.

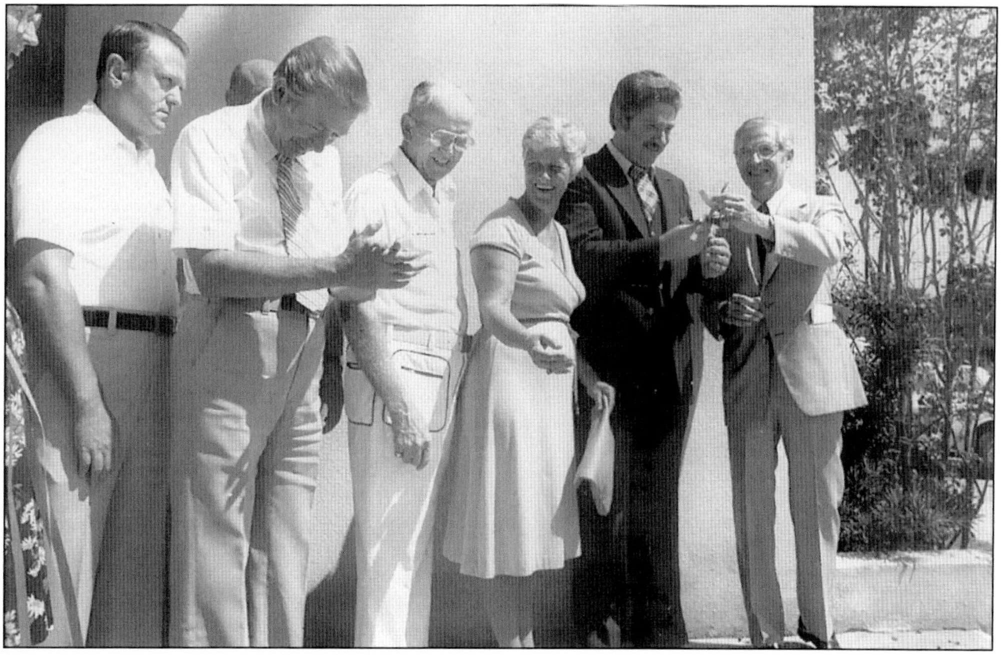

SHERIFF IN TOWN 1981. The Flagler County Sheriff's office established a physical presence in Palm Coast by opening a substation built next to the existing Palm Harbor Emergency Service building. Pictured at the ribbon cutting, from left to right, are Claire Rule, Joe Church, county commissioner Merhl Shoemaker, (hidden in back) civic association president Ken Hawthorne, *News-Tribune* reporter Jim Miskelly, woman's club president Fran McLamb, Flagler County sheriff Dan Bennett, and ICDC president Alan Smolen.

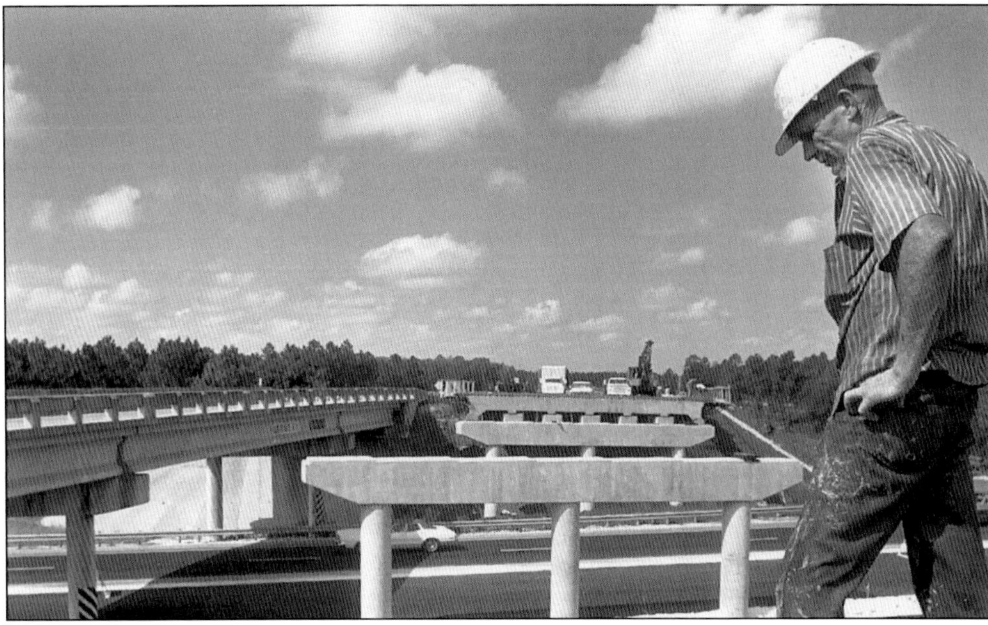

WHAT'S NEXT? FALL, 1980. An unidentified worker seems to be contemplating his next step in the completion of an interchange at the overpass of 1-95. ICDC contributed more than $3.3 million to a partnership with the state in what Alan Smolen called, "an uncommon example of a public convenience being constructed with private funds." Leaders envisioned a stimulus to economic growth. Most Palm Coasters were just happy to finally have direct access to their community.

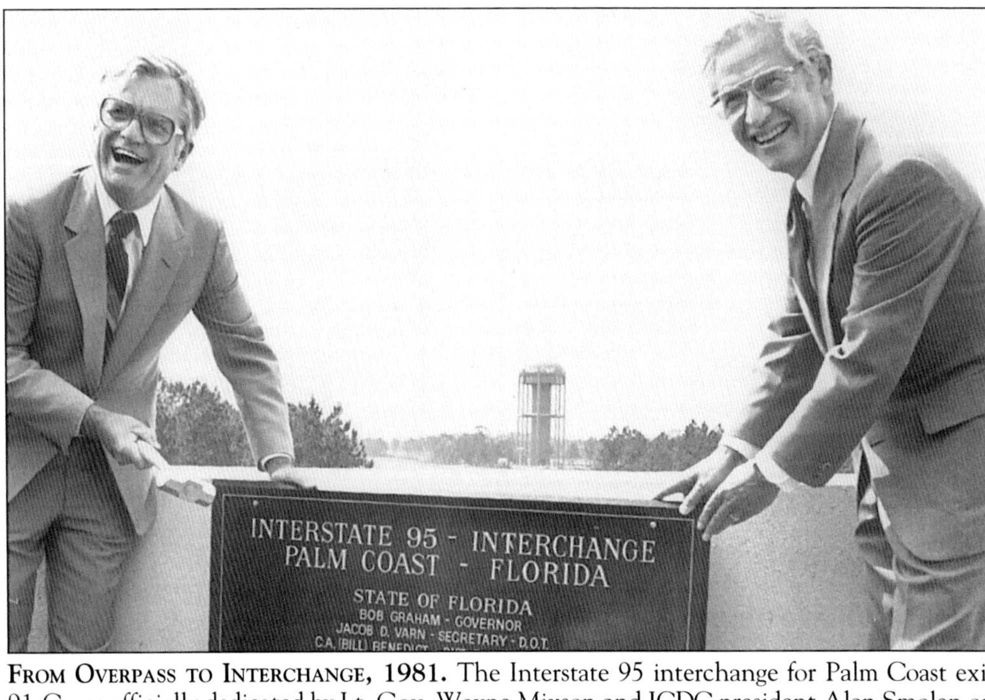

FROM OVERPASS TO INTERCHANGE, 1981. The Interstate 95 interchange for Palm Coast exit 91-C was officially dedicated by Lt. Gov. Wayne Mixson and ICDC president Alan Smolen on May 21, 1981.

Three

A Perfect Place to Live

Ten years after ITT's original purchase of the empty land, the frontier/pioneer period of Palm Coast history was essentially over. Civilization had come to Palm Coast in the form of a Publix/Eckerd anchored shopping center and a direct connection to the interstate highway system. In 1982, Florida New Homes and Condominium Guide *analyzed the community and came to the conclusion, "It may just be the perfect place to live." With the basics in place, could Palm Coast improve even further?*

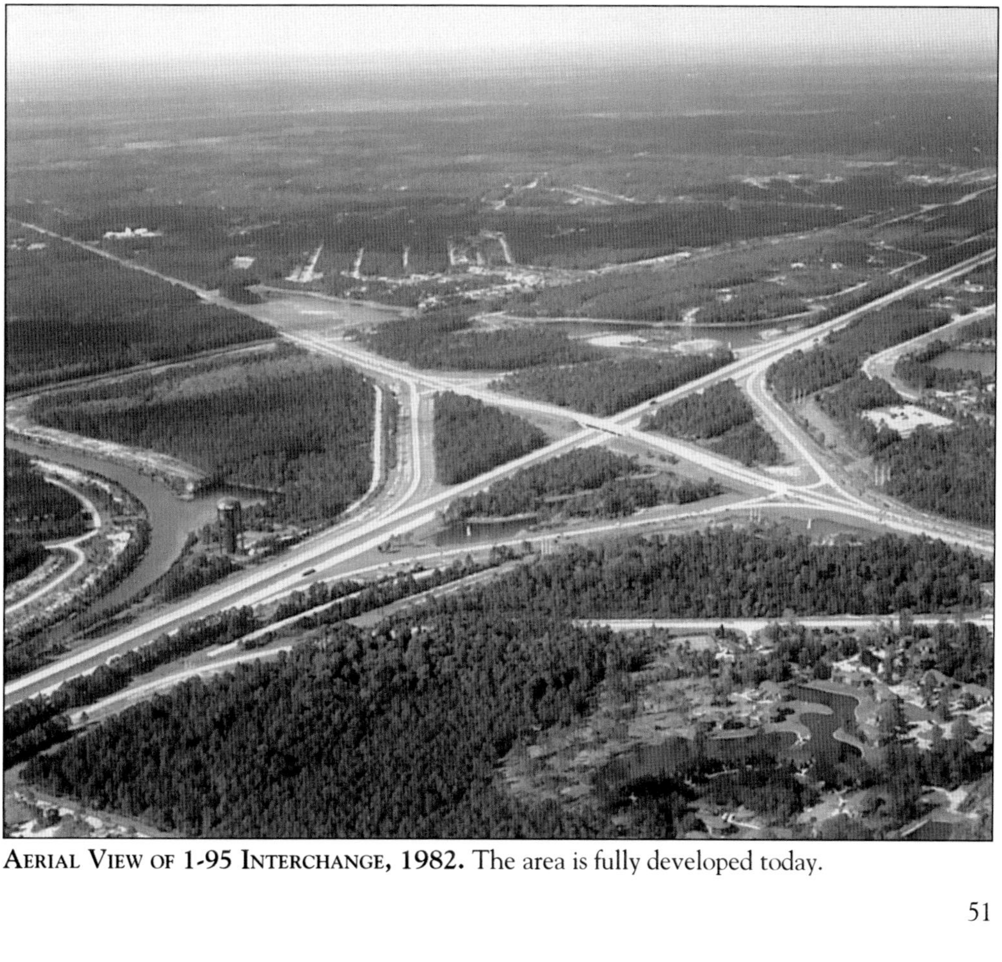

Aerial View of 1-95 Interchange, 1982. The area is fully developed today.

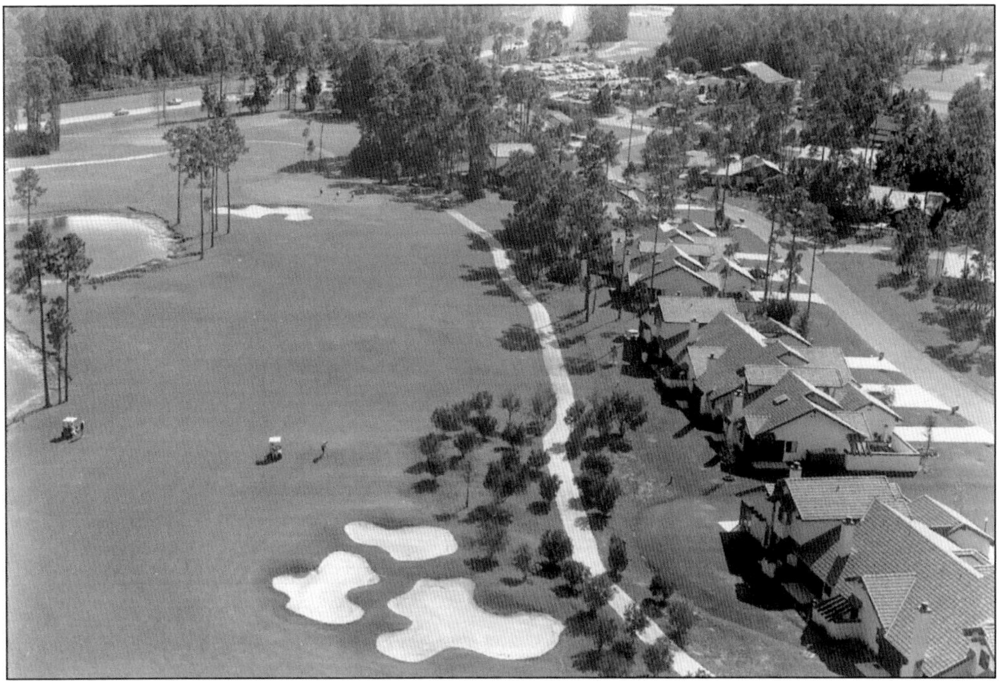

Second Golf Course, 1980. The Arnold Palmer and Ed Seay–designed Pine Lakes Country Club course, open since 1980, was officially dedicated on August 21, 1981. The 7,074-yard PGA course meanders along the newly built Pine Lakes section of Palm Coast.

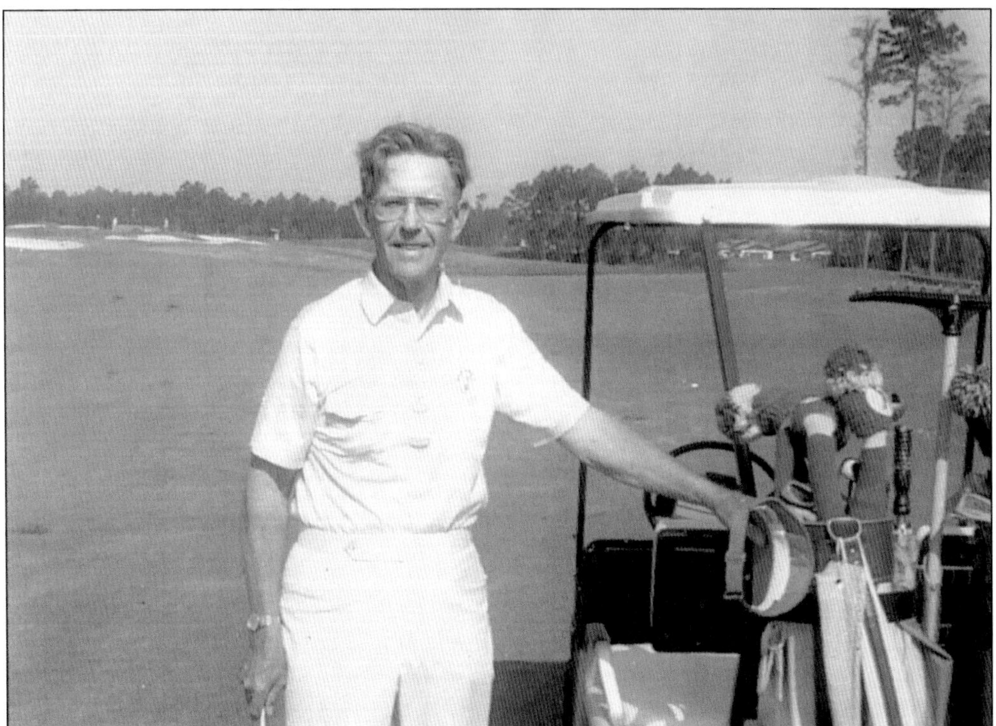

Larry Lane. A golfer, musician, singer, and recording artist, Larry loved Palm Coast.

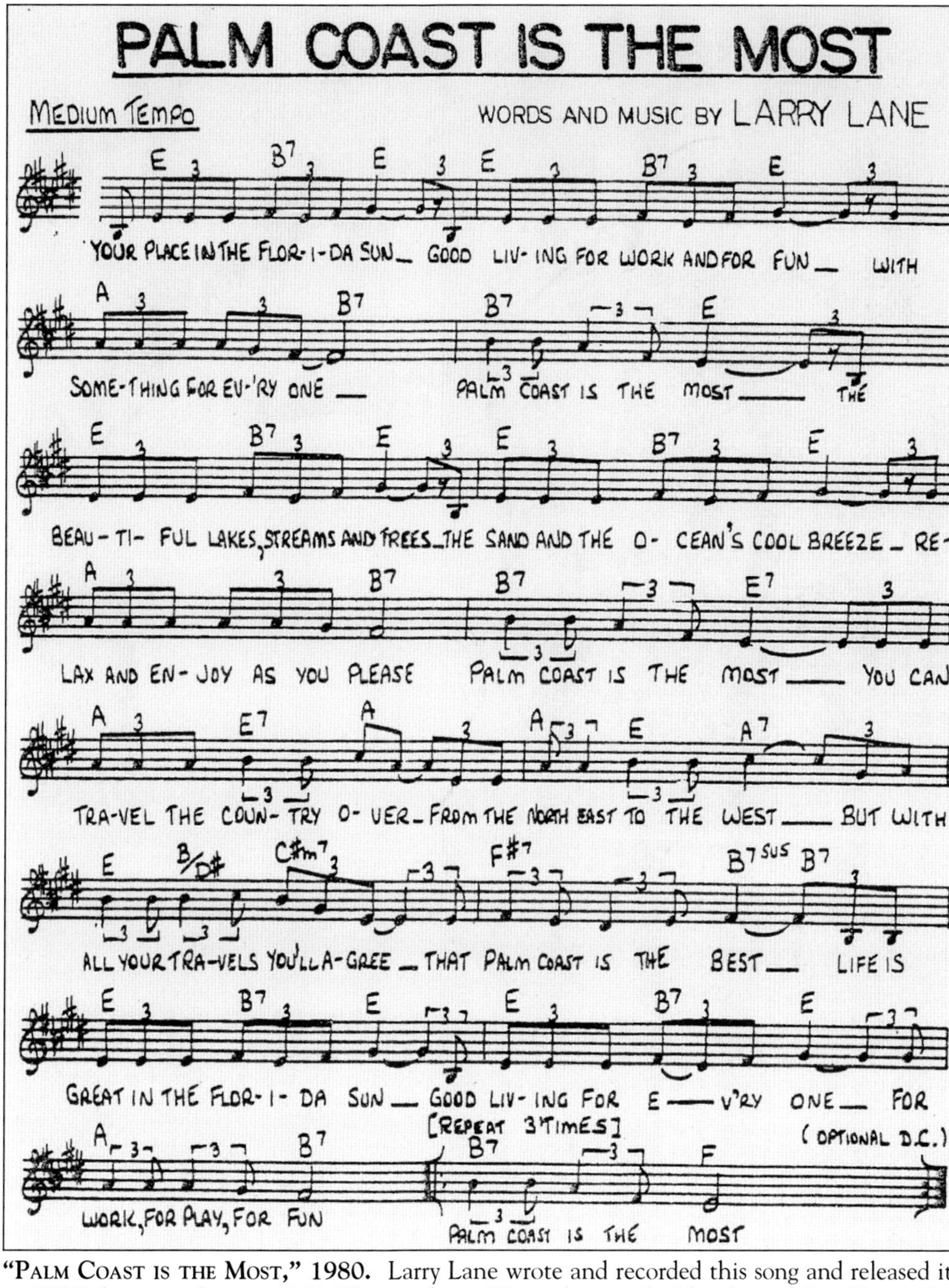

"Palm Coast is the Most," 1980. Larry Lane wrote and recorded this song and released it to ICDC for general use in 1981. The words are "Your place in the Florida sun/ Good living for work and for fun/ With something for everyone/ Palm Coast is the most./ The beautiful lakes, streams, and trees/ The sand and the ocean's cool breeze/ Relax and enjoy as you please/ Palm Coast Is The Most./ You can travel the country over/ From the North East to the West/ But with all your travels you'll agree/ That Palm Coast is the best./ Life is great in the Florida sun/ Good living for ev'ryone/ For work, for play, for fun/ Palm Coast is the most.

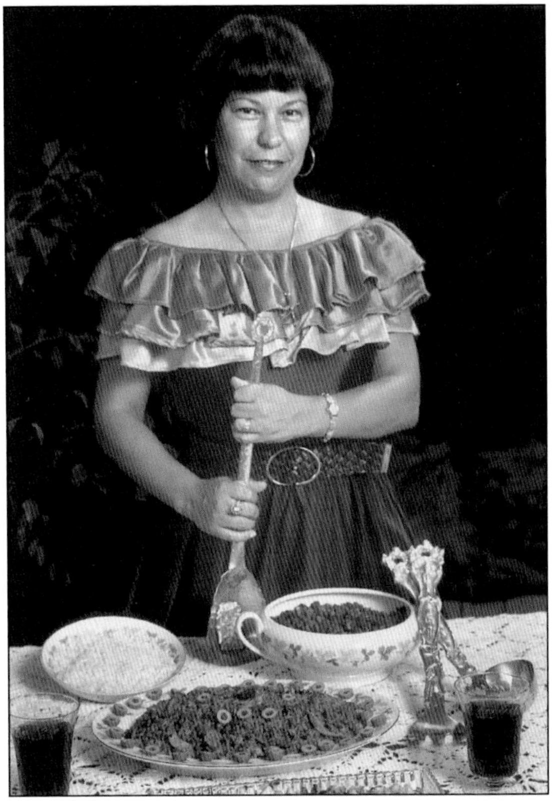

International Flavor 1978–1992. The Palm Coast International Festival had its beginning in 1978 when Mrs. Fanny Herrera sought to bring together the diverse cultures of the many other Palm Coast residents whose ancestors traced back to foreign lands. She organized the first festival on the weekend nearest Columbus Day as a tribute to the United States.

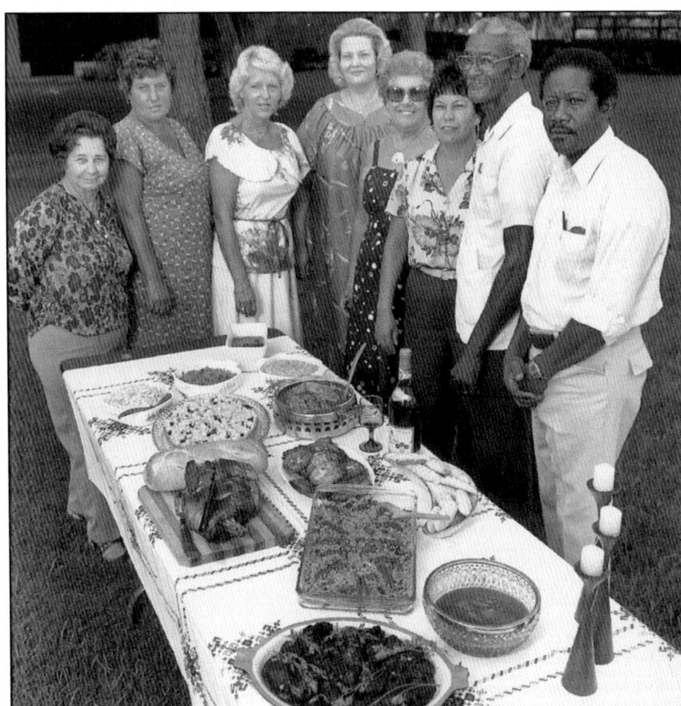

Festival Continued. It features the food and native dress of the different nations of the world. Attendees pictured in this photograph, from left to right, are Connie Horvath, Erica Shoeps, Ursula Gittler, Margie Jusino, Carmen Border, Fannie Herrera, Alfredo ?, and Bert Hunt.

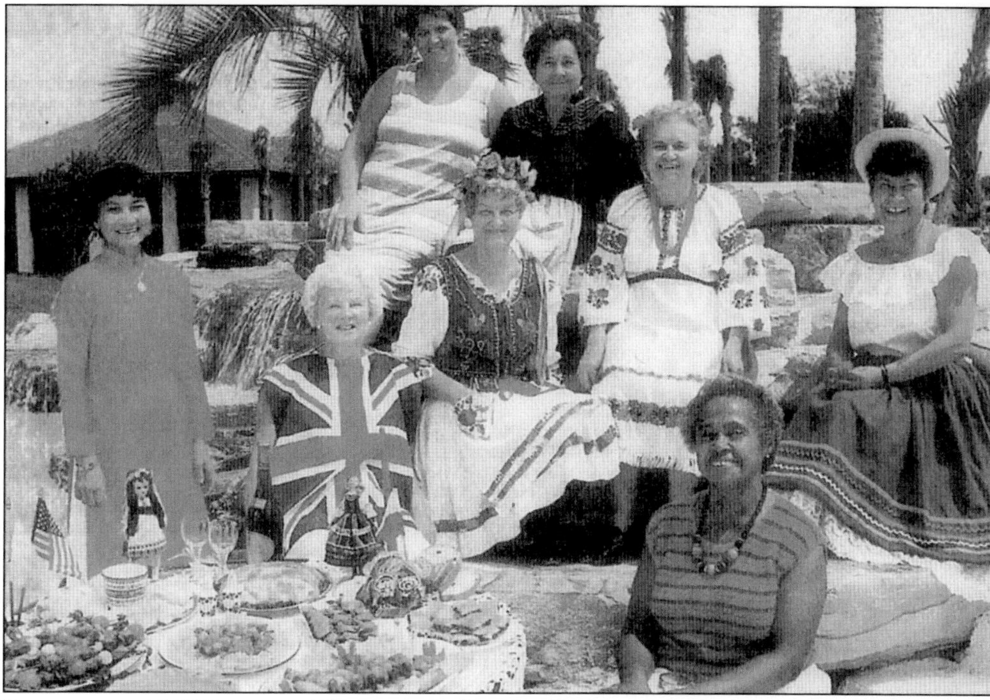

Preview for 1985 Festival. Shown poolside at the Harbor Club Vacation resort in Palm Coast are (in front) Pearl Owens (Afro-American Caribbean Cultural Heritage Organization) with sweet potato pie; (middle row) Marie Cox (Vietnam) with cha glo, Miriam Rich (England) with eccles, Ann Morrow (Poland) with braided bread, Mary Mandrich (Ukraine) with varenyky potato dumplings, and Fanny Herrera (Colombia) with pinchakebob; (back row) Rosa Pascazio (Italy) with calzone and Connie Horvath (Hungary) with Gulyas.

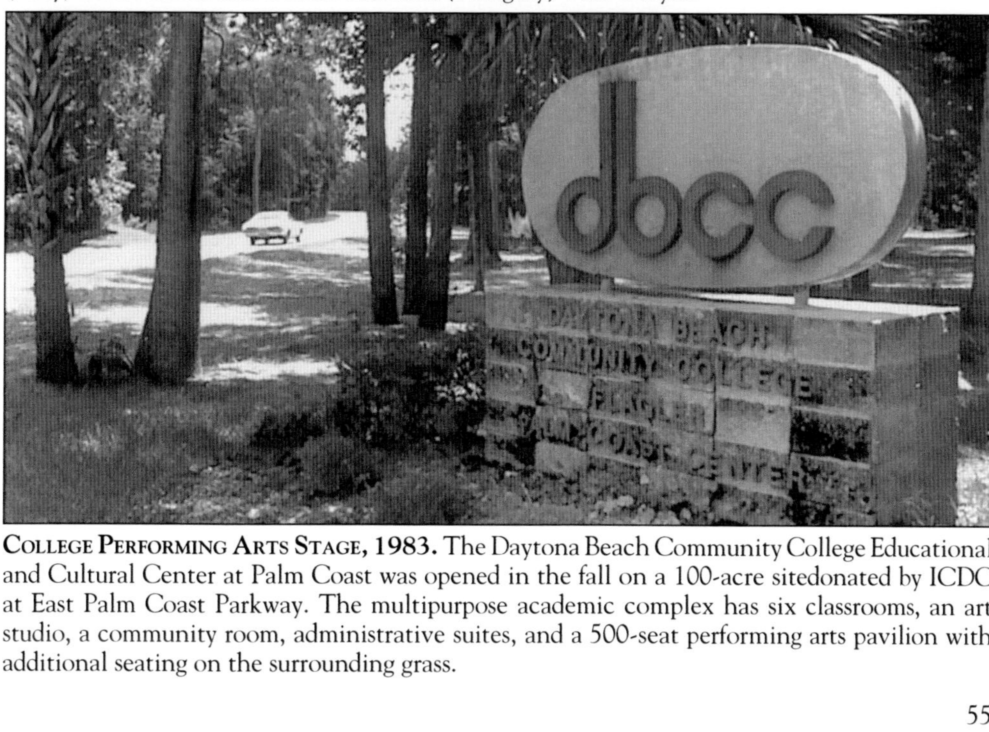

College Performing Arts Stage, 1983. The Daytona Beach Community College Educational and Cultural Center at Palm Coast was opened in the fall on a 100-acre sitedonated by ICDC at East Palm Coast Parkway. The multipurpose academic complex has six classrooms, an art studio, a community room, administrative suites, and a 500-seat performing arts pavilion with additional seating on the surrounding grass.

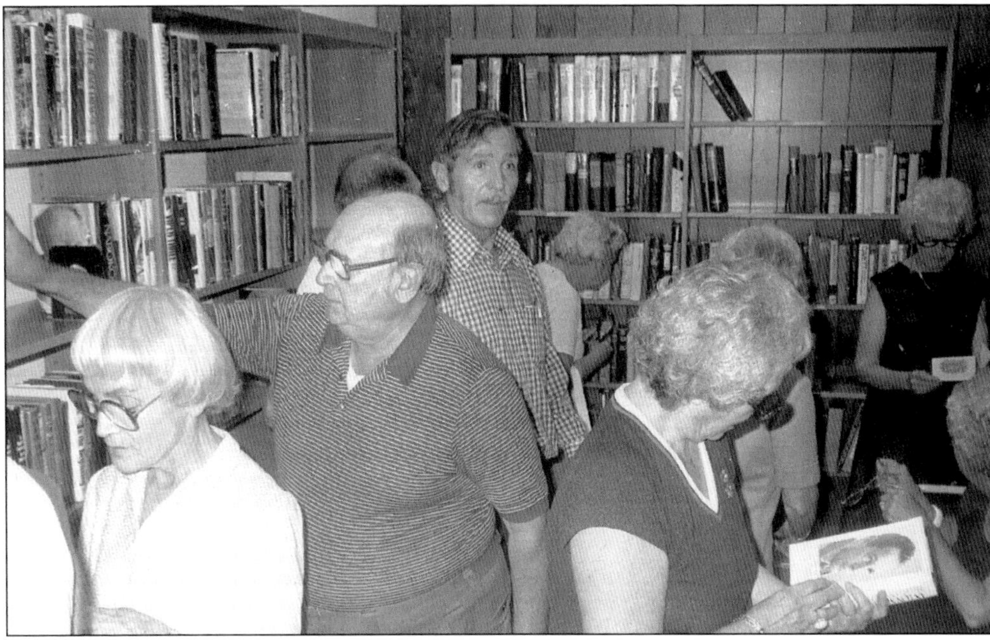

BOOKS FOR PALM COASTERS. A small Flagler County Branch Library opened in May of 1980. Pictured are Frances Wadsworth, Mr. and Mrs. Milton Werby, John Young, and Winnie Flanagan.

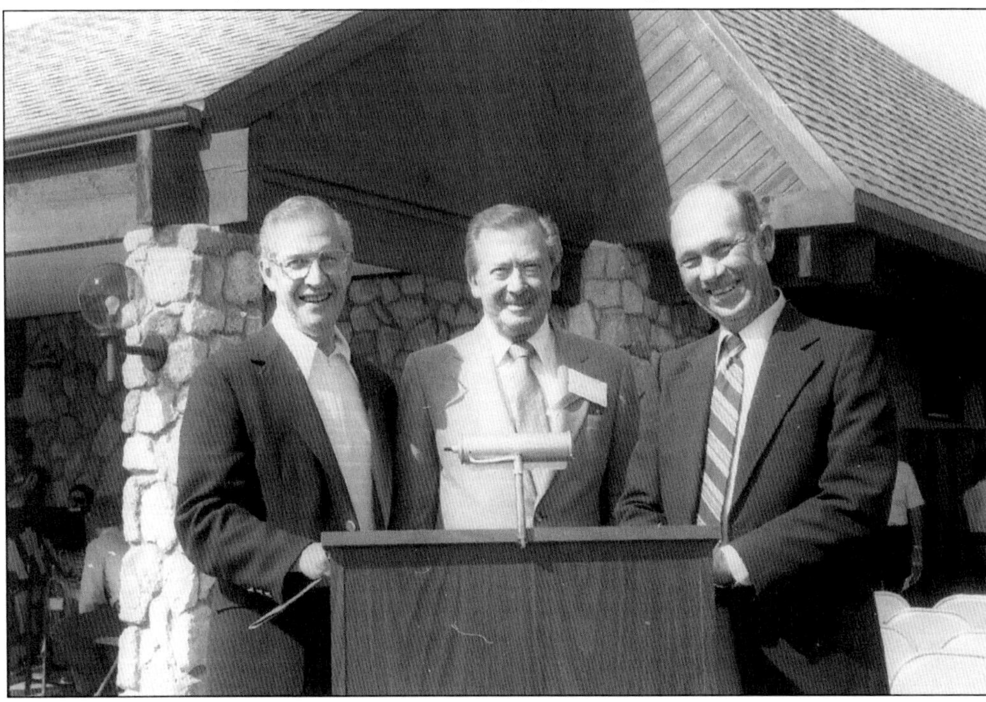

FIRST LIBRARY DEDICATION, FEBRUARY 11, 1984. The present City Hall building was the site of Palm Coast's first adequate library. The county had bought the building but everything else was owned by the Friends of the Library. Shown here is ICDC president Alan Smolen, Friends of the Library president Merhl Shoemaker, and County Commission chairman, Tommy Durrance.

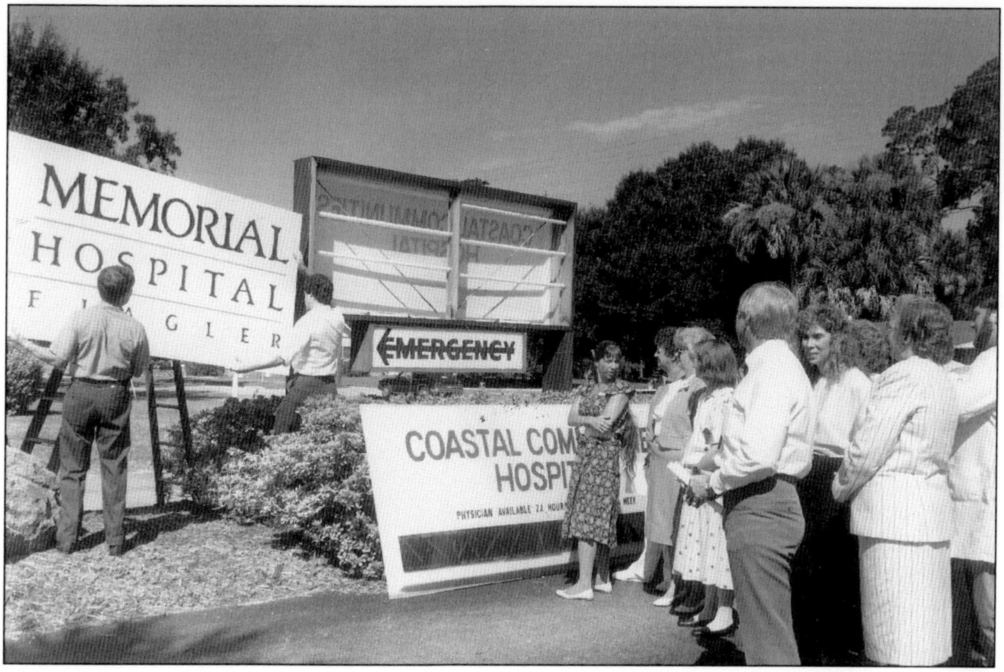

NEW HOSPITAL, FEBRUARY 19, 1989. Department heads look on as the sign is changed from Coastal Community Hospital to Memorial Hospital/Flagler. Acquisition by a larger hospital chain promised improved services and facilities.

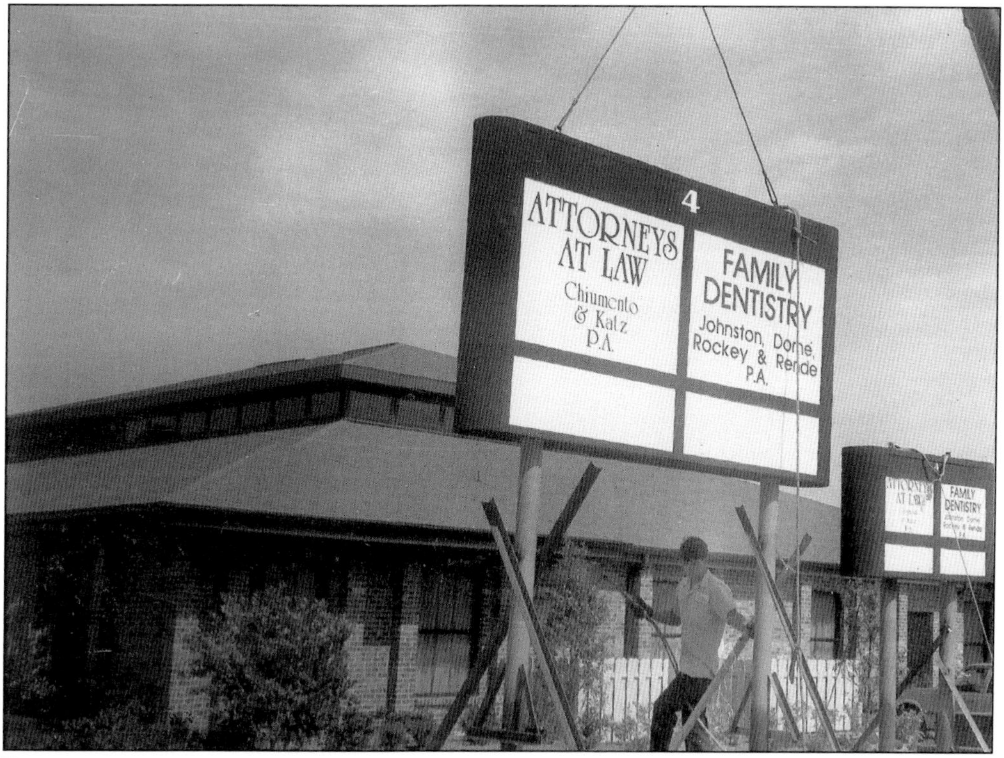

BUSINESS IMPROVING, MARCH, 1988. Early pioneer business providers expanded their facilities.

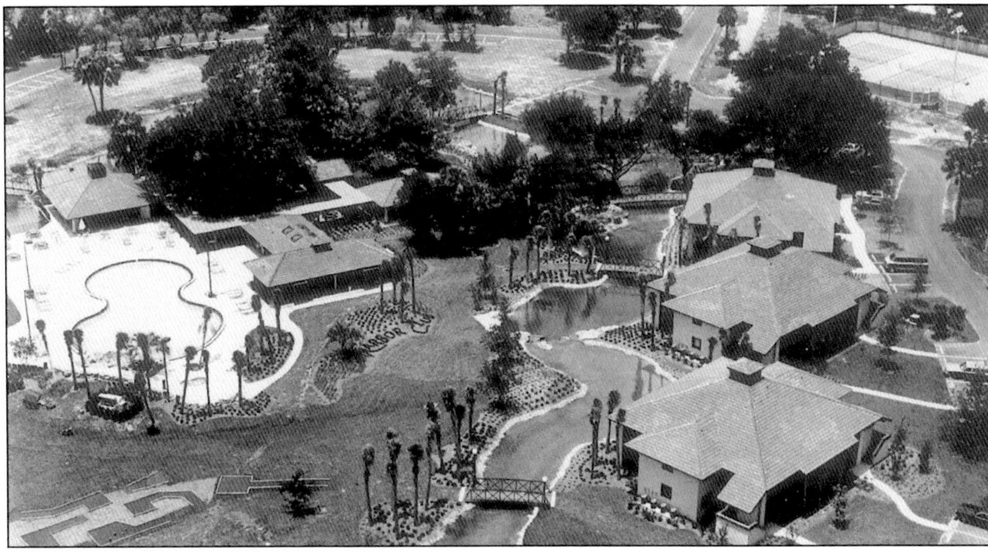

First Vacation Ownership Resort, 1985. The Harbor Club was designed with nothing but vacation in mind. Owners or guests bring nothing but themselves as even silverware and linens are provided. Located just off the Intracoastal Waterway, the club is an environmental paradise with a freshwater stream encircling the resort's private amenity island. Pedestrian bridges lead you to the free form pool, indoor/outdoor spa, health club facility, and pavilions for teens and children. Fine dining and every conceivable popular outdoor activity are right nearby.

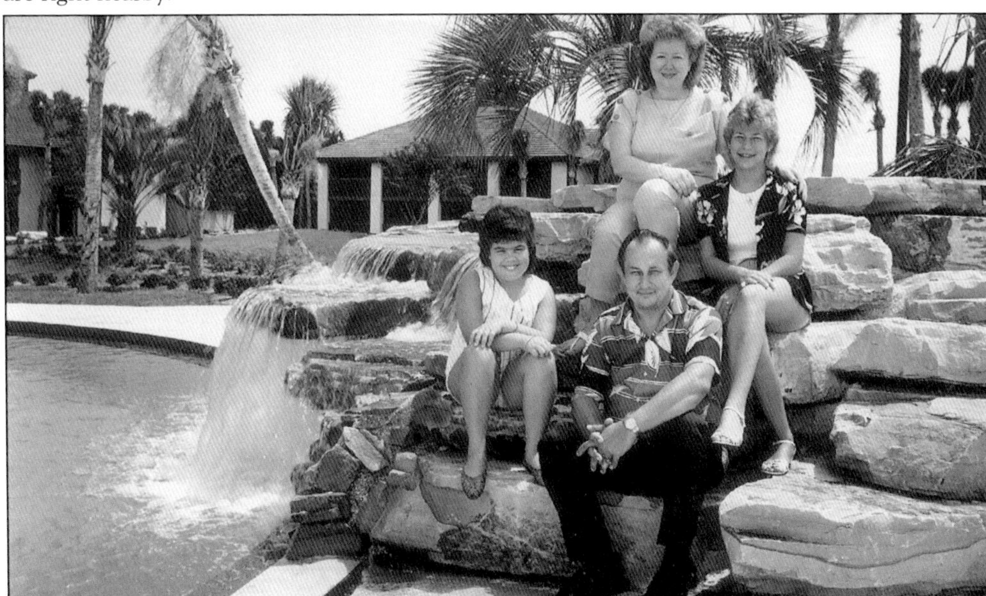

Promotional Photo. The Harbor Club used the photo and text below as advertisement: "Kankakee Family in Florida. John and Jane Doe, with daughters Jan and Joann, of Kankakee, recently spent a week of sun and fun at The Harbor Club, a vacation-ownership resort in Palm Coast, Florida on the state's northeast coast. To their friends back home, the Doe's send this vacation portrait and a few short words: golf, tennis, the beach and sunshine at a private Florida resort are tough, but we're making the best of it. Be home soon."

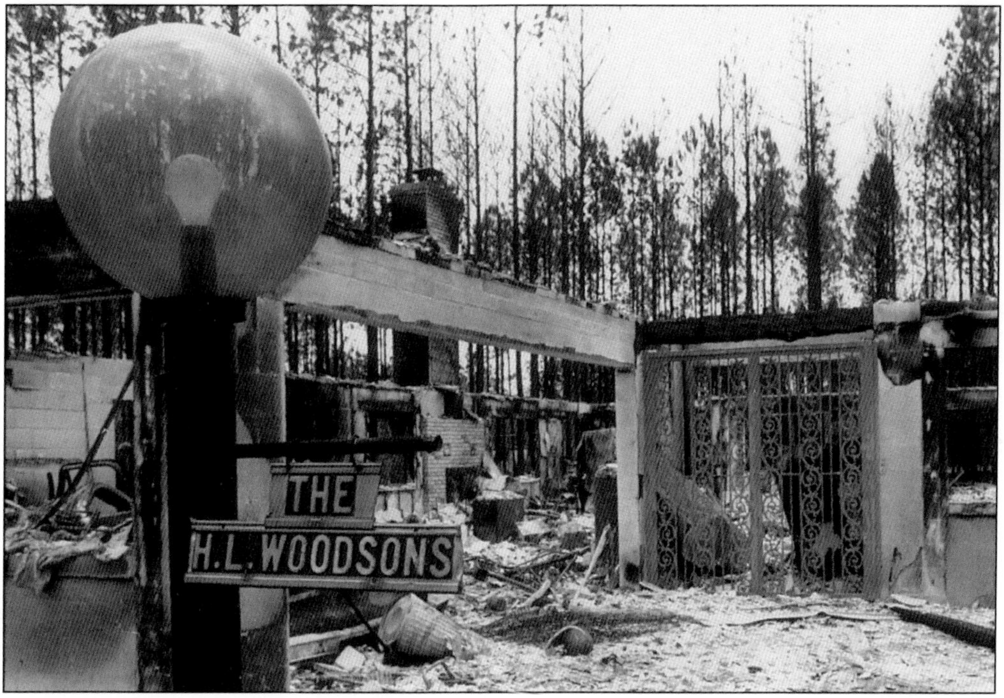

Disaster by Fire, 1985. Even in paradise there was a snake. After years of building, the 1985 fires showed that there could be destruction in Palm Coast, as endured by the Woodson family.

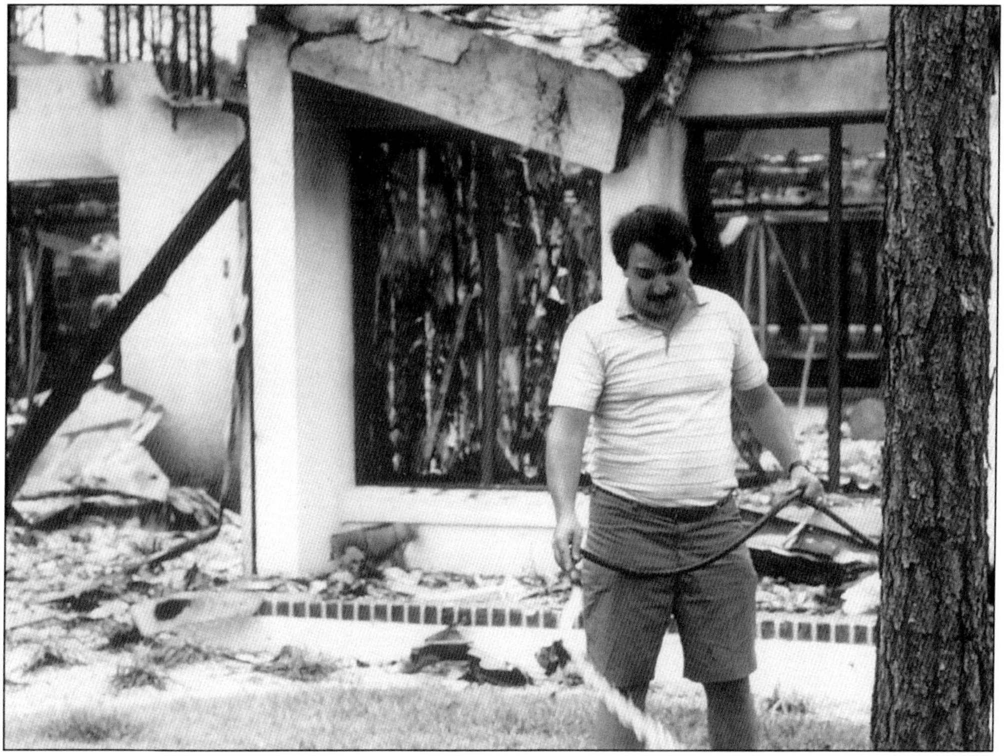

Resident Dousing Embers. The house above was rebuilt and is lived in today.

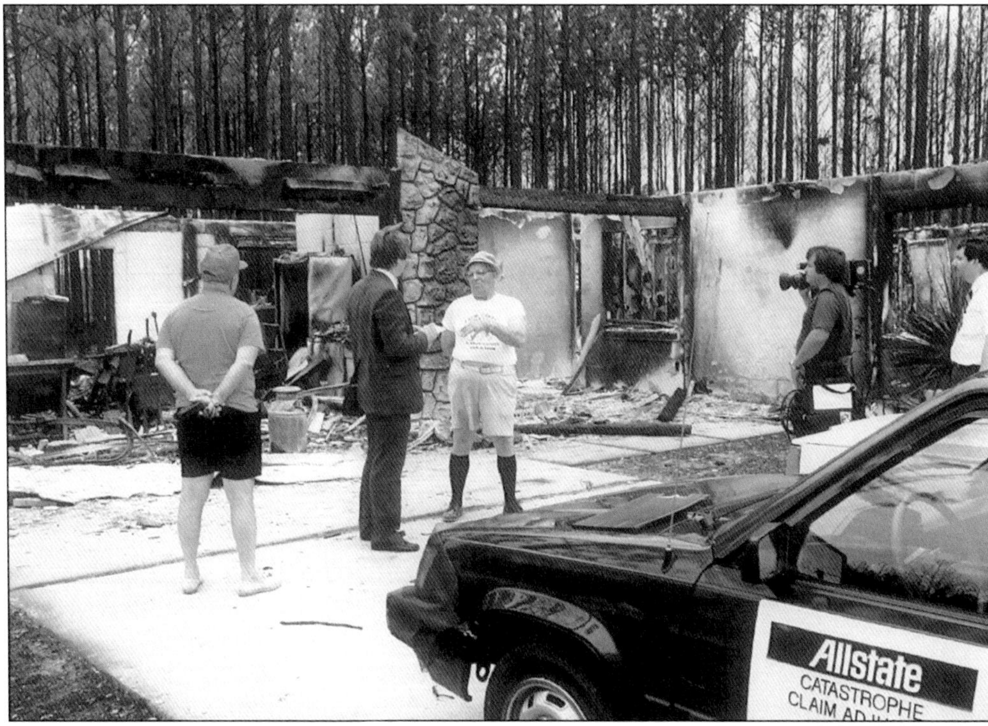

INSURANCE. Residents reported that fire loss claims were promptly adjusted and paid.

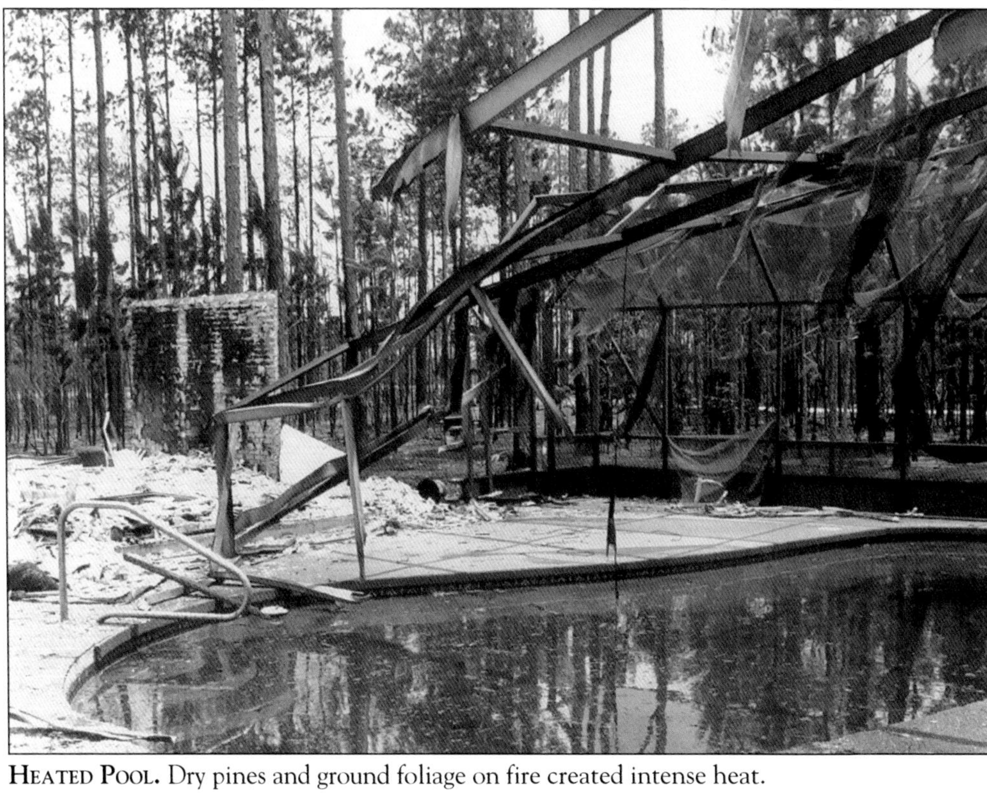

HEATED POOL. Dry pines and ground foliage on fire created intense heat.

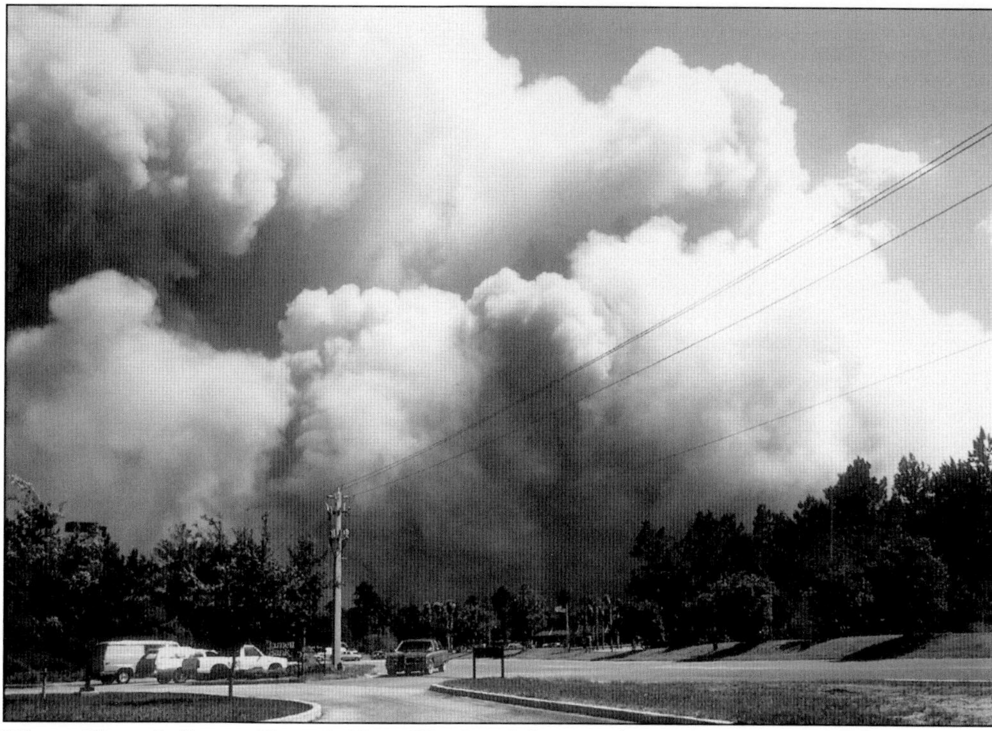

Where There's Smoke There's Fire. Wind and flying embers selected areas of destruction.

Smoke Everywhere. Poor visibility and smoke inhalation made life difficult.

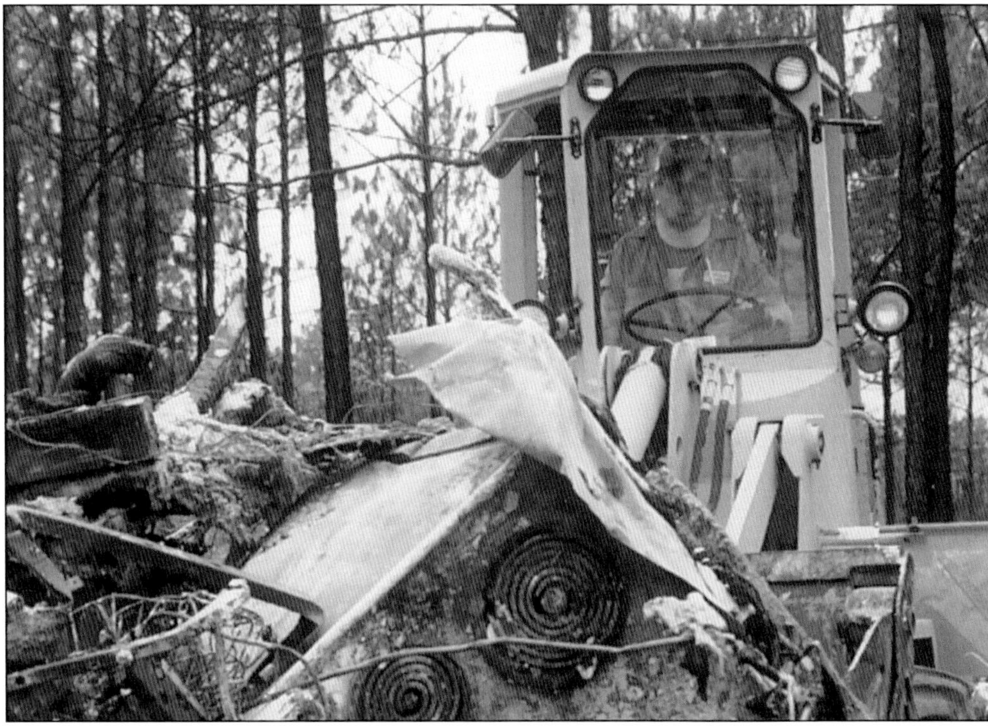

Cleaning up to Rebuild, 1985. It was time to forget the loss and move forward.

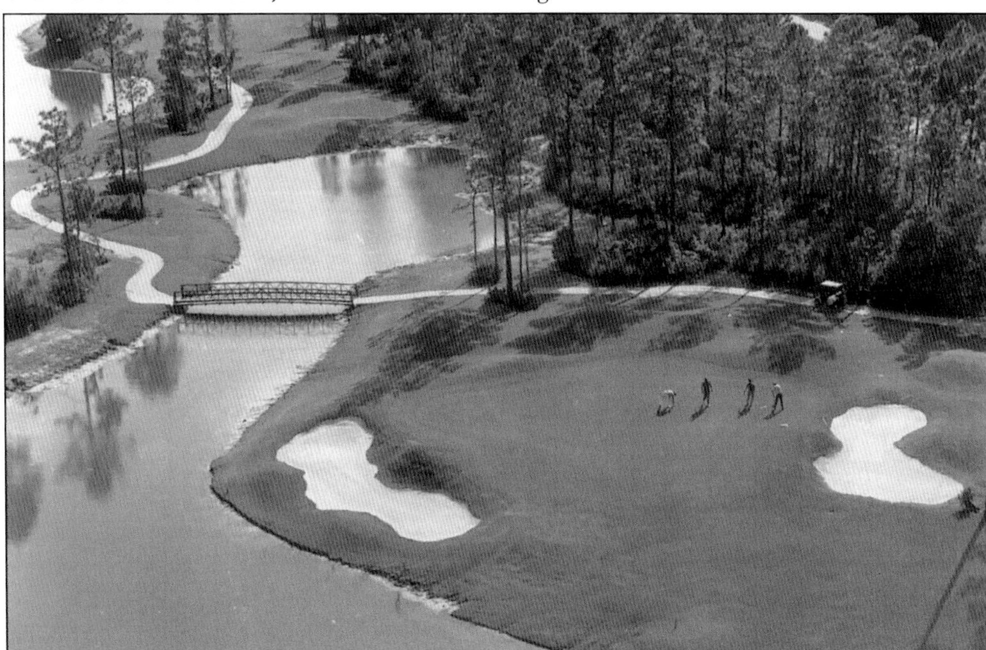

Third Golf Course, 1985. Matanzas Woods is the second Arnold Palmer and Ed Seay–designed golf course in Palm Coast. Weaving its way for 6,985 yards through the pines and palmettos in the northwestern section of the community, the area has recovered from a fire that swept through a portion of it in 1998.

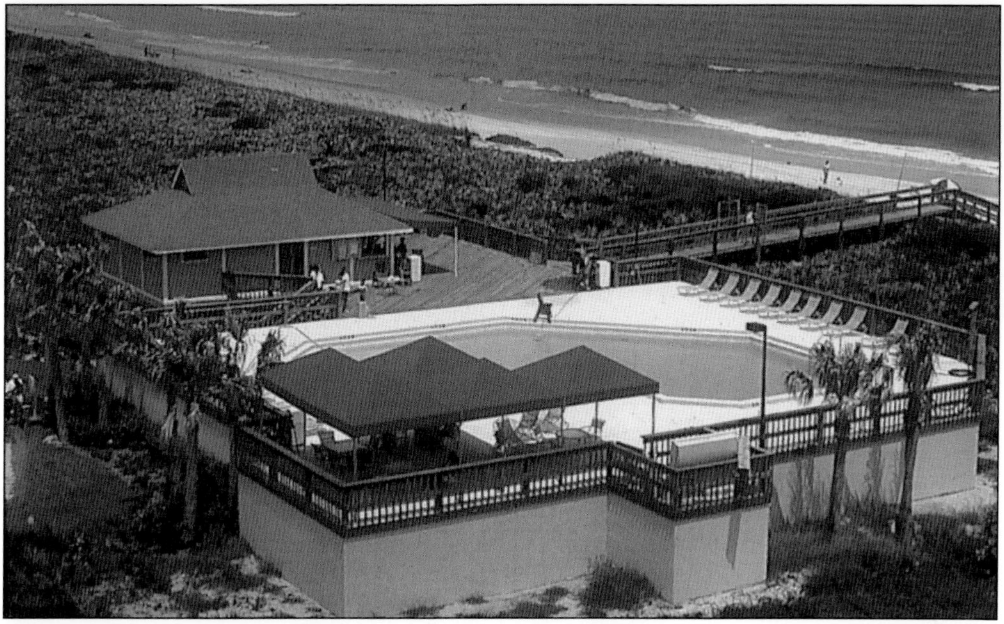

Swim—Ocean or Pool, 1985. The SunSport Beach Club was private, secluded, and the perfect place to enjoy a lazy afternoon with family and friends to swim in the pool or the ocean. It was torn down to make way for the new Ocean Hammock development and golf course.

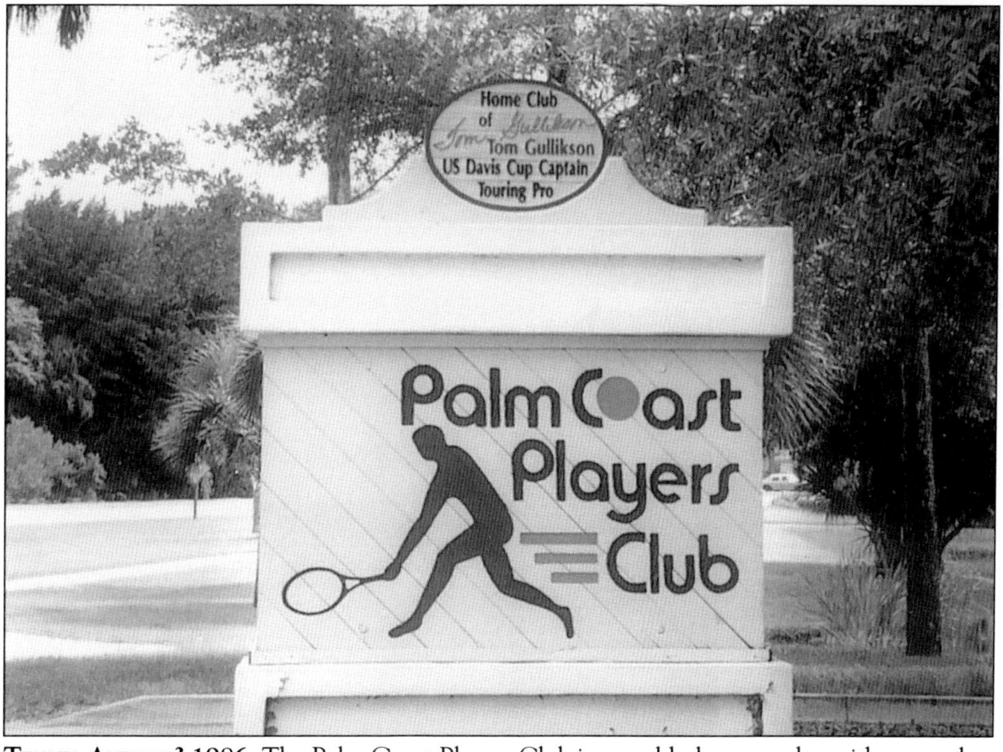

Tennis Anyone? 1986. The Palm Coast Players Club is a world-class complex with grass, clay, and hard surface courts—18 in all—plus practice and racquet-ball courts, a seasonal swimming pool, and a two-story clubhouse.

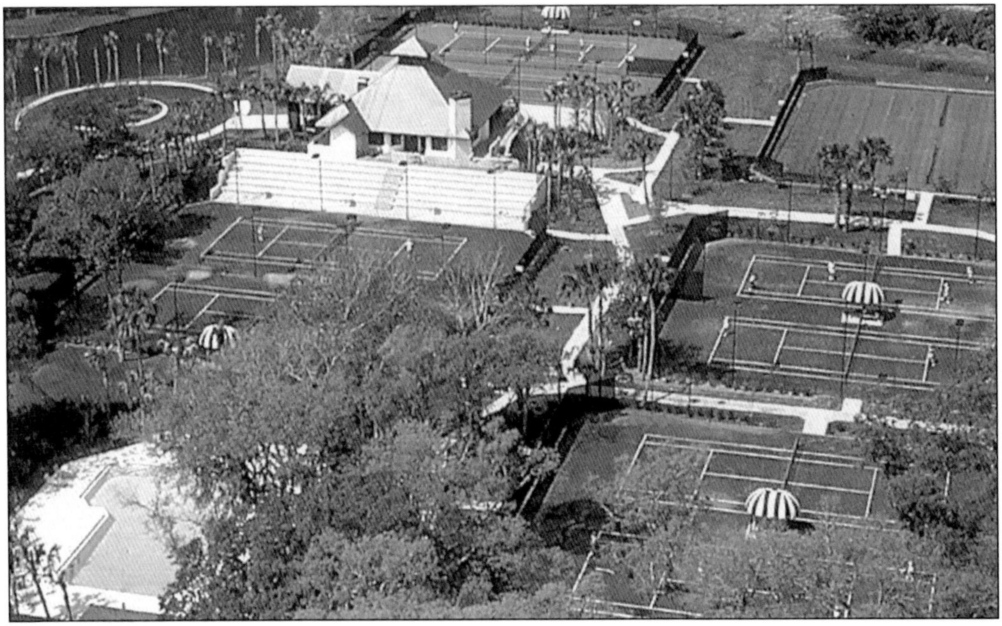

"1987 Best New Courts of the Year." The award was given to the Players Club by *Tennis Industry Magazine*.

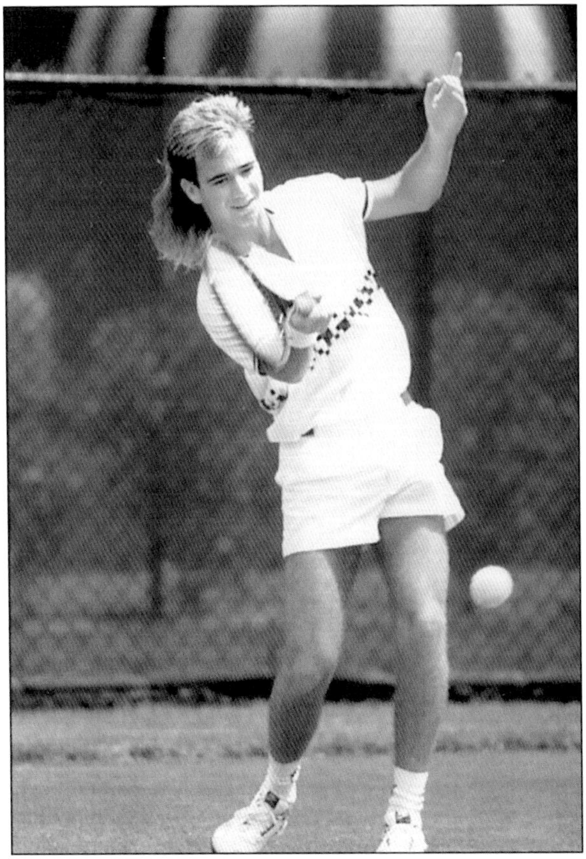

Do You Know This Man? In June of 1987, young Andre Agassi, wearing significantly more hair than he does today, practiced on the grass at the Players Club along with Michael Chang.

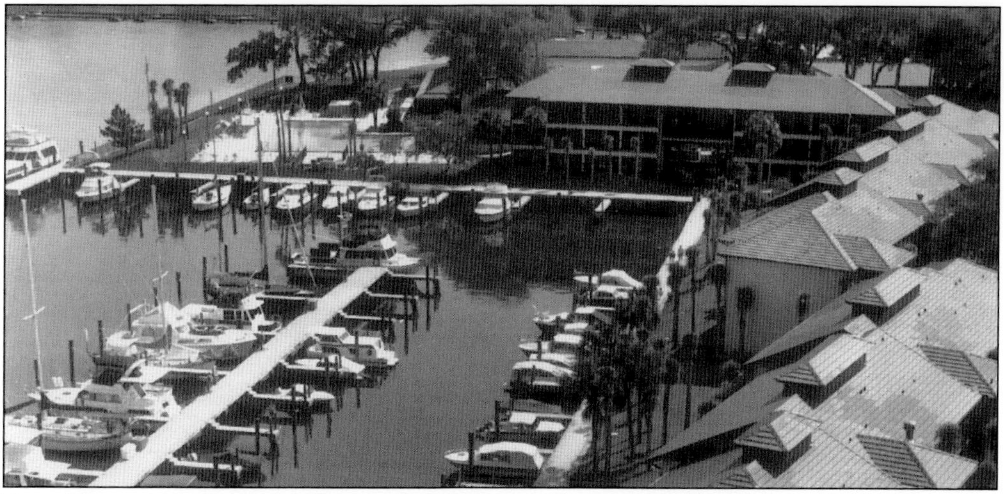

FIRST HOTEL, 1987. Pictured here is the Sheraton. The original Sheraton Motel by the Ocean was scheduled for renovation, but it was torn down instead. Work had begun on the Hammock Dunes Bridge and on oceanfront land developed by ITT's Admiral Corporation. Sheraton, another ITT subsidiary, opened the new hotel in Palm Coast, expanding the yacht club site. The Harbor Restaurant was remodeled to accommodate 235 people, and a meeting and banquet space was created for 400 more. The two-story hotel is surrounded by the Palm Coast Marina and Ships Store, the Harbor ClubVacation Resort, and the nearby Players Club, which replaced the Palm Harbor Tennis Club's courts.

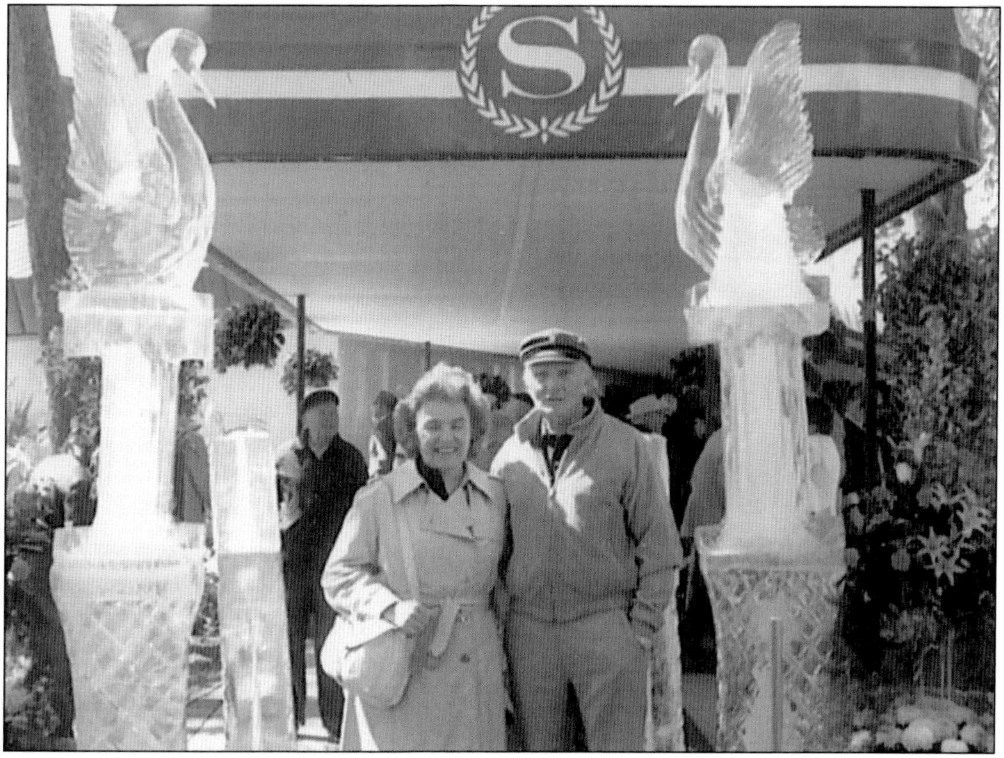

JOHN AND THERESA SCHWARTZ. The Schwartzes are pictured standing by the entrance to the new Sheraton on the Intracoastal Waterway.

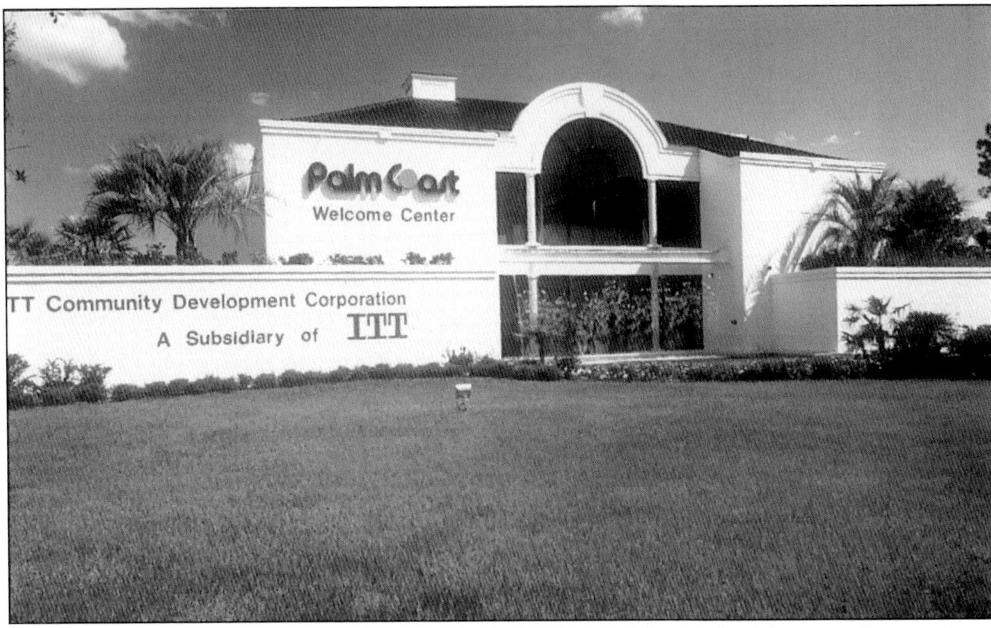

Welcome Center, 1987. ICDC constructed this beautiful new building on the southeast corner of Old Kings Road and Palm Coast Parkway to attract visitors just as they exited I-95 going east.

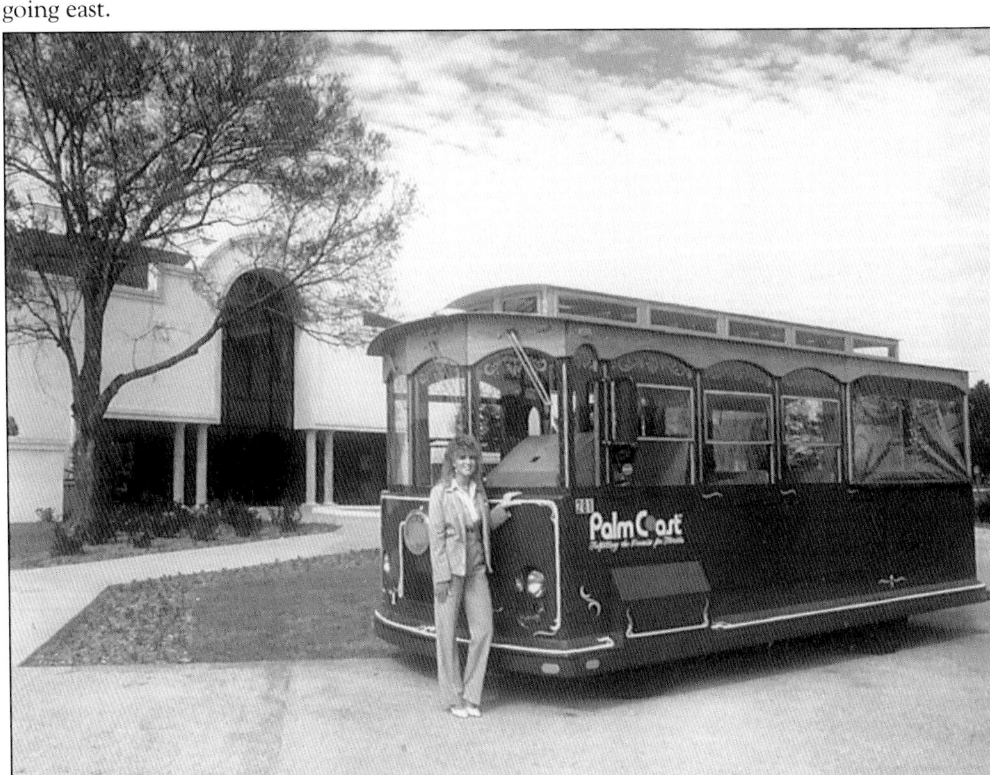

Taxi Anyone? Clients could be taken by this attractive bus/trolley from the welcome center to the tower/model sales area and on a tour of Palm Coast.

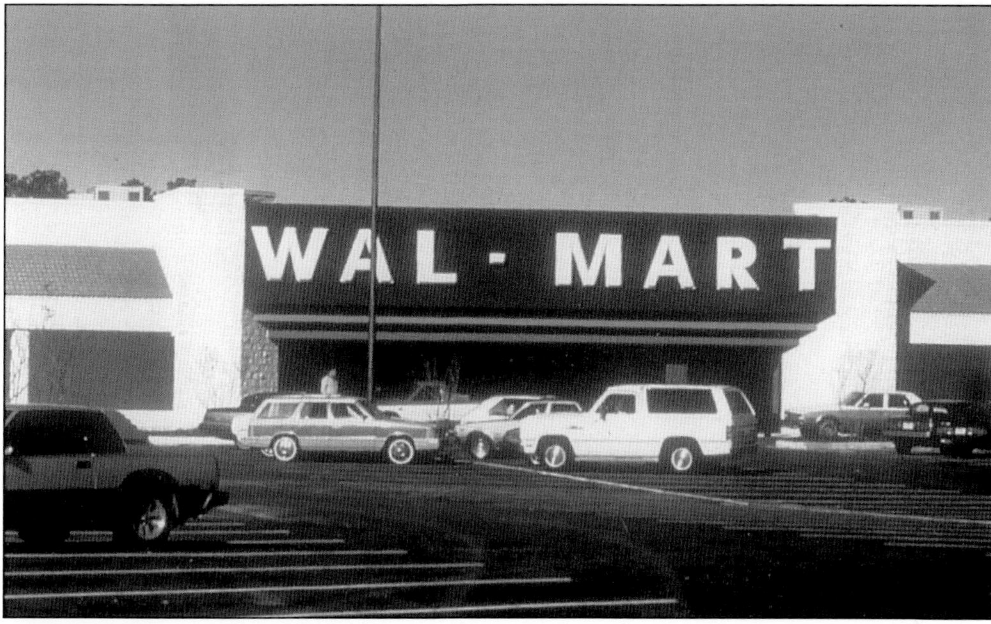

GROWTH, 1987. Our first Wal-Mart, located in the present Staples/Scotties shopping area, proved to be too small and the present super center opened in town in 1995.

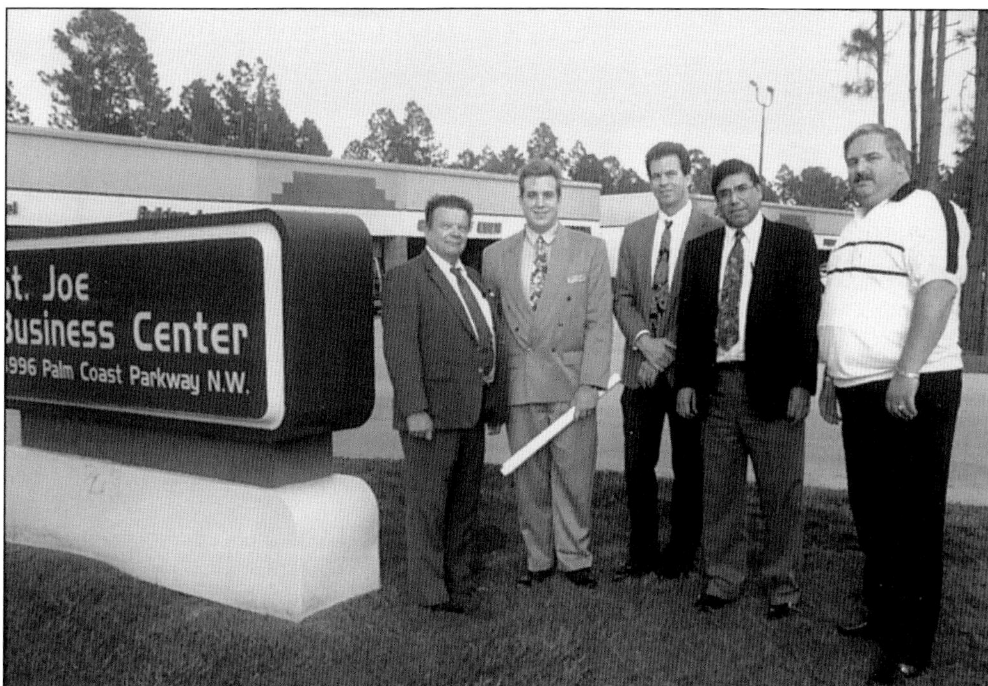

NEW BUSINESS AND SHOPPING CENTER, 1987. Shown here are realty executives Mr. Nieminen and son Scott, Palm Coast Holdings commercial salesman Dave Lusby, unidentified, and Ron Szymanski.

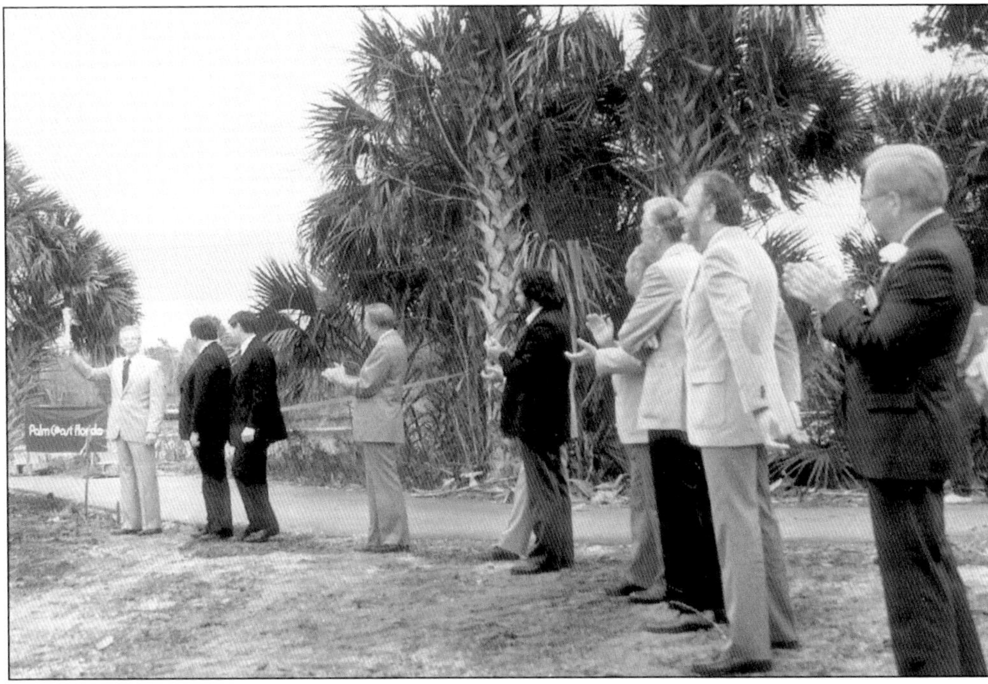

The Hammock Dunes Bridge Groundbreaking, February 1987. Alan Smolen holds high the torch for the bridge he had promised "In My Time" when he became president of ICDC in 1975.

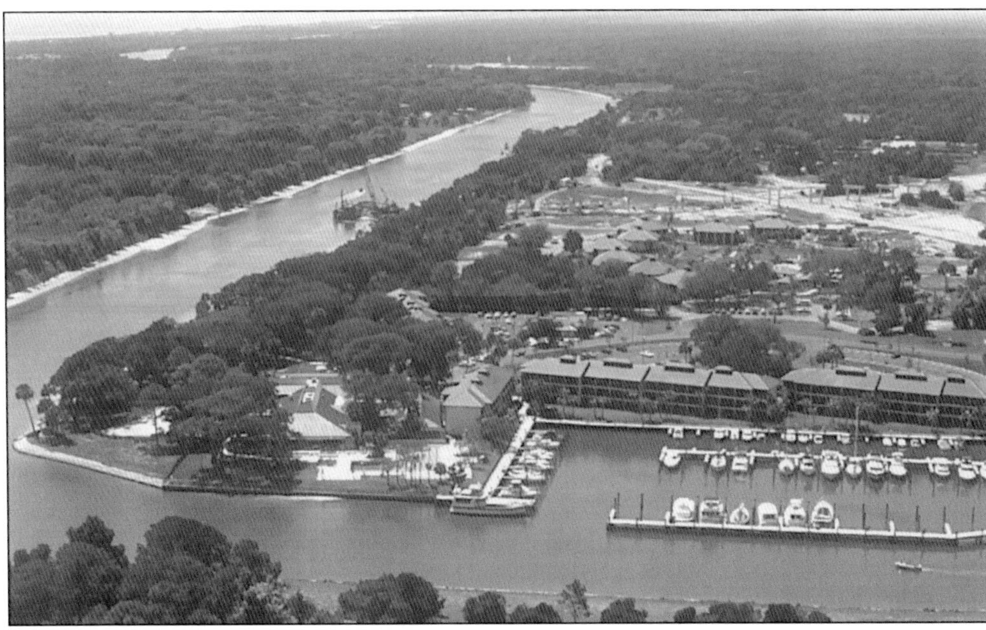

Preparation, 1987. In this aerial photo looking south, the ground has been cleared, the first road abutments have been constructed, and the dredge and derrick in the Intracoastal Waterway signal the impending start of the long awaited Hammock Dunes Bridge. Further north are the Harbor Club, Sheraton, Main Canal, and the land upon which Marina Cove was to be built.

Building. The bridge would include two traffic lanes, two 10-foot auxillary lanes, and a separate pedestrian bicycle lane. The dunes community development district was created by the state to build and operate the bridge. It issued $16.3 million in revenue bonds to be paid over the years by bridge tolls.

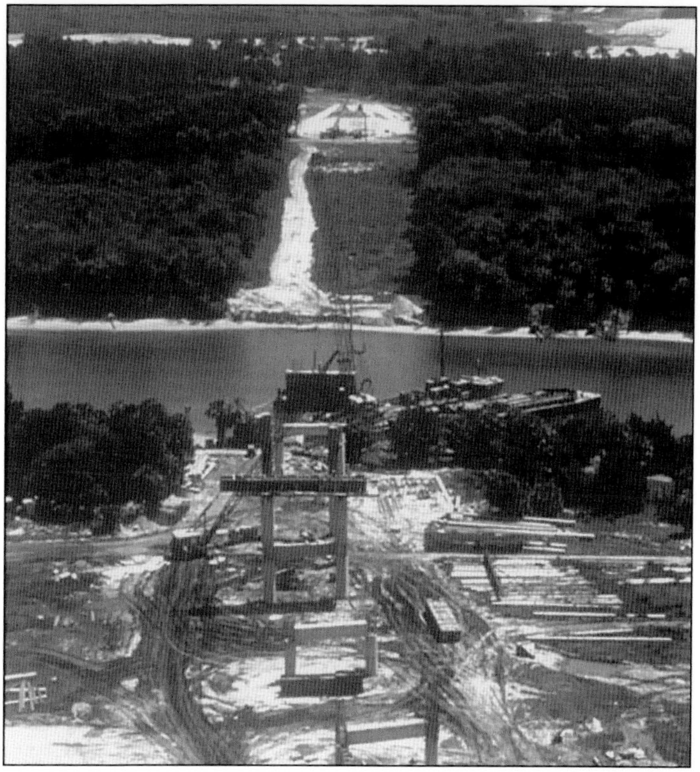

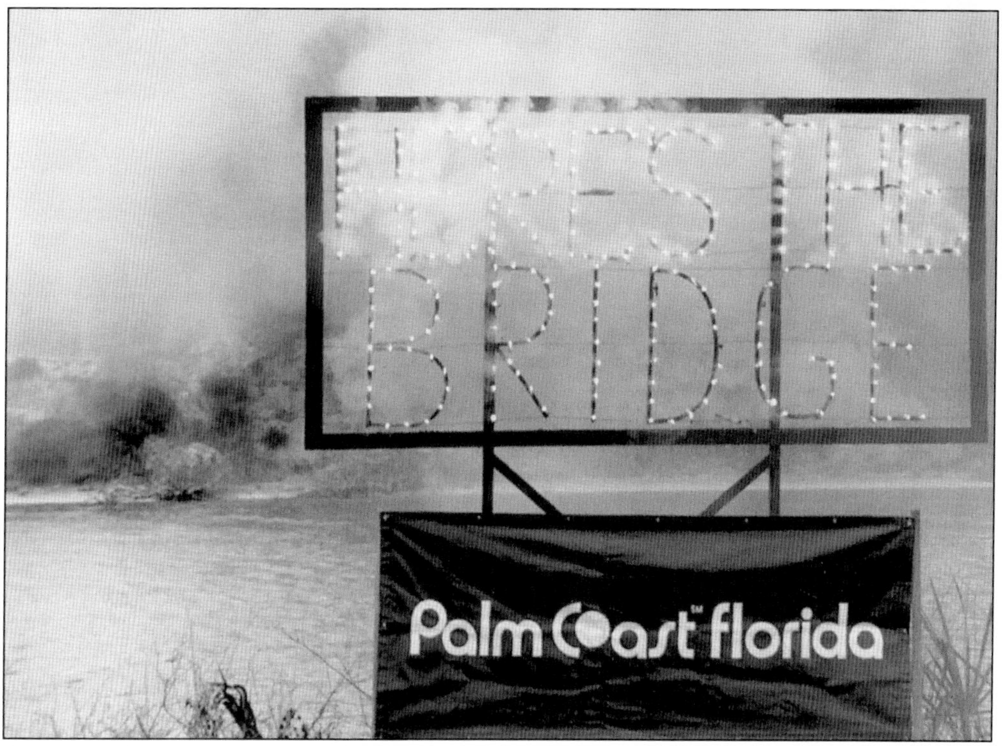

Fireworks. This set piece proudly announces "Here's the bridge."

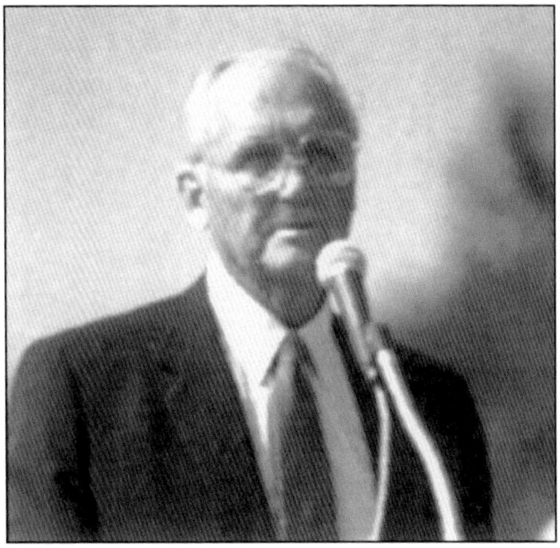

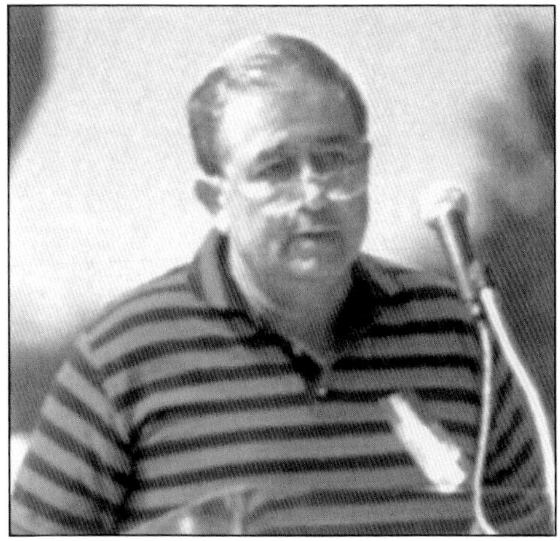

Bridge Dedication, July 3, 1988. U.S. Representative Bill Chappell was the keynote speaker. ITT Corporation president "Pete" Thomas said, "What began as an ITT project has become a collaboration between the developer, public agencies, and the people."

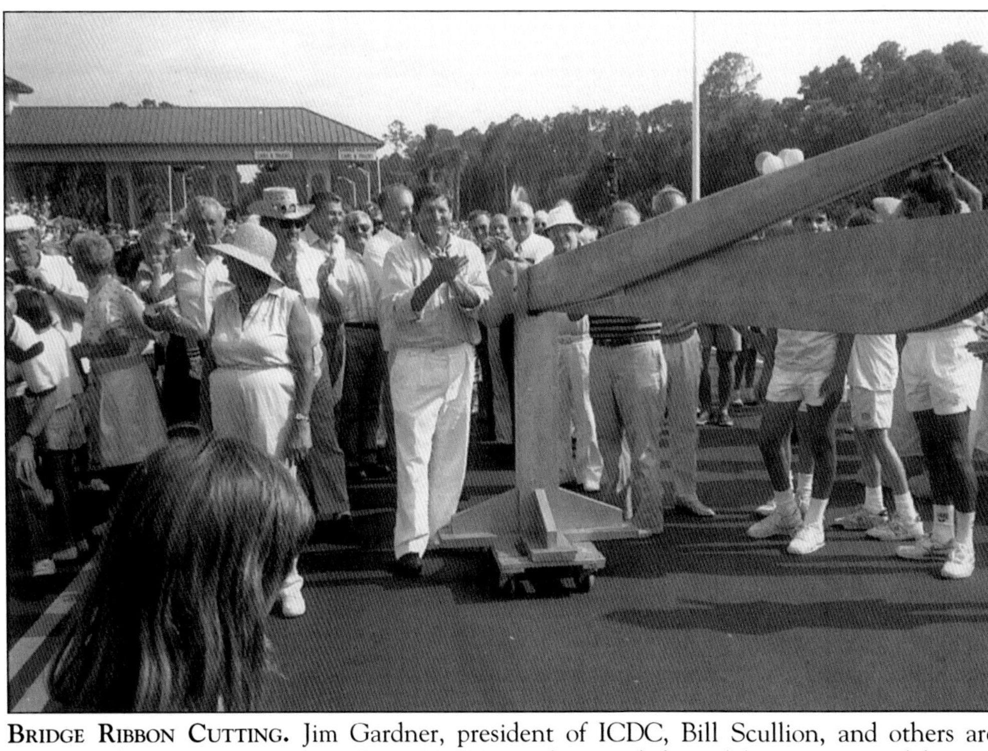

Bridge Ribbon Cutting. Jim Gardner, president of ICDC, Bill Scullion, and others are shown with appropriate scissors. Over 20,000 people attended an elaborate party celebrating the opening of the $10.1 million bridge with a long parade and night time fireworks in a huge outpouring of community spirit.

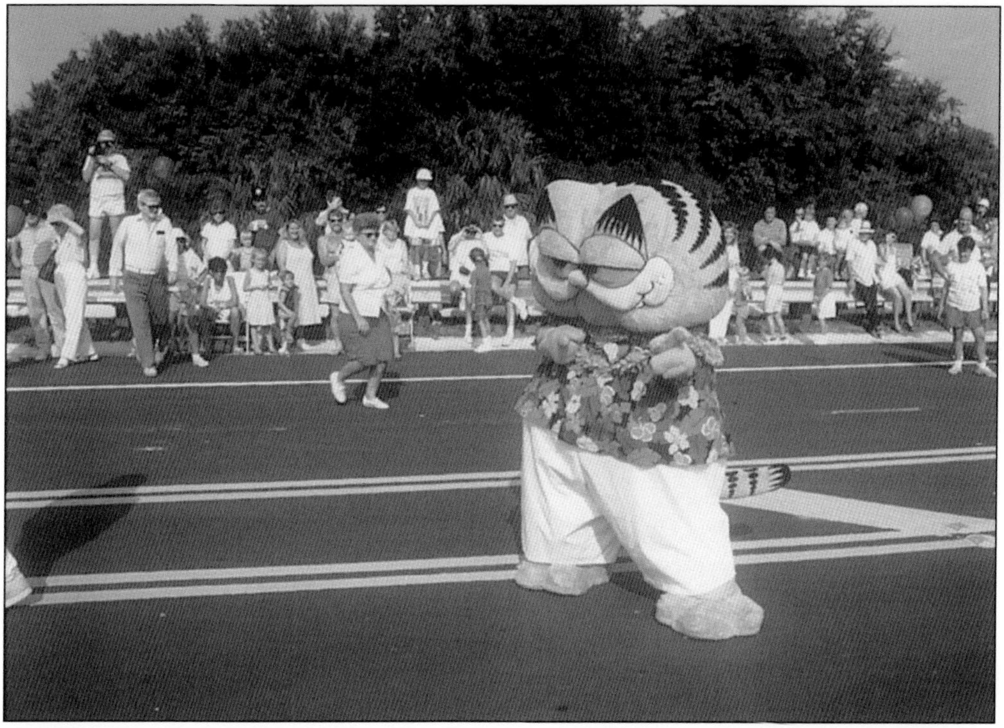

GARFIELD LEADS THE PARADE. The ICDC Palm Coast symbol participated in the parade.

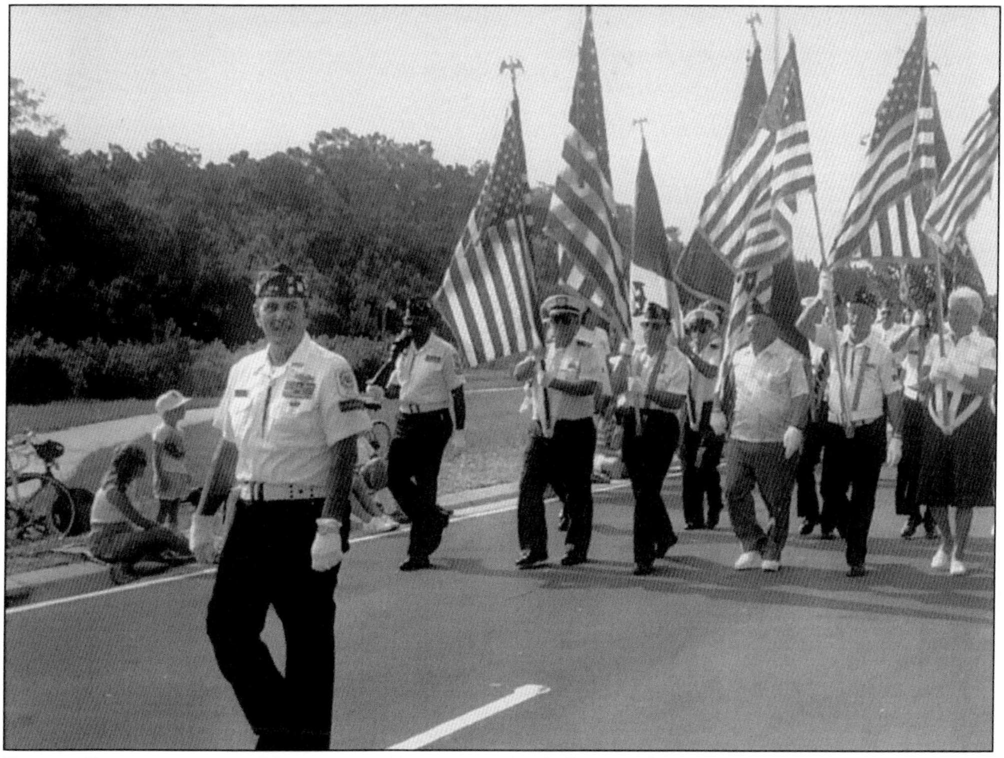

FLAGS. Flags were carried by veterans' groups to lead the parade.

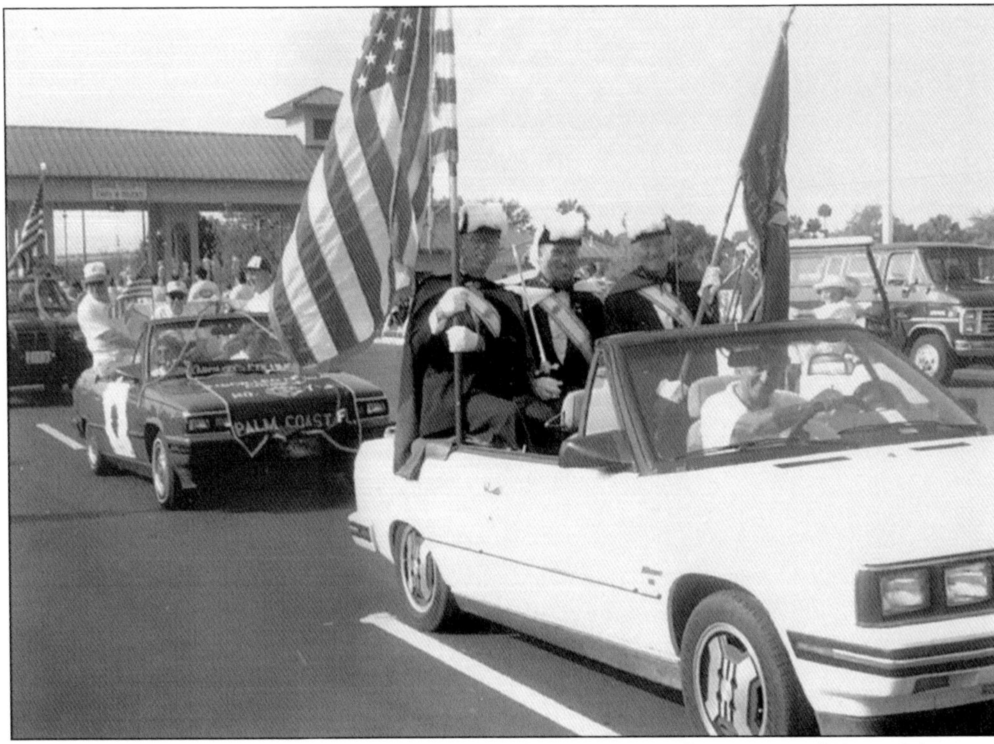

KNIGHTS OF COLUMBUS. Grand Knight Robert Richstatter, Barry Ferguson, and Victor Mazzarini were in the parade.

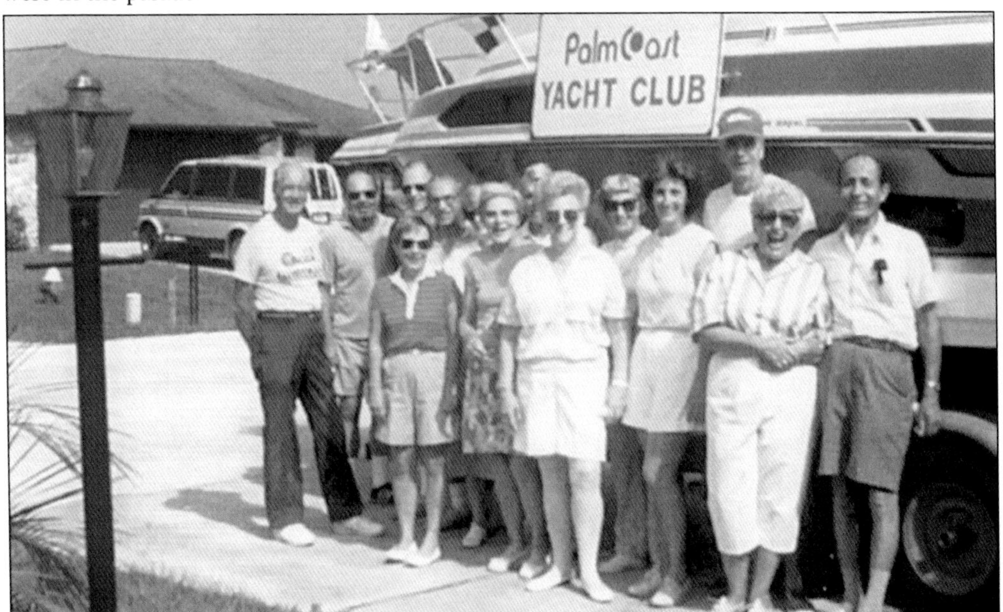

PALM COAST YACHT CLUB. The boat *Just Because*, owned by Jack and Barbara Abadji, had just crossed the new bridge on a trailer. Ray Thompson, Chuck Johnson, Ida Bertsch, Edna Johnson, Shirley and Howard Haury, Joan and Custy Guiness, Don Graham, and Marion Hofmann are all shown here.

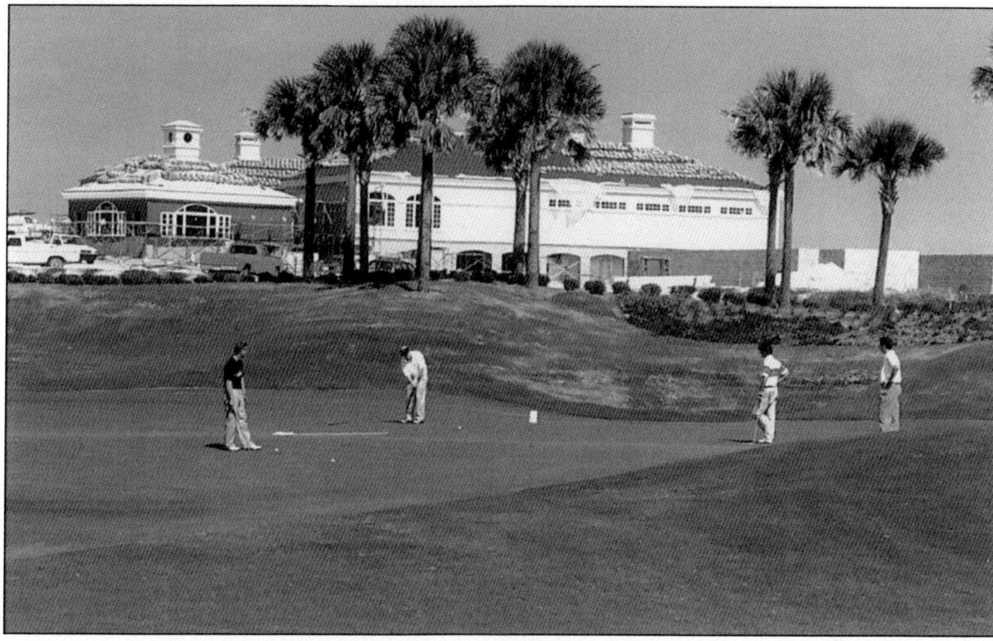

FOURTH GOLF COURSE, 1989. Hammock Dunes Links course was designed by Tom Fazio. The 6,802-yard, ocean-side course was paired with the "only clubhouse directly on the ocean in Florida" at that time. The $6 million building and golf course opened March 16, 1991. Pictured above is the 18th hole and clubhouse with Mediterranean-style architecture.

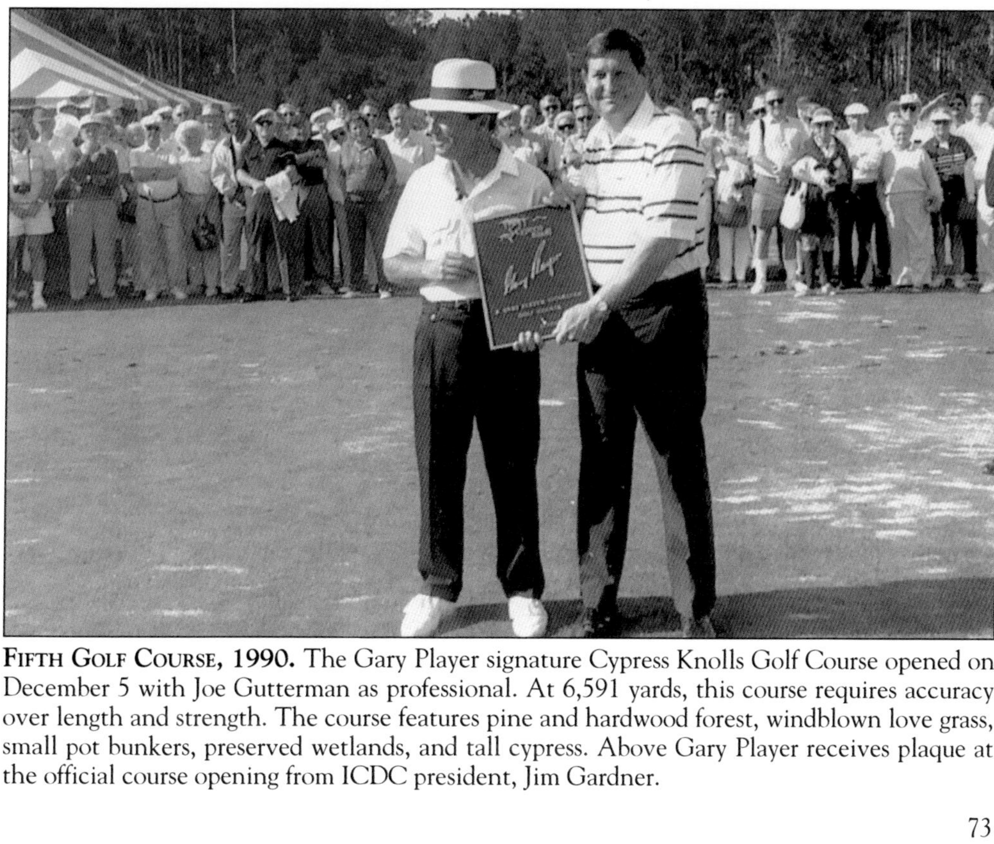

FIFTH GOLF COURSE, 1990. The Gary Player signature Cypress Knolls Golf Course opened on December 5 with Joe Gutterman as professional. At 6,591 yards, this course requires accuracy over length and strength. The course features pine and hardwood forest, windblown love grass, small pot bunkers, preserved wetlands, and tall cypress. Above Gary Player receives plaque at the official course opening from ICDC president, Jim Gardner.

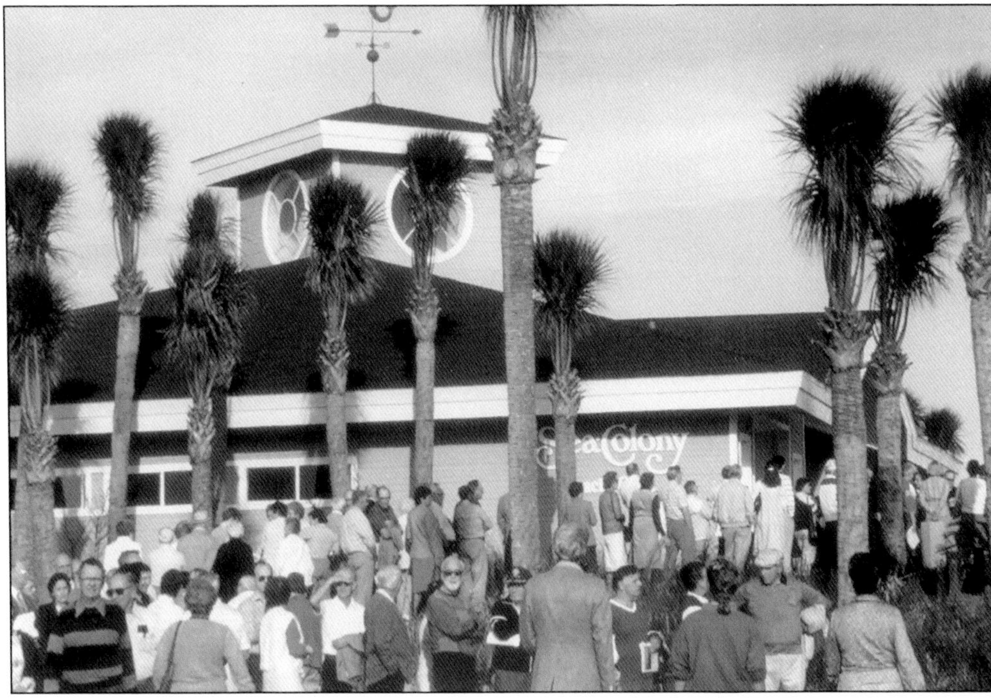

Sea Colony, 1986. The sea colony consists of New England–style houses on the ocean on A1A north of the bridge. Pictured here is an early sales reception.

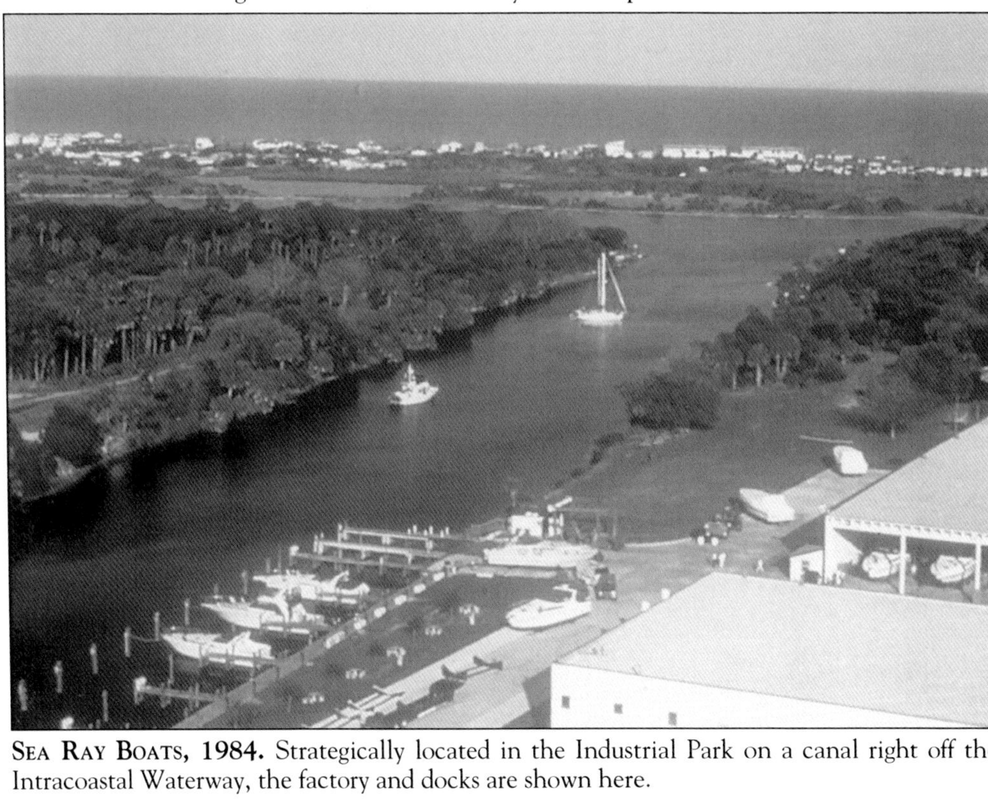

Sea Ray Boats, 1984. Strategically located in the Industrial Park on a canal right off the Intracoastal Waterway, the factory and docks are shown here.

BIKE PATHS THROUGHOUT COMMUNITY, 1988. Concrete paths were built to connect shopping areas and activity centers with every developed neighborhood in Palm Coast. Today the paths interlace the entire community for use by pedestrians, bikers, and carts. They are tied into an elaborate system making the A1A coastal corridor available from one end of Flagler County to the other.

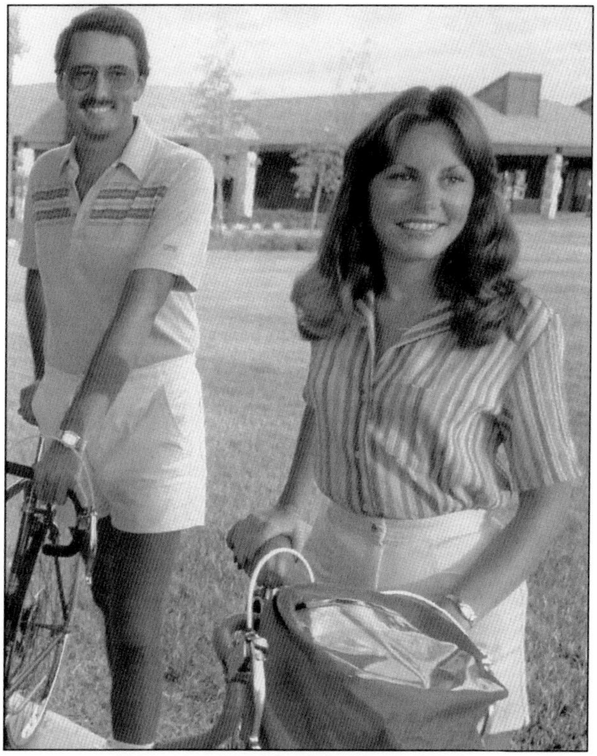

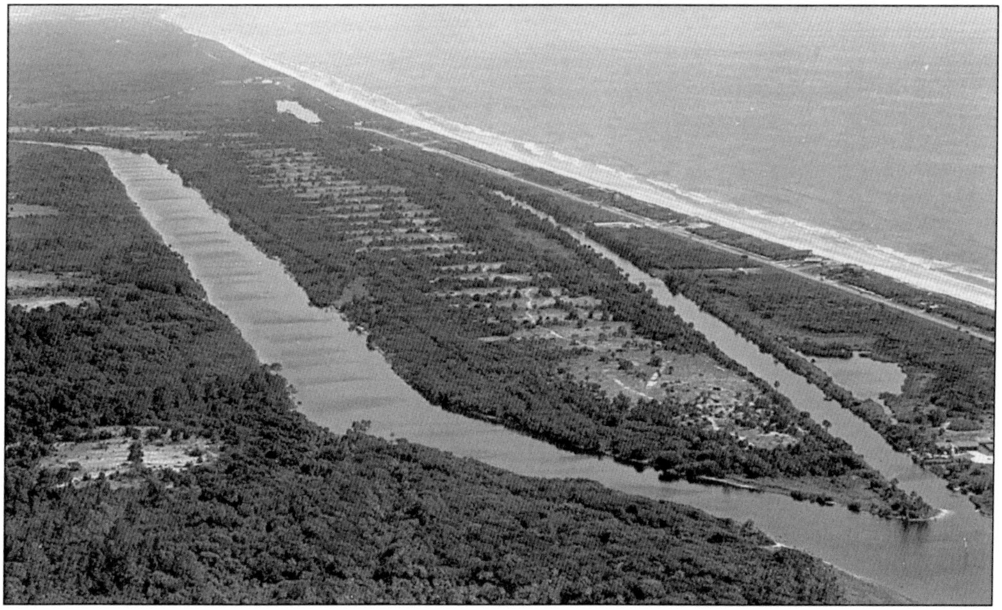

HAMMOCK DUNES PREPARATION. The ICOC Admiral Corporation had been doing environmental studies and planning the area shown above since the early 1980s. As shown here, the Island Estates area between the old unused East Coast Canal and today's Intracoastal Waterway has just been cleared before development. The area shown is part of the longest area of undeveloped coastline in Florida. ITT Subsidiary ICDC took great care in the environmental design for the area and its golf course.

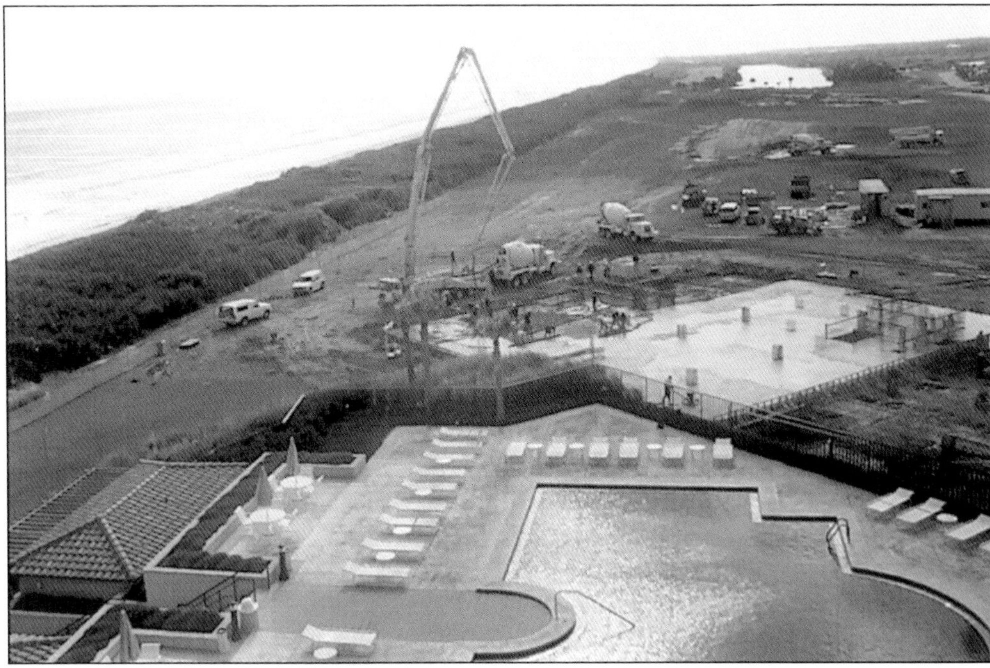

CONSTRUCTION. The old Sheraton was completely demolished and a new larger and more beautiful edifice was being erected.

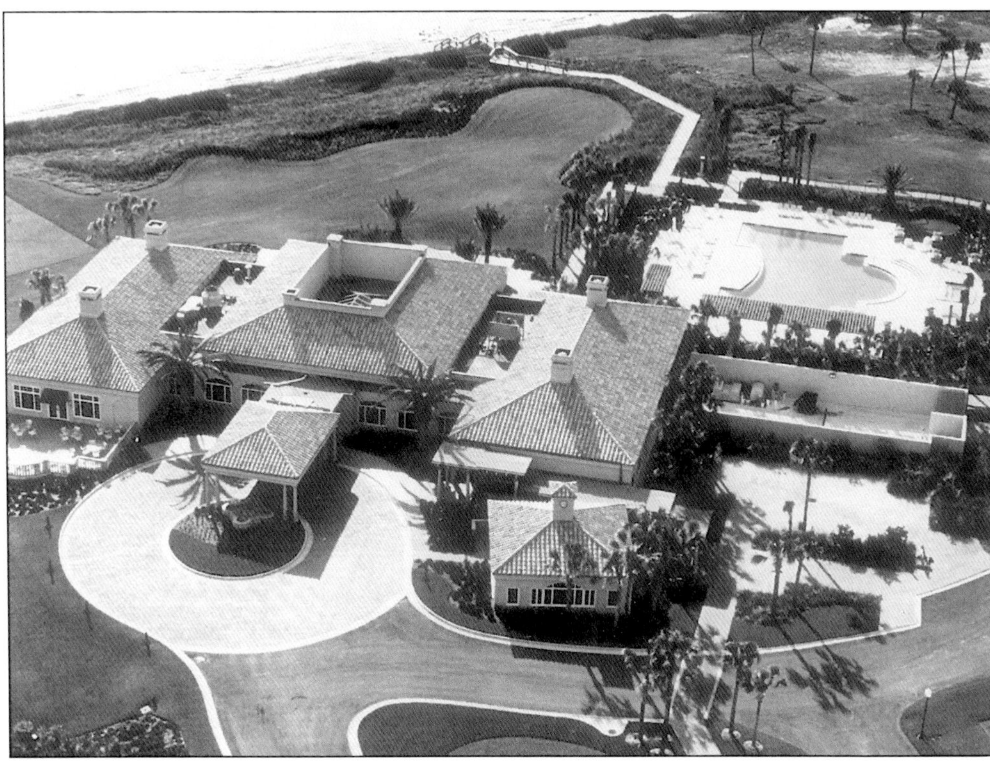

THE RESULT. This beautiful clubhouse was completed in 1989.

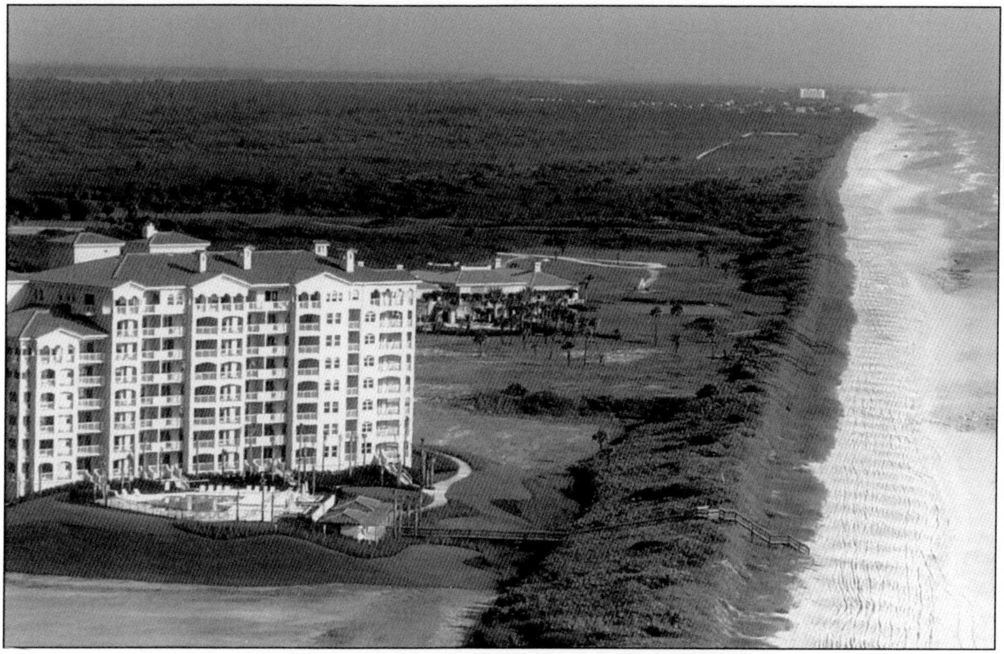

SURF CLUB, 1992. Bob DeVore, president of ITT Community Homes, was responsible for this 96-unit, V-shaped condominium that had all rooms facing the ocean. Notice the extensive area by the ocean providing habitat for the endangered Florida Scrub Jay. The Surf Club on route A1A is teamed with Lakeside by the Sea, which has its own boat club on the Intracoastal Waterway, as the most northern Palm Coast development.

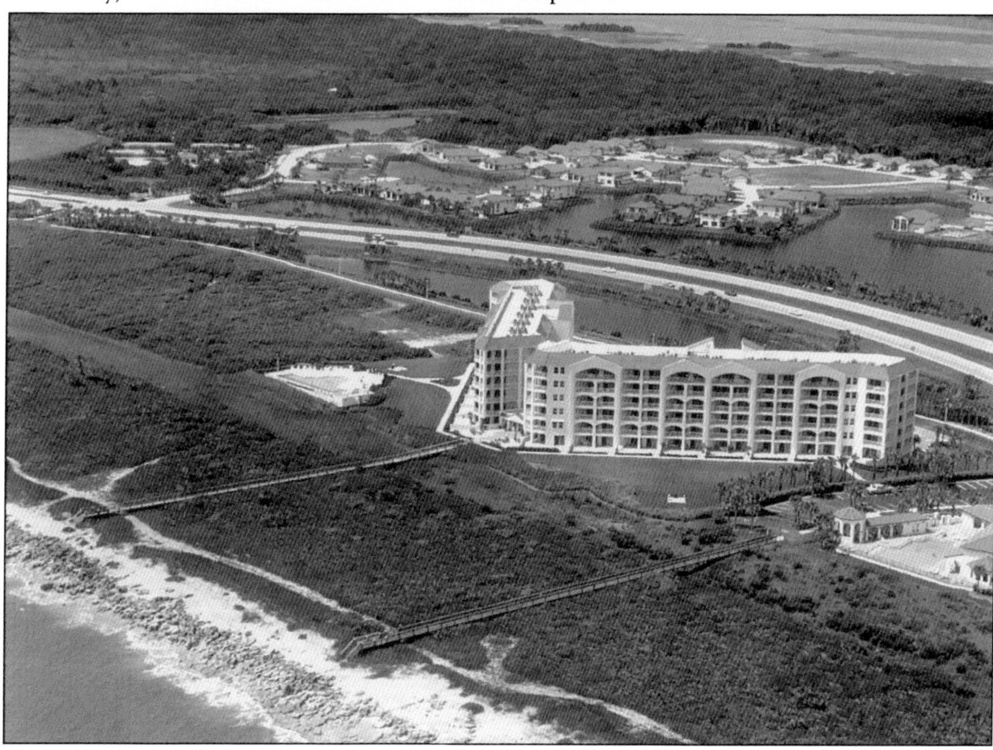

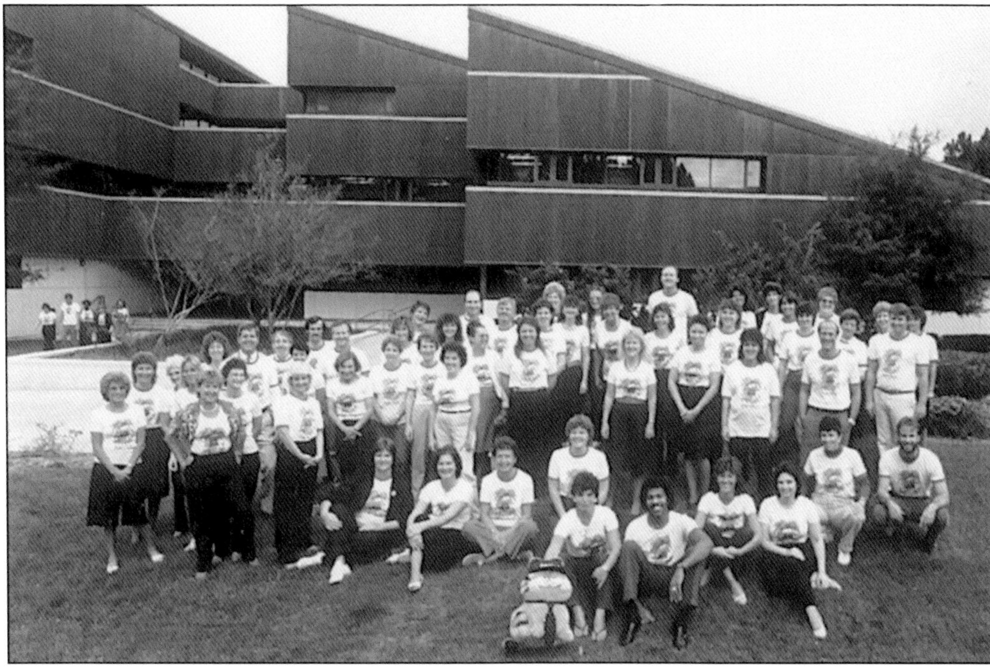

PALM COAST'S LARGEST EMPLOYER, 1969–1995. Hammock Dunes was the last major project undertaken by the corporation before they sold most of their substantial remaining holdings in 1995. The following photographs depict ICDC employees from 1980 on. Many are still active in the Palm Coast community today. Not all names are listed on some pictures. Shown above are the staff at ICDC headquarters on Garfield T-Shirt Day, October 4, 1985.

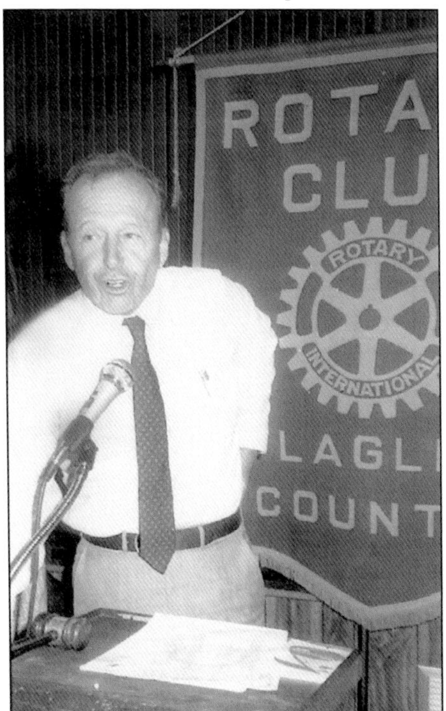

JERRY FULL 1980. During the early 1980s, it was common to see and hear Jerry reporting new ICDC developments to the community. Here, Rotarians heard about the new hotel, tennis club, and golf courses, as well as the beautification of Palm Coast Parkway. Jerry was elected to Palm Coast's first city council. It is still common to see Jerry at meetings discussing Rails to Trails and a number of environmental issues.

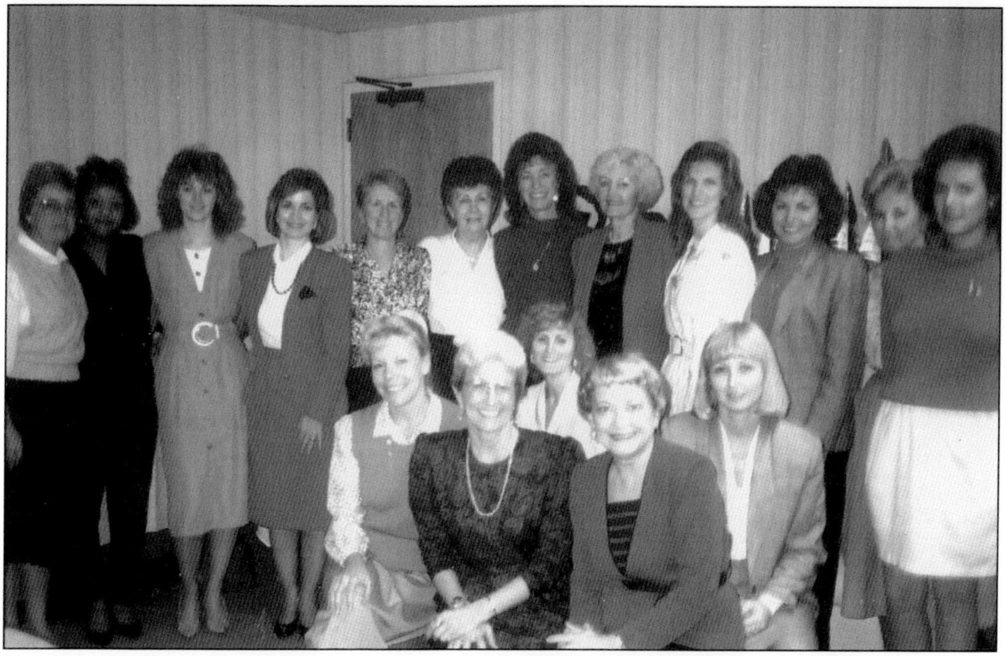

THE SENIOR EXECUTIVE SUPPORT GROUP, DECEMBER 1990. Members of the group pictured above, from left to right, are Priscilla Hooper, Pam Thompson, Lisa Bryl, Janice Bosworth, Irene Missbach, Lillian Megonegal, Becky Bearrs, Micette Stapp, Libbie Butler, Vicki Root, Jan Voelker, Marianne Murphy, Kathy Ross, Jean Hill, Arlene Wilson, Dorothy Zierk, and Barbara Peacock.

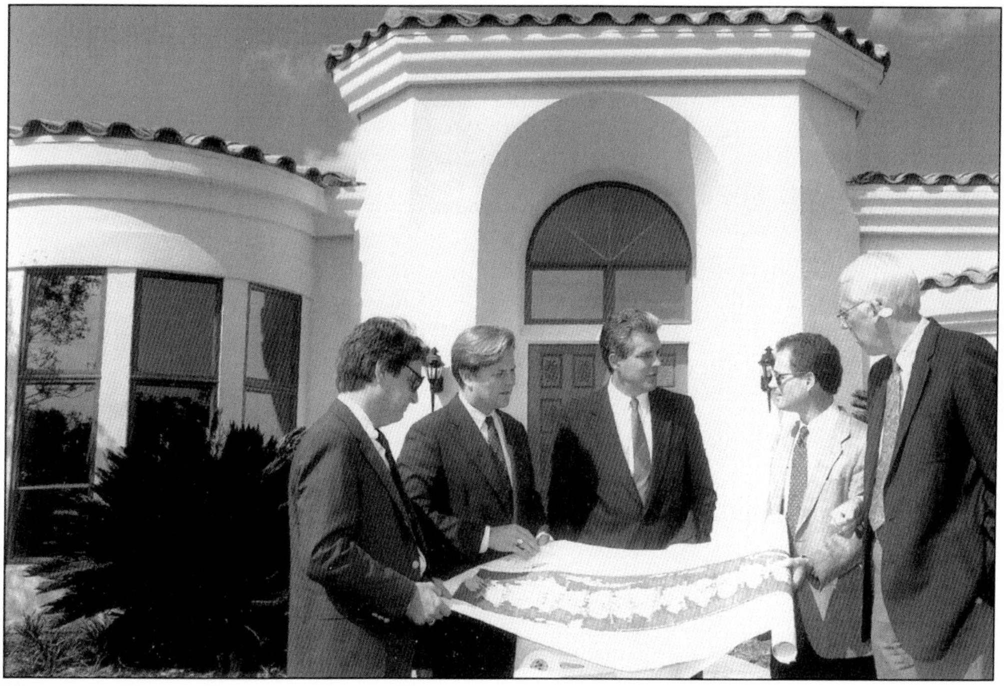

HAMMOCK DUNES PLANNING SALES TEAM AT GRANADA. David Root, Michael Wiles, John Schlegel, and Don Magee are shown here.

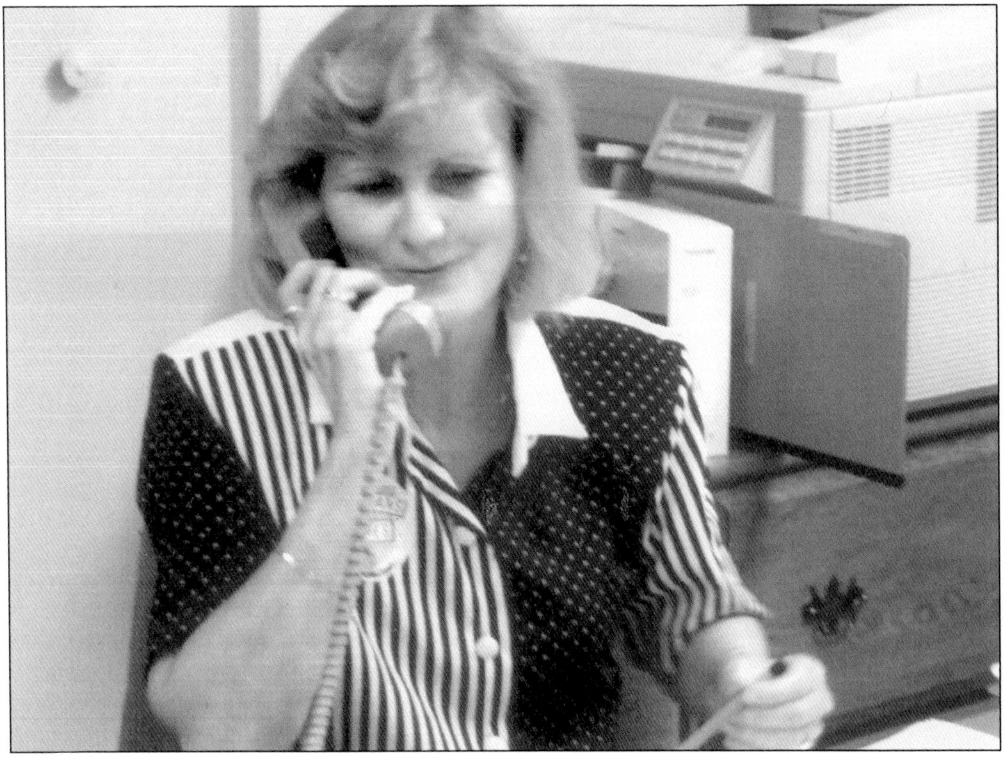

Arlene Wilson. Starting at ITT-CDC in Miami in 1977, Arlene moved to Palm Coast as administrative secretary to President Alan Smolen in 1978 until his retirment in 1985. She continued with President Jim Gardner until he retired in 2000, and she was one of two employees remaining when ITT-CDC completely closed its doors in March 2001.

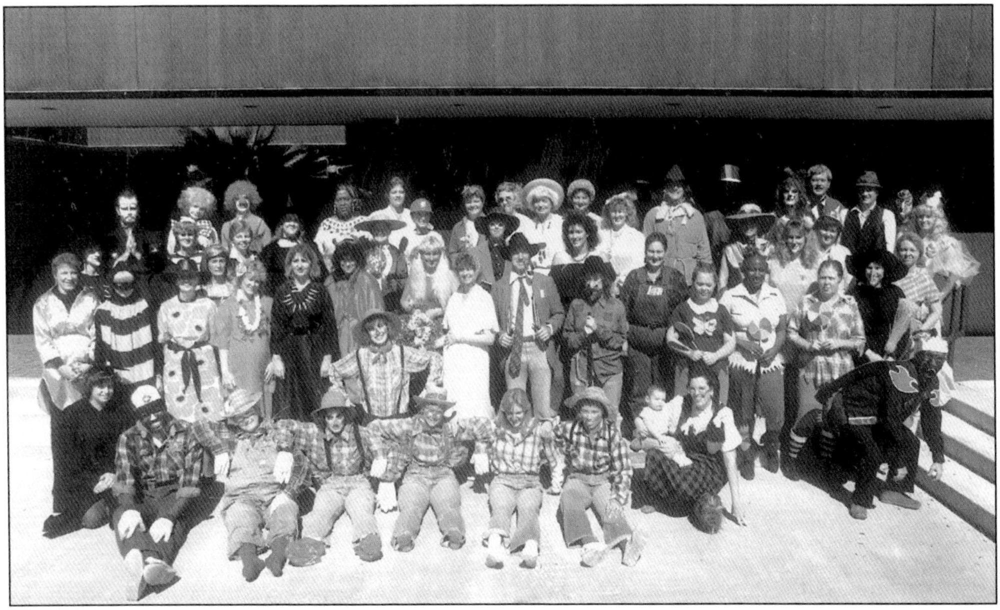

ICDC Employee Halloween Party 1988. Cal Massey in a white face appears in the top upper left of this picture.

Four

The People

Their Organizations and Activities

From the start, ITT had provided the physical facilities and the philosophy of a socially and environmentally balanced planned community. The pioneer settlers had encountered early challenges and overcame them with enthusiasm and spirit. Thus far the book has emphasized ITT's completion of Palm Coast's physical facilities. It is now time to examine the initiative and spirit of the people, working together in organizations or as individuals, to continue building an active, diverse, interesting, and vital community. Could the prophesy "It may just be the perfect place to live," be fulfilled?

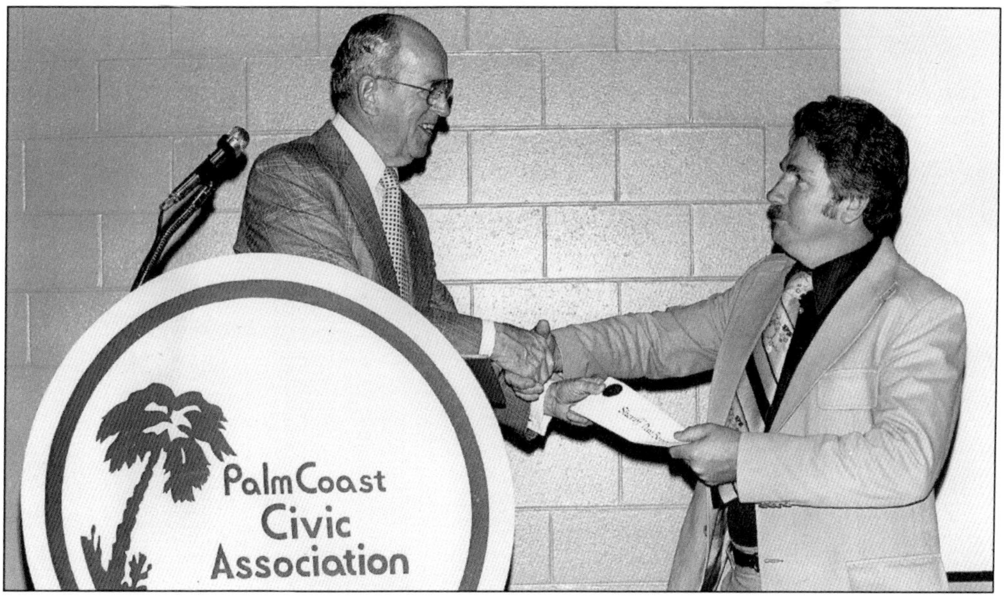

Palm Coast Civic Association, July 1972. The first organization formed by Palm Coast residents was designed to enhance residential life. Only 50 houses had been completed when 20 homeowners organized a committee to draw up the civic association's constitution and by-laws. The organization's purpose was to provide a means for residents to gather and discuss ideas and programs for improving their community. Their objectives included maintaining and increasing property values; providing civic functions, social activities, entertainment, recreation, nuisance control, and beautification of property; and to serve as a liaison with the developer. Interest in politics soon followed. Bill Loeb served as the first president, Cliff Parr was vice president, Charles Konopasek was treasurer, and Bernadette Collier was secretary. Here, 1978–1979 Palm Coast Civic Association president Jim Miskelly honors Sheriff Dan Bennett.

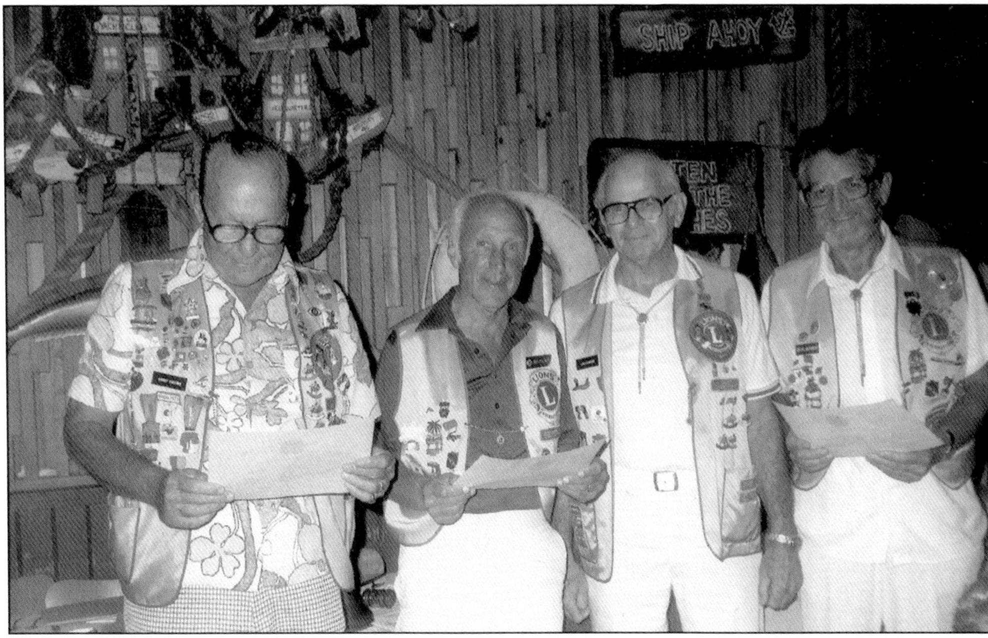

Lions Club, 1973. The purpose of the Lions Club is to contribute to the growth and general welfare of members and of the local community. Early support was directed towards Boy Scouts and Girl Scouts, the Council on the Aging, and the Special Olympics. Above, President Elwood Harkins presents a Golden Chain Award for outstanding community work to Richard Perlman, Leonard Flanagan, and Edmund Klukowski in September 1982.

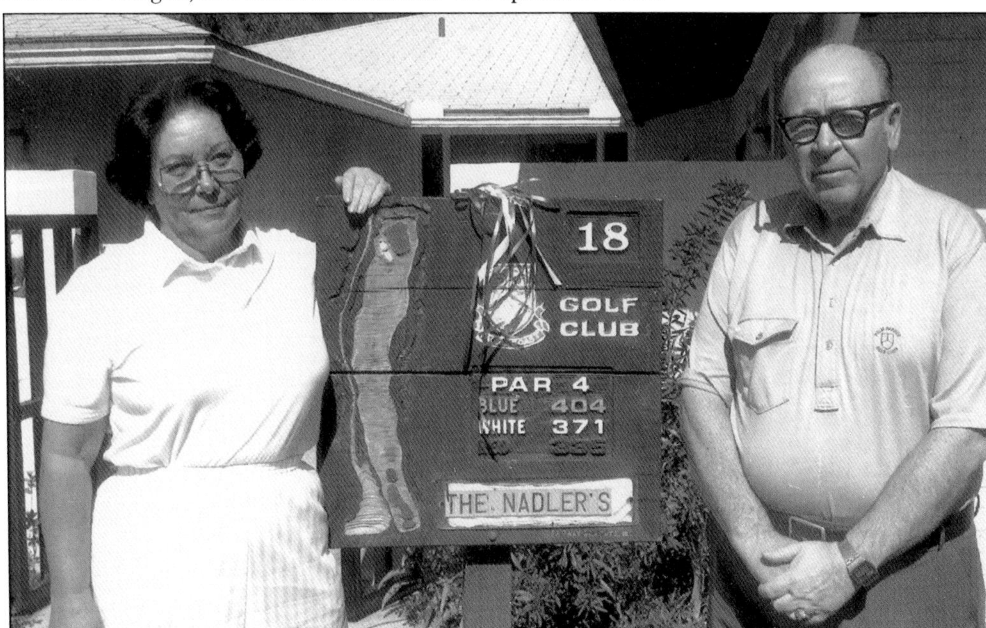

Palm Coast Men's and Women's Golf Associations, 1973. The associations serve to promote fellowship, improve member's golf games, establish lasting friendships, and enjoy the game of golf. Jim Miskelly, a reporter of the local golf scene for many years, provided this picture of typical golf association members. Jack and Elfi Nadler pose outside their home in 1991.

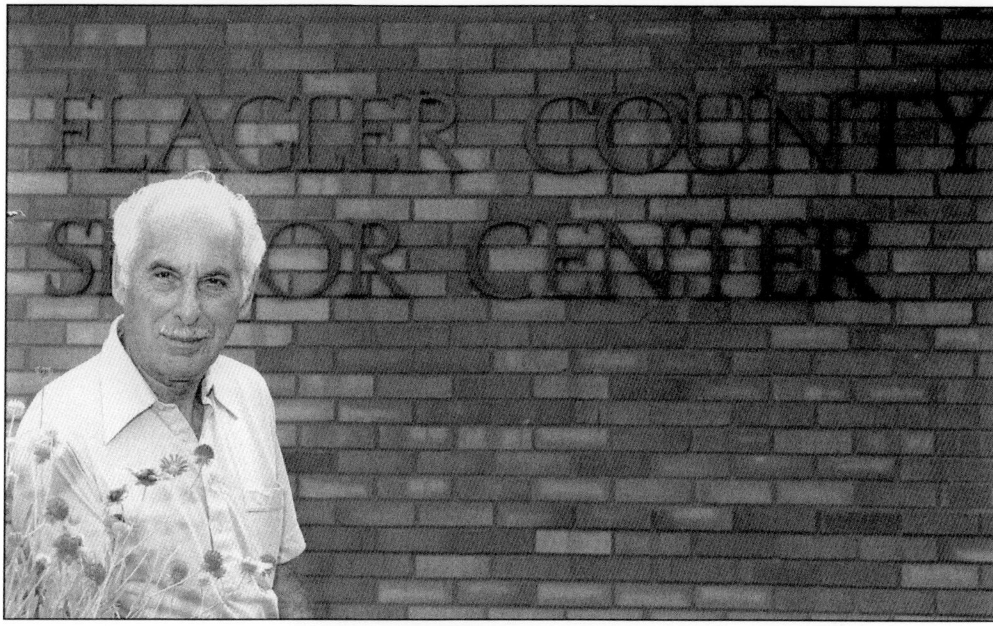

FLAGLER COUNTY COUNCIL ON AGING, 1974. The council was a group formed to offer a broad variety of vital services to the aging and the handicapped regardless of age. As a private and public citizen, David I. Siegel worked steadfastly for senior issues. The Center for Senior Services now bears his name after being dedicated to him on April 21, 2003.

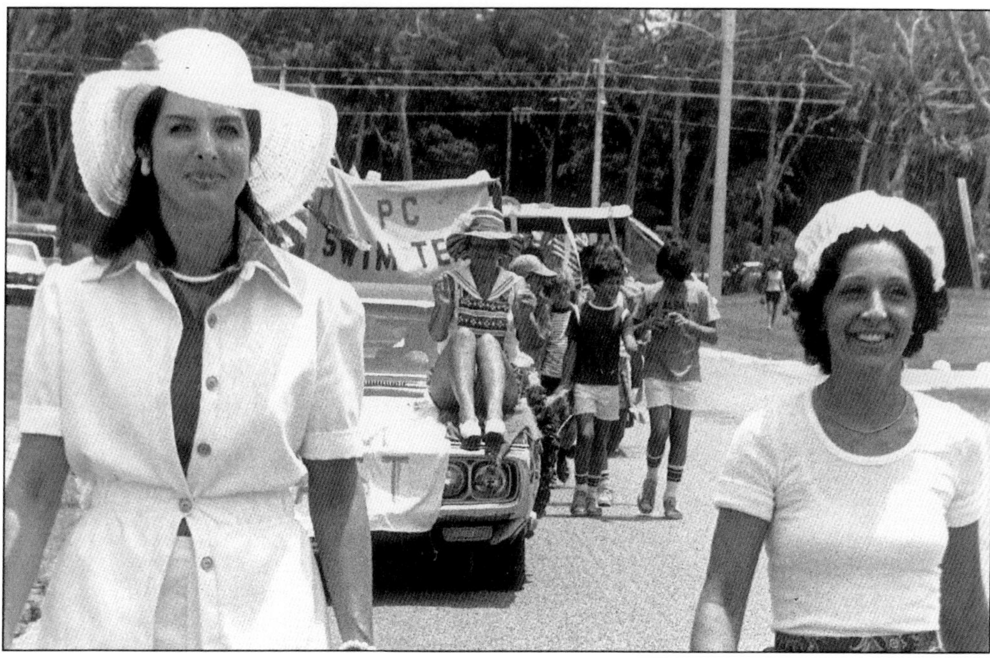

PALM COAST WOMAN'S CLUB, 1974. This group was formed to foster the development of educational, literary, scientific, and philanthropic programs to make Palm Coast a better place to live. They assisted in the formation of the regional library system and awarded fine arts scholarships to Flagler/Palm Coast High School students. Shown here are President Pat Cafaro, Executive Vice President Madeline Lee, and Ann Morrow (on car) in the Bicentennial Parade.

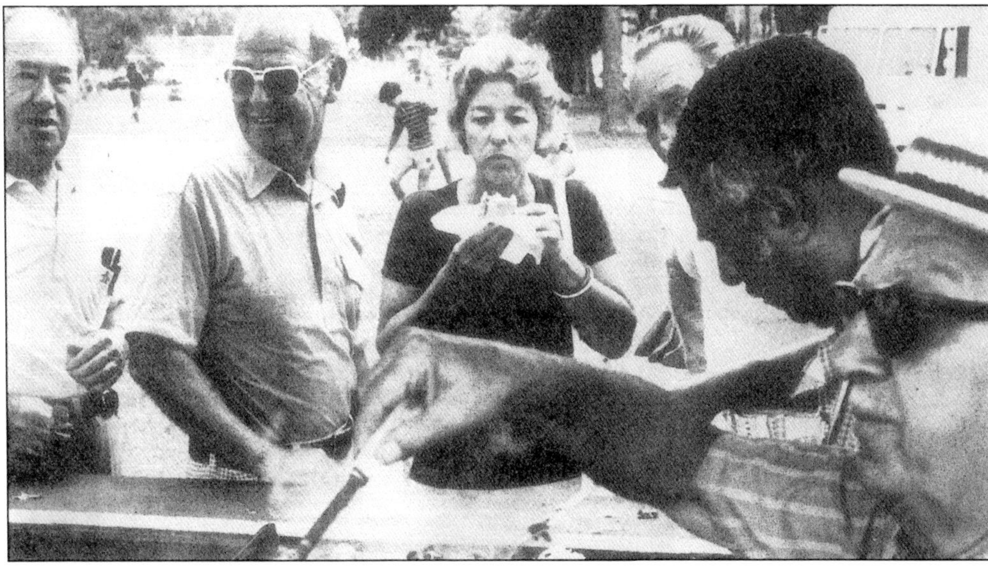

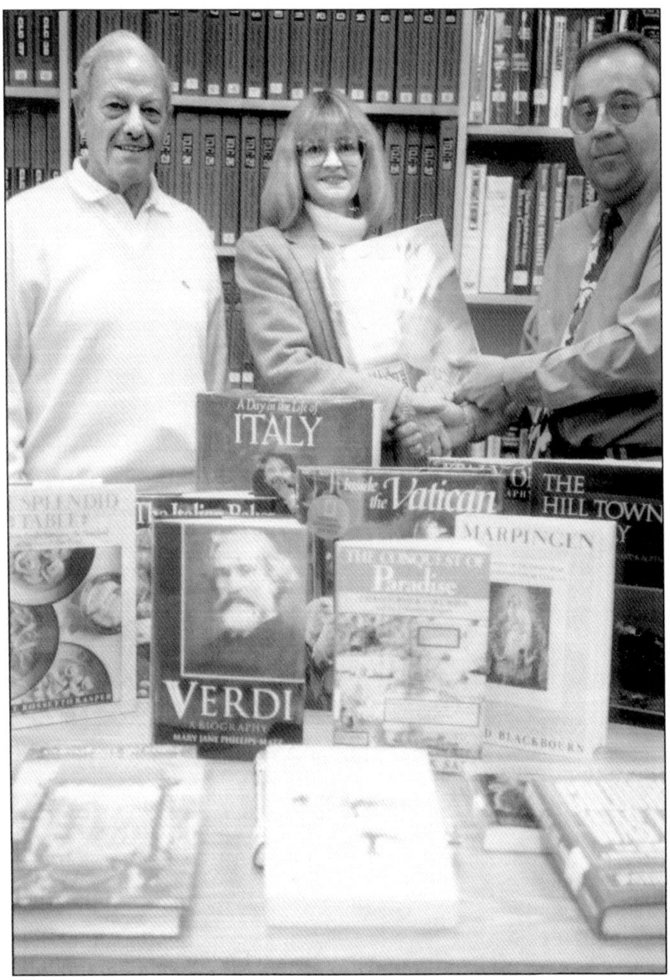

ITALIAN AMERICAN CLUB, 1974. This group served to provide a means to form endearing friendships, promote better understanding of the Italian-American heritage, and cooperate in building a better community through direct involvement in charitable efforts. The group was formed by Carmine Izzilo, Nunzio Palladino, John Ruggeire, Sam Merenda, and Tom Albano with Michael Chiumento as acting legal advisor. The organization's annual three-day "Festa Italiana" in the spring draws visitors from throughout the region. Pictured in 1995 making the Italian-American Club's annual donation to the library of books reflecting the Italian culture are Orlando "Al" Nunziata, the Heritage Committee; Roberta Shaw, librarian for book selection; and Alphonse Ripandell, president IASC.

PALM COAST TENNIS ASSOCIATION, 1974. To promote active organized participation in tennis, to assist the community in acquiring proper facilities for the sport, and to provide opportunities for tennis friendships was the mission of the association. Pictured in August 1976 are the following: Joe Beyta, Betty Armstrong, Ann Tillard, Marie Savino, Will Berkit, Ed Zenobi, Bob Armstrong, and Tom Thornton. They are shown at the four courts of the Yacht Club, before they were replaced by Sheraton Hotel parking.

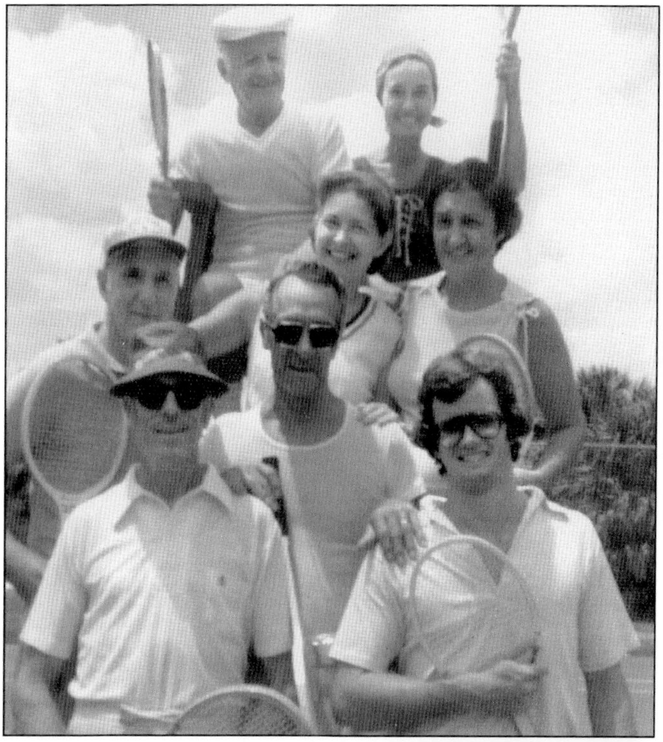

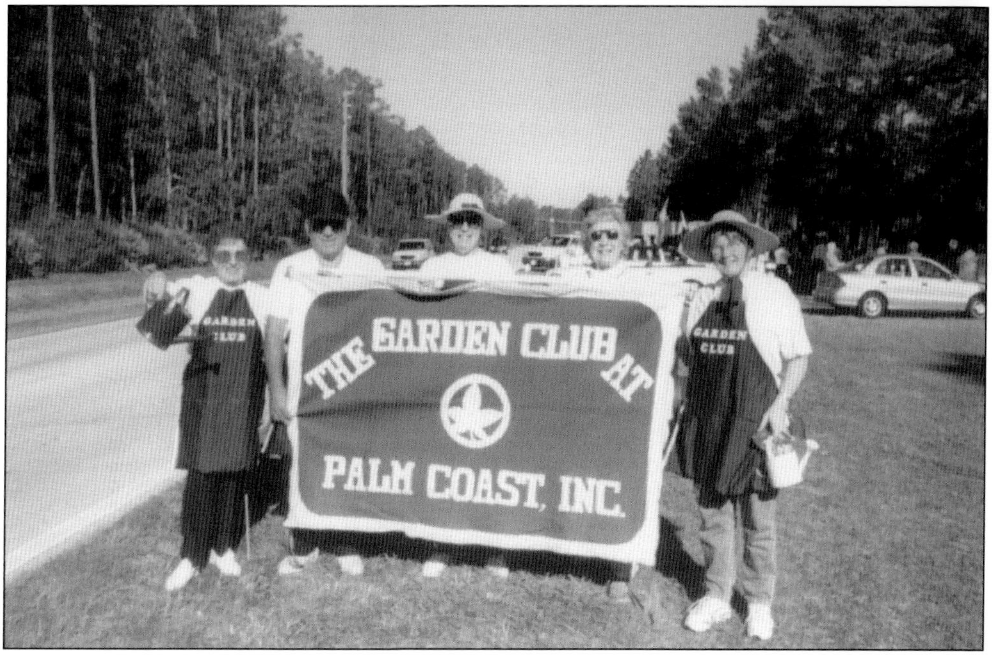

GARDEN CLUB OF PALM COAST, 1974. This group served to encourage interest in all phases of gardening and to promote beautification of the community. In June 1976, the first club officers were Dolph Smally, president; Lester Barr, vice president; Margaret Davie, secretary; and Alfred Ingham, treasurer. Pictured here are Bea Silvester, Barbara Sulser, Miriam Rich, Bev Martinolick, and Roy Schaffer.

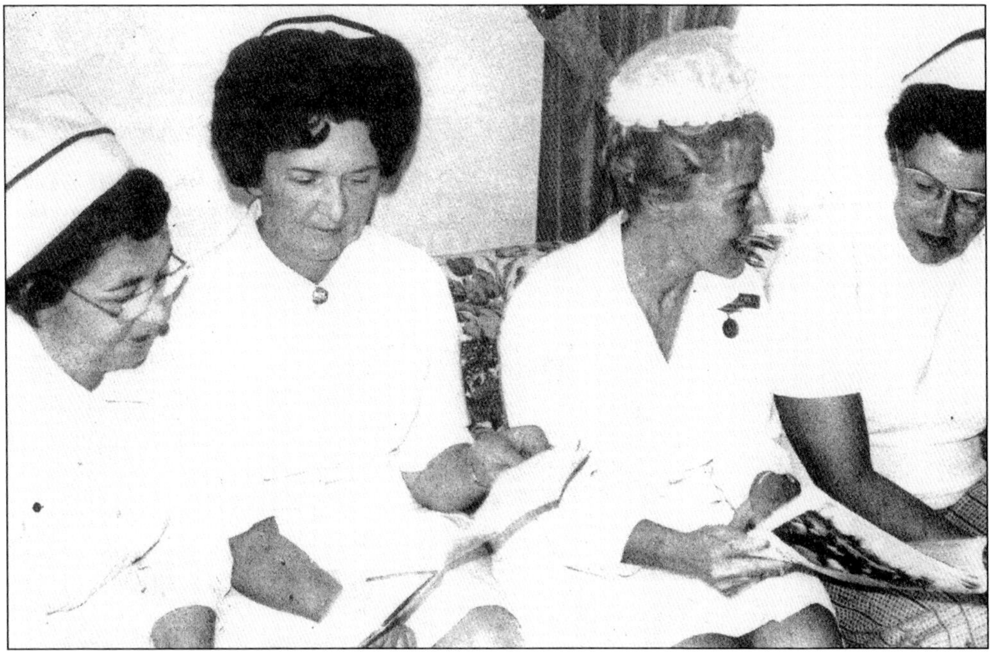

PROFESSIONAL NURSES OF PALM COAST, 1975. In January, the new officers discussed their plans for the coming year. They were, from left to right, Augusta Dunn, secretary; Isabella Kempa, vice president; Mary Pauly, president; and Mary Beattie, treasurer.

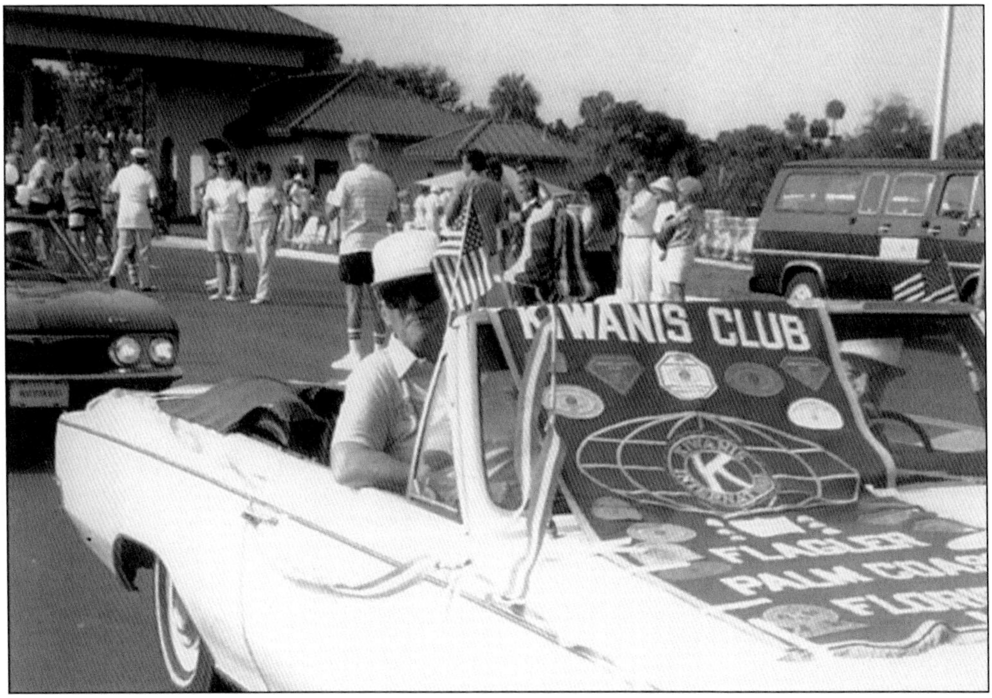

KIWANIS CLUB, 1977. The club is a world wide service organization for men desiring personal involvement in the leadership and improvement of their communities. Members are here shown participating in the bridge opening in 1988.

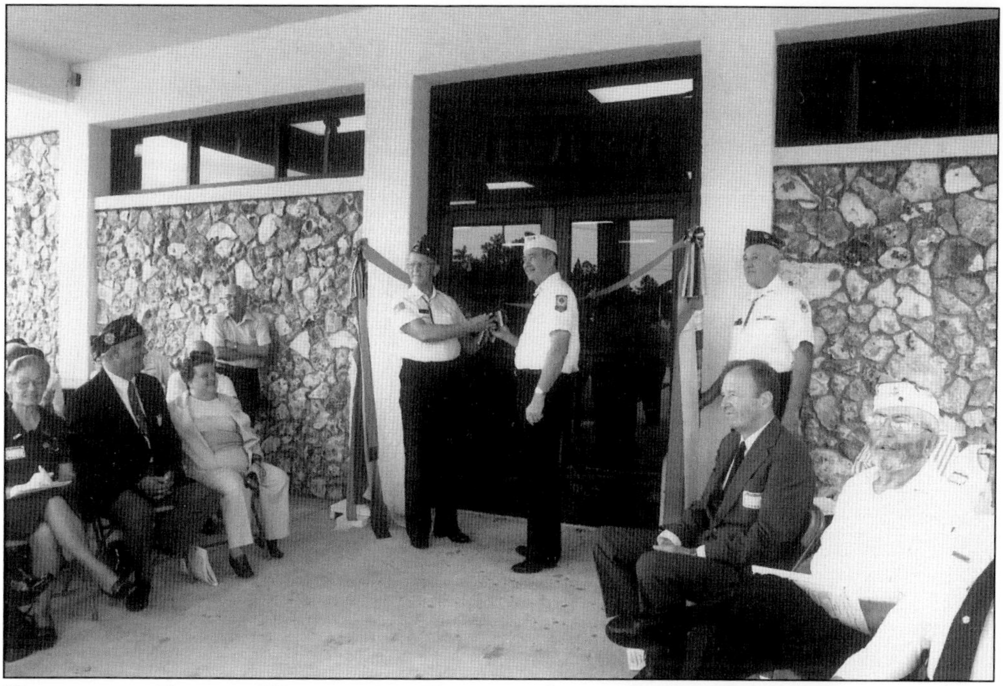

Veterans of Foreign Wars, 1976. They served to assist U.S. War Veterans and spread Americanism and patriotism. Pictured here is the grand opening of the Post 8696 building and social hall on Clubhouse Drive. The only participants identified are Ed Flad and Jerry Full.

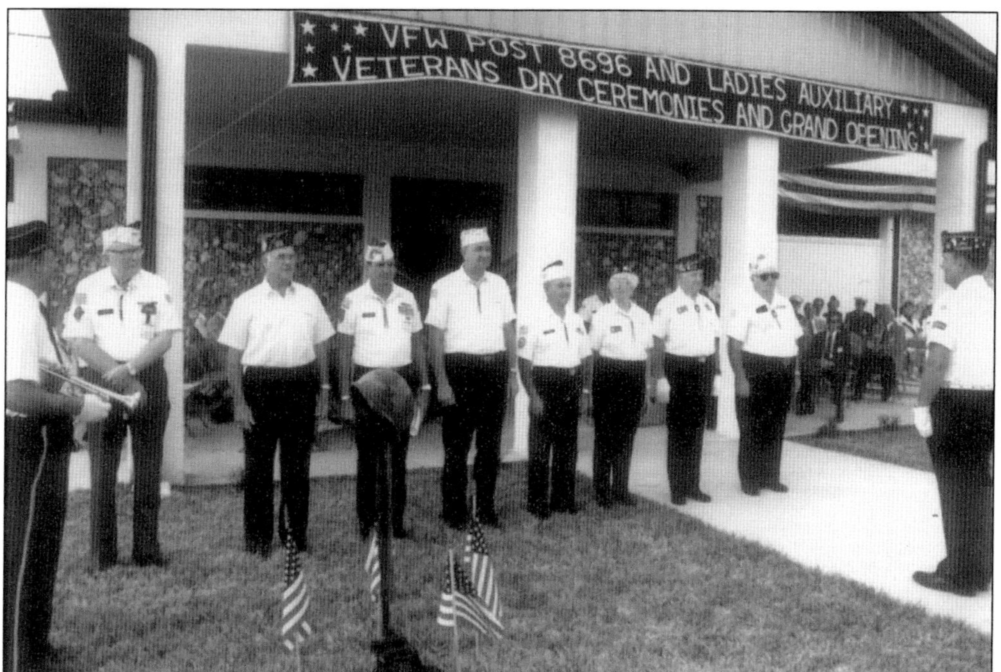

VFW Opening. Veterans honor their fallen comrades.

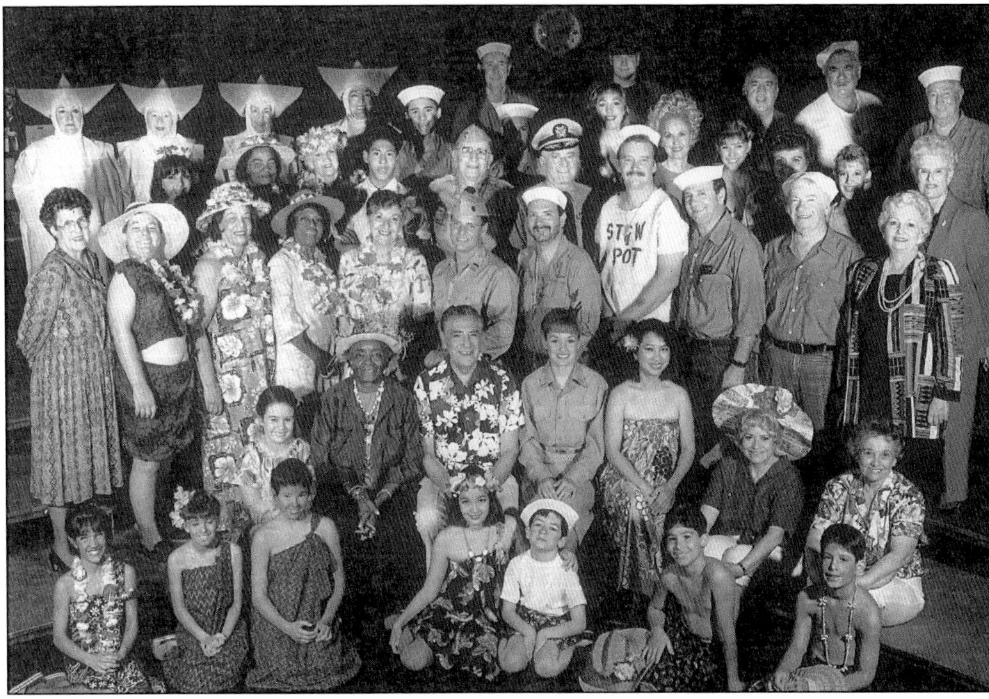

Little Theater of Palm Coast, 1977. The theater provided cultural entertainment for area residents. Olive Harkins was the first director/president. The first performances were in the YMCA/Community Center. The group purchased land in 1998 and hopes to build a theater facility soon. Pictured above is the cast of *South Pacific*.

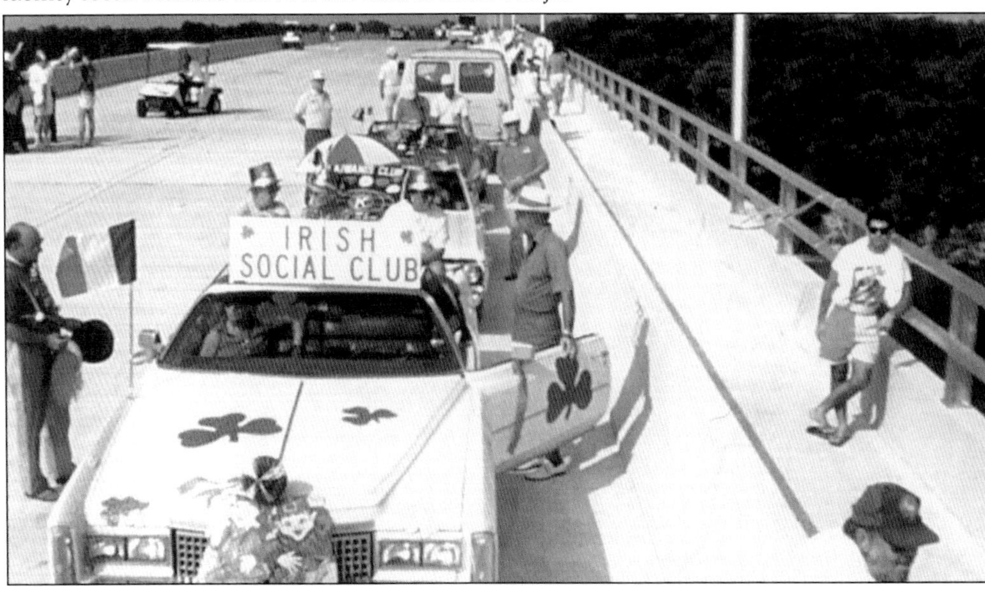

Irish Social Club, 1979. This is a group who strives to offer social enjoyment and help to the needy. The club offers membership to those who are either Irish or would like to be. Area Irish Americans and Ancient Order of Hibernians brought the first St. Patrick's Day Parade in all of Florida history to Palm Coast in March of 1973. Here they are shown as part of the bridge parade in 1988.

Boy Scouts, 1970–1980s. This organization aids in the development of youth to assume future responsibilities as adults. Palm Coast Cub Scouts Den 2 pose during the Boy Scout oath in March 1978. Members, from left to right, are Ed Herrera, Jason Grace, Eddie Brown, Jason Jastremski, Brian Gynizio, and Michael Chiumento.

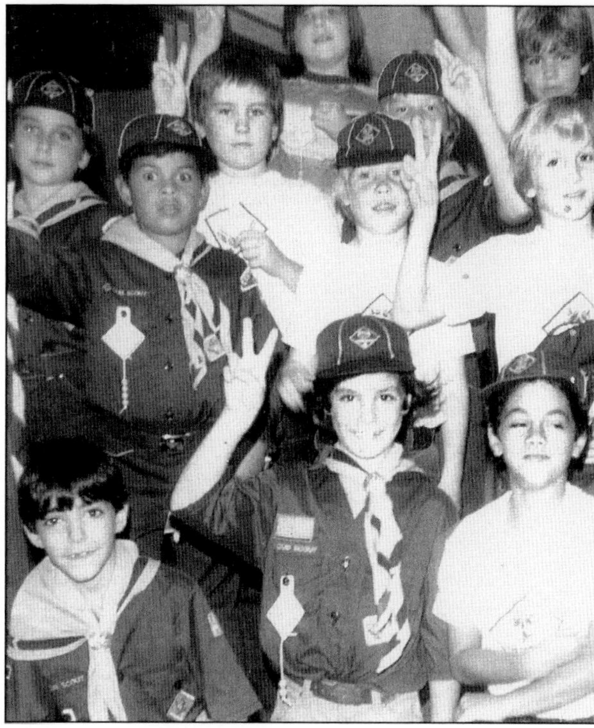

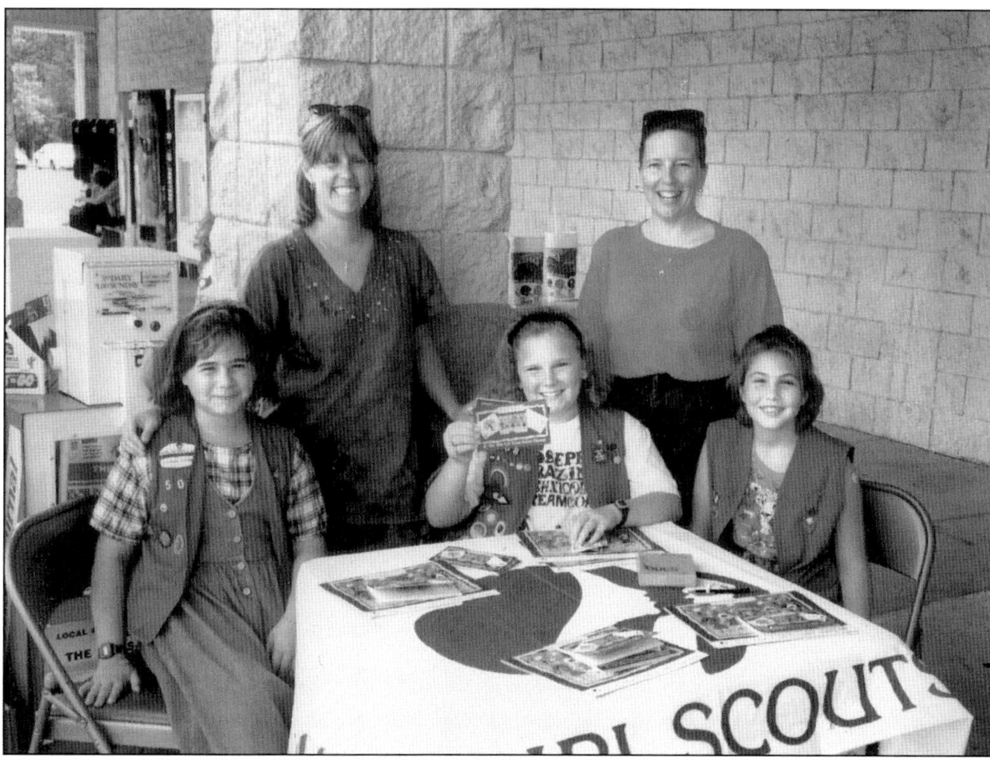

Girl Scouts. Unidentified Girl Scouts and leaders sell cookies at Winn-Dixie.

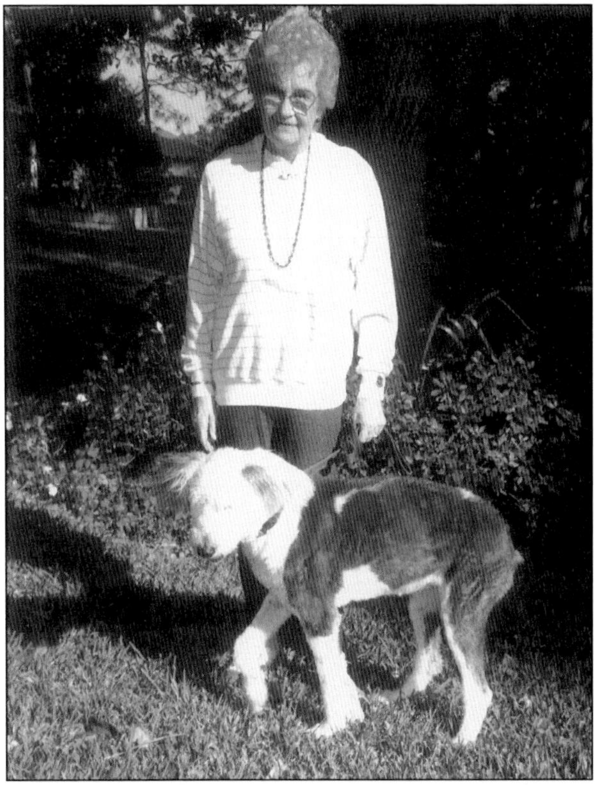

HUMANE SOCIETY, 1982. Pictured here is Hanneke C.A. Frederik, who, with co-founder Ken Dawson and an ICDC grant, began Palm Coast's first animal shelter.

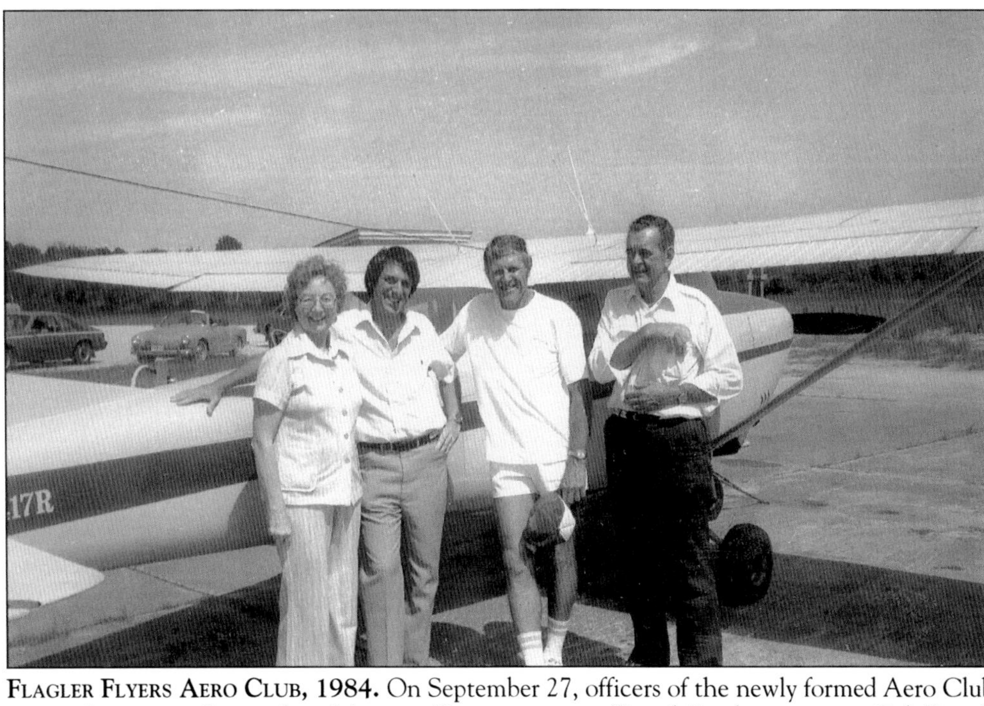

FLAGLER FLYERS AERO CLUB, 1984. On September 27, officers of the newly formed Aero Club met at the airport. Pictured are Margaret Davie, secretary; David Geszler, treasurer; Bob Siegel, president; and Bill MacVay, board member.

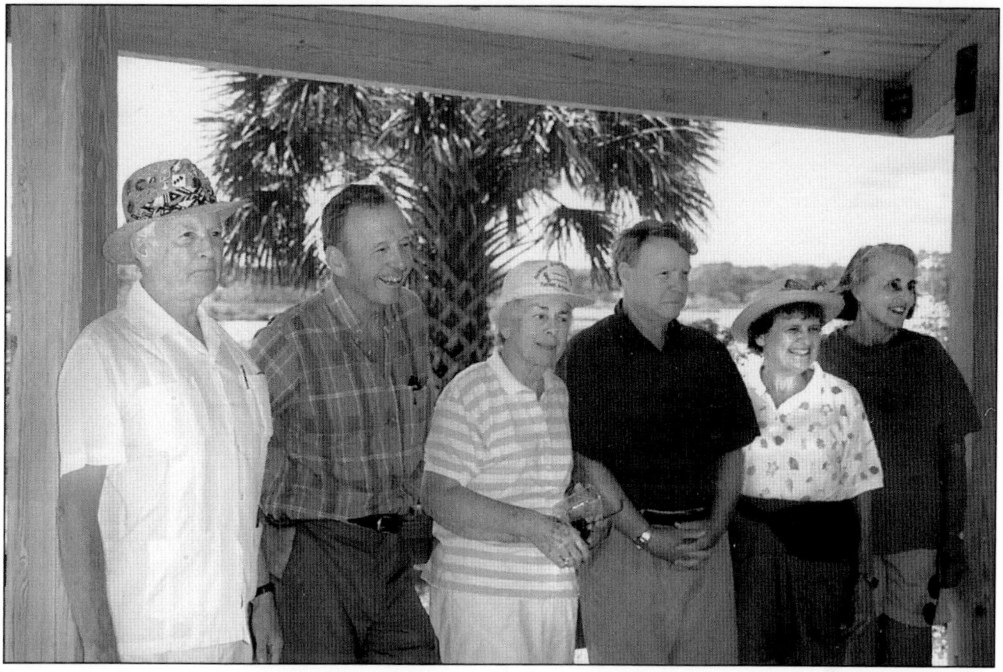

AUDUBON SOCIETY. Preserving the wildlife and habitat necessary for our balanced co-existence with nature is this group's goal. Former president Jerry Full poses with an unidentified group at nature trail on Intracoastal Waterway in Flagler Beach.

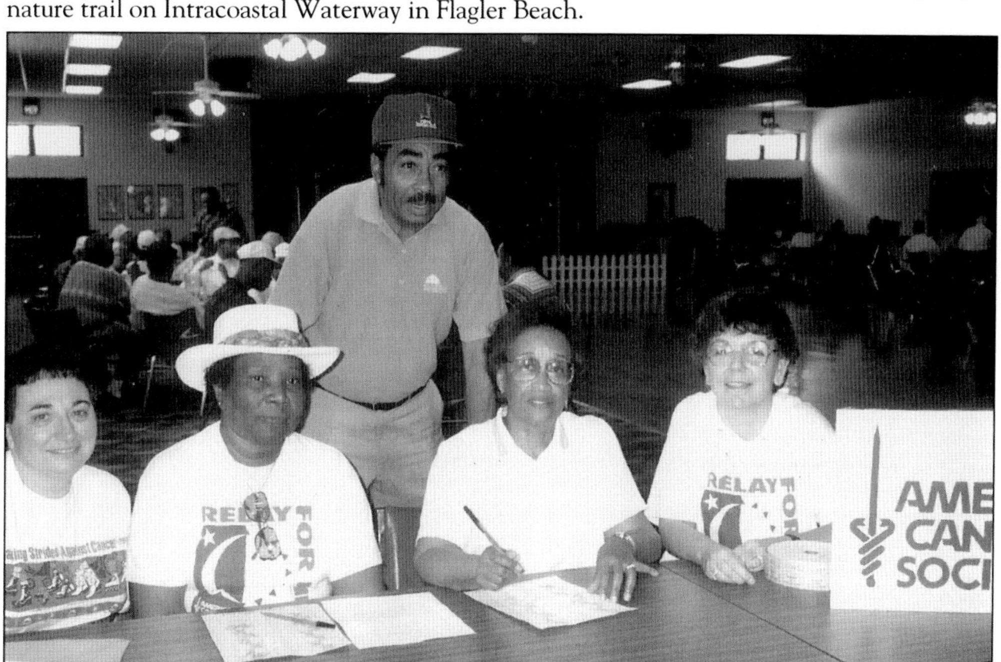

AMERICAN CANCER SOCIETY. This society supports cancer research, aids local victims with medication and transportation as needed, and raises funds to aid the national effort. Pictured are Marie Devine, Ada McCain, Muriel McCoy, Joanne Dors, and Roscoe McCain (standing) at the VFW Hall in the early 1990s.

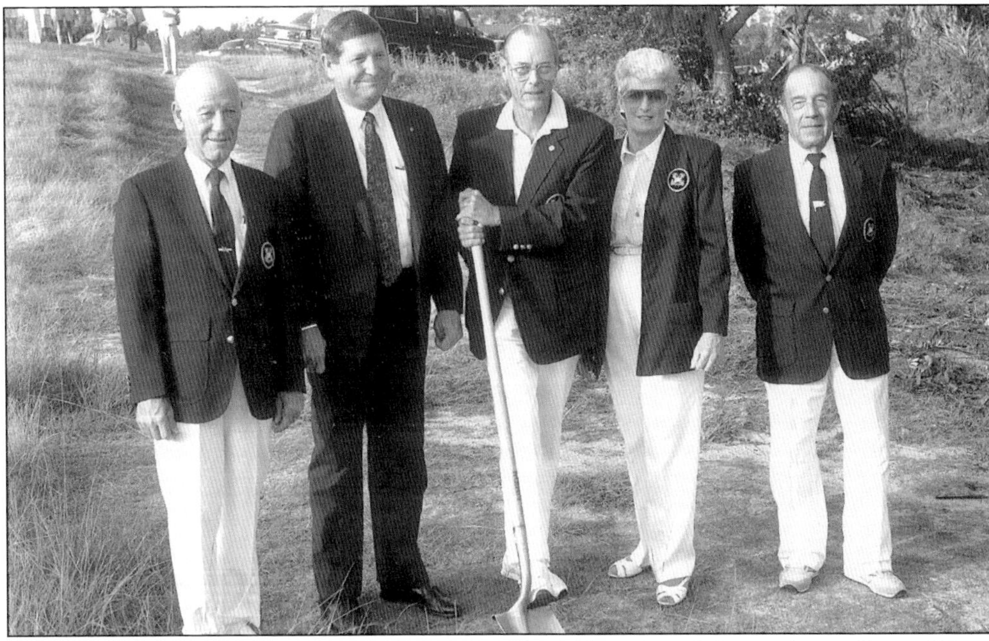

Palm Coast Yacht Club Ground-Breaking. Shown here from left to right are Briggs Edney, vice commodore; Jim Gardner, ICDC president; George Hoffman, commodore; Dell Trayer, rear commodore; and Ted Hess, fleet captain. The first Palm Coast Yacht Club was built by ICDC at the intersection of the Intracoastal Waterway and the main canal to be a civic and social center for the entire community. The new PCYC is a privately built, members-only boating club.

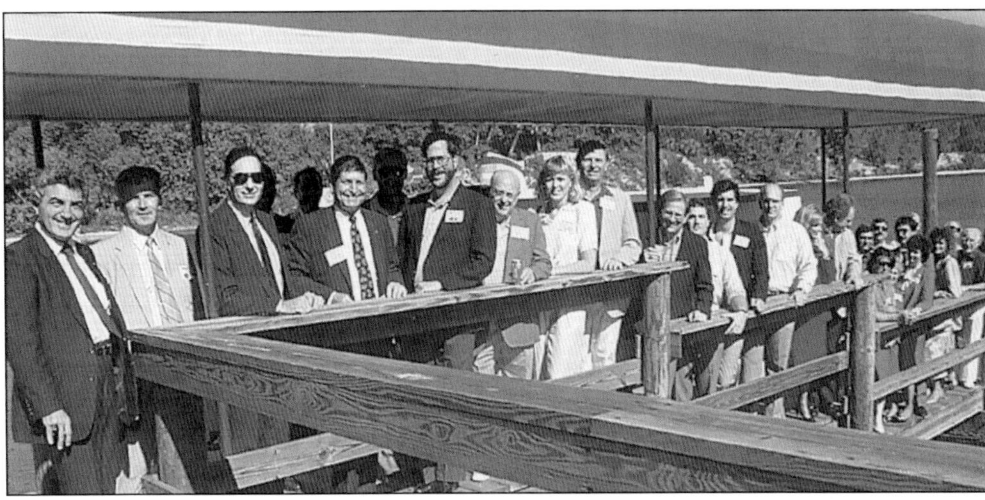

Flagler County Chamber of Commerce, 1969 to Present. The group is always interested in improving the business climate of the entire community. Here, the chamber gets ready for an Intracoastal Waterway boat tour. Flagler County business leaders hosted an entourage from the Florida Department of Commerce in August 1988. Sponsored by the Flagler County Chamber of Commerce, ITT-CDC, Flagler/Palm Coast Homebuilders Association, Marineland, and the Committee of 100, the three-day tour offered state industrial development officials a first-hand look at a community and county "on the verge of taking off in an economic boom," said Steve Mayberry, director of economic development. His prediction was accurate.

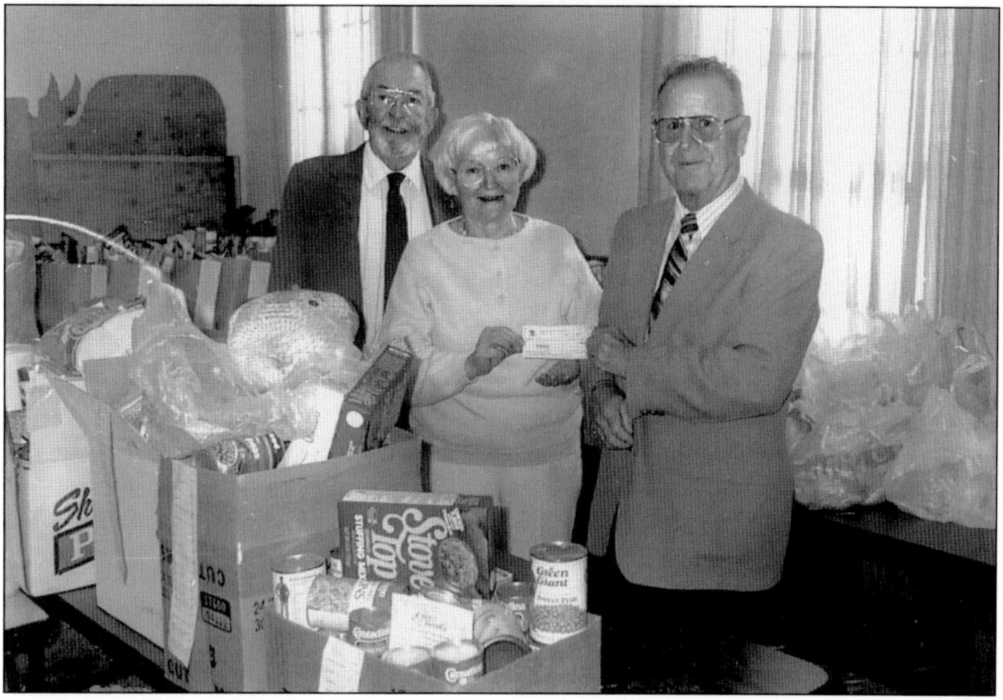

CHARITY AT HOME, 1990. When the United Church Women undertook a project to aid the needy at Thanksgiving, they received some help from the Kentucky Colonels, a national charity organization. Grace Lorenz, coordinator for church women, accepts a check from Col. Shelton Barber while Col. Virgil Green, chairman of the contributions committee looks on.

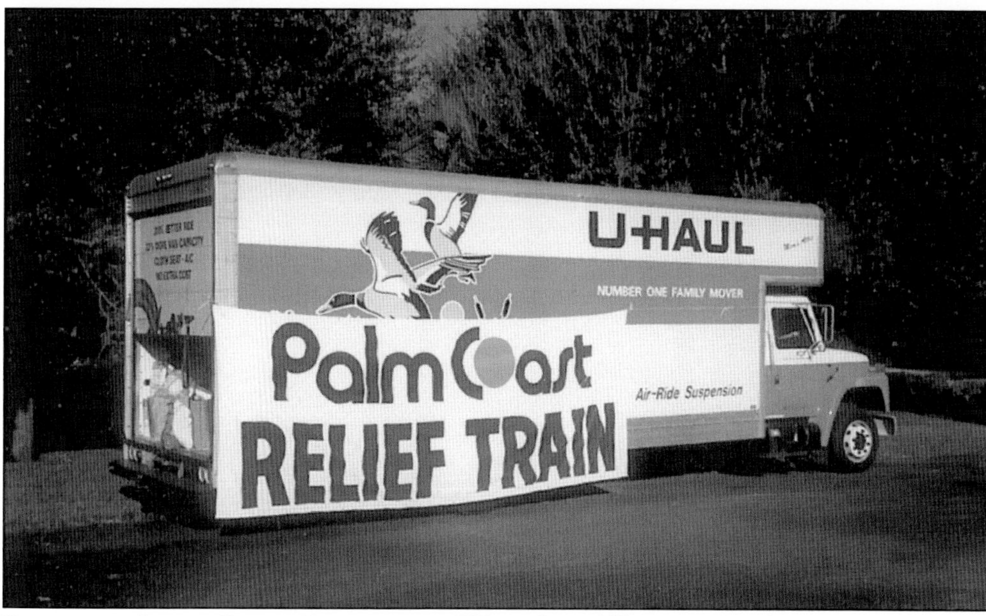

EMERGENCY AID TO OTHER COMMUNITIES. When the wildfires struck Palm Coast in 1985 and again in 1998, fire departments from all over the U.S. sent men and equipment to help the community. When hurricane Andrew unleashed its devastation, Palm Coasters sent emergency relief to Homestead, Florida.

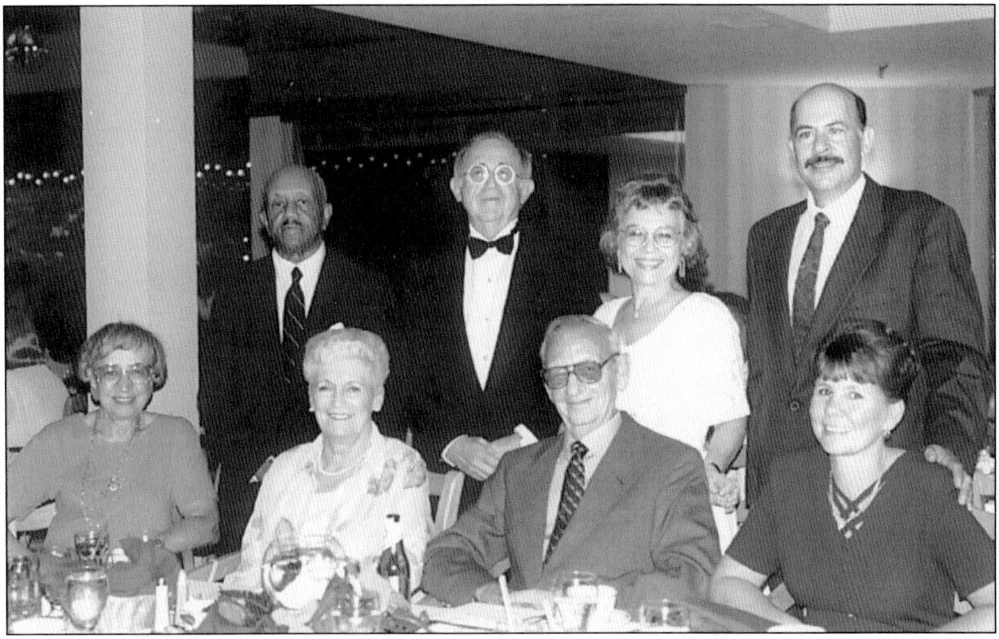

Flagler County Education Society, 1999. Fundraising and support to Palm Coast schools and education system is the group's purpose. This occasion is the the Flagler County Education Dinner Dance honoring Shirley and Sam Newton. Pictured are (front row) Theta Wilson, Dell Trayer, Tom Trayer, and Cathy Cerreta; (back row) Joe Jennings, Education Foundation president Arnold Levy, Muriel Levy, and Steven Cerreta.

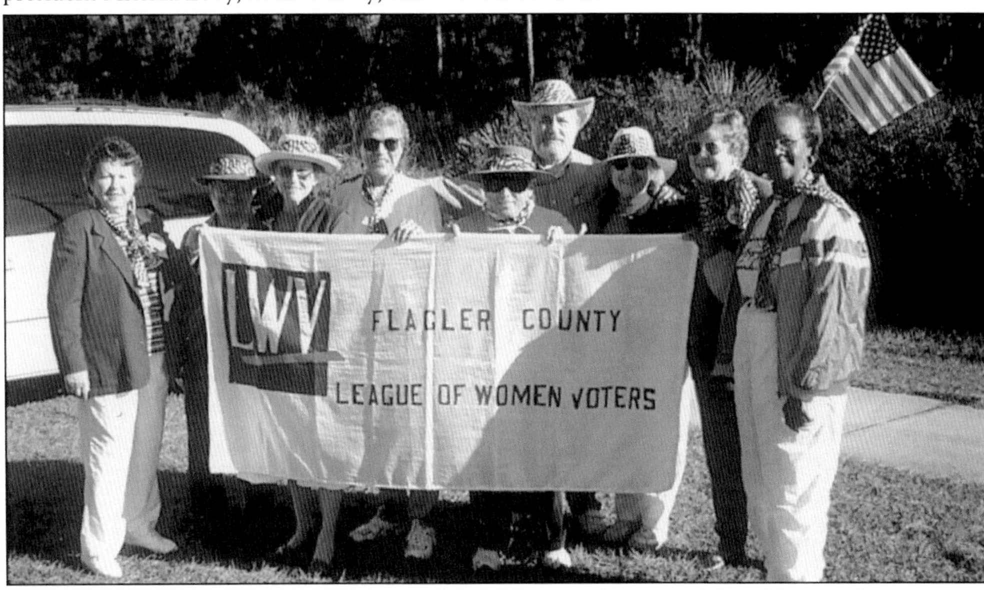

League of Women Voters. The members meet to discuss public affairs and give voters an impartial analysis of the issues and the opportunity to evaluate their elected officials. Representing the league in the December 2, 2000 Palm Coast Holiday Parade were, from left to right, Janet Spurlock, Benita Sirkin, Wilma Vogt, Phillipa Bergin, Art Sirkin, Joel Rosen, Muriel Levy, Anne Nardi, and Willa Prince. Not shown was League of Women Voter president Mary Ann Clark.

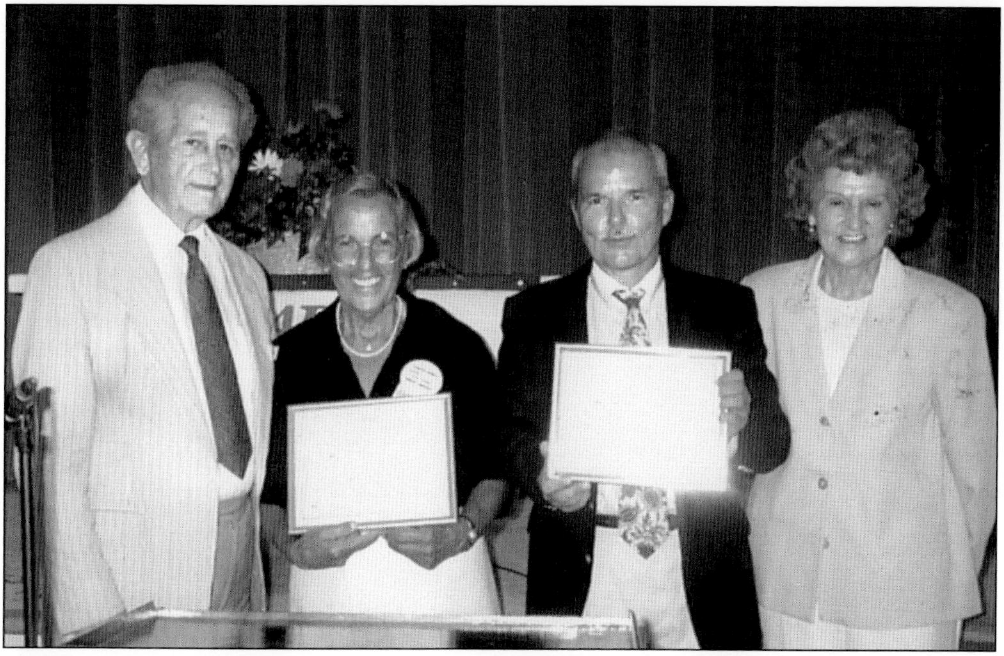

AARP. In this 1995 picture are John Evans, program chair; Sandra Rose Friedman, president of the Friends of the Library; Doug Cisney, library director of the Flagler County Public Library; and Kay Tobia, president of the local branch of AARP. Doug and Sandra Rose were being awarded certificates of appreciation for presenting a program about the library.

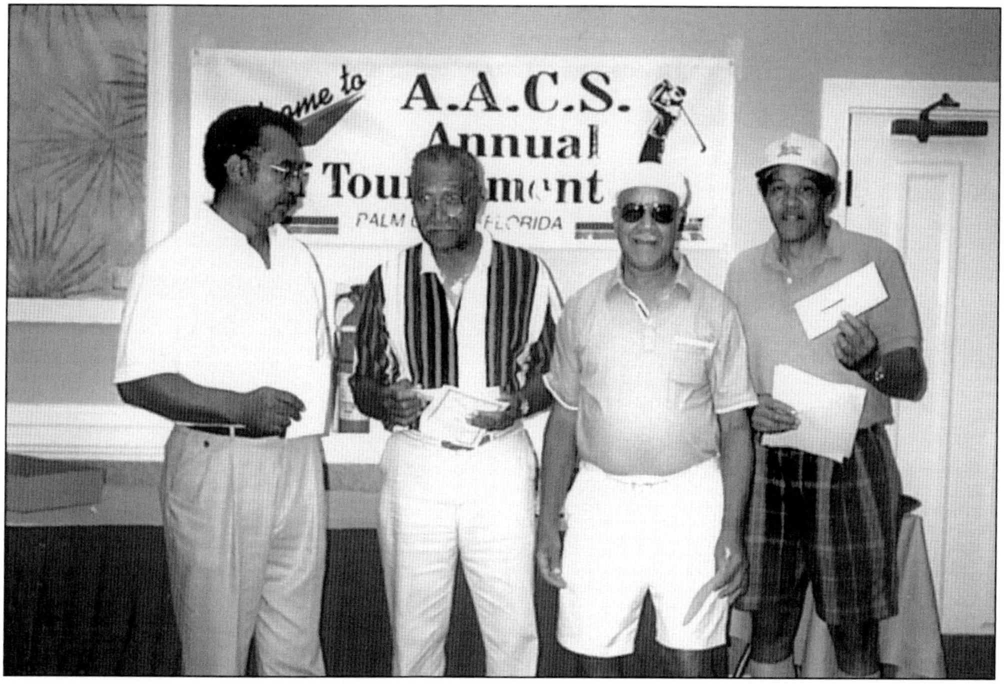

African-American Cultural Society, 1996. Pictured at the annual Charity Golf Tournament in May 1996, members from left to right are Lawrence Wettlin, Rod Murell, Johnny Maze, and Herbert Bethel.

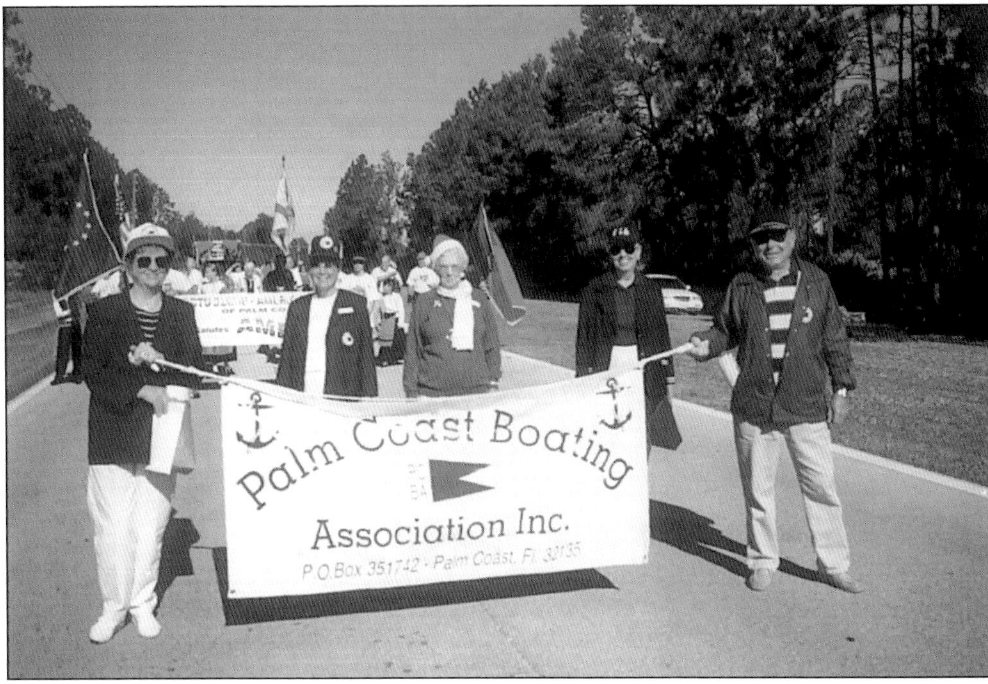

Palm Coast Boating Association. The association was represented in the December 2000 annual parade by Bea Silvestri, Barbara Sulser, Miriam Rich, Bev Martinolick, and Roy Shaffer. Other boating associations include the Palm Coast Cruisers, Anchor Boat Club, and PCYC.

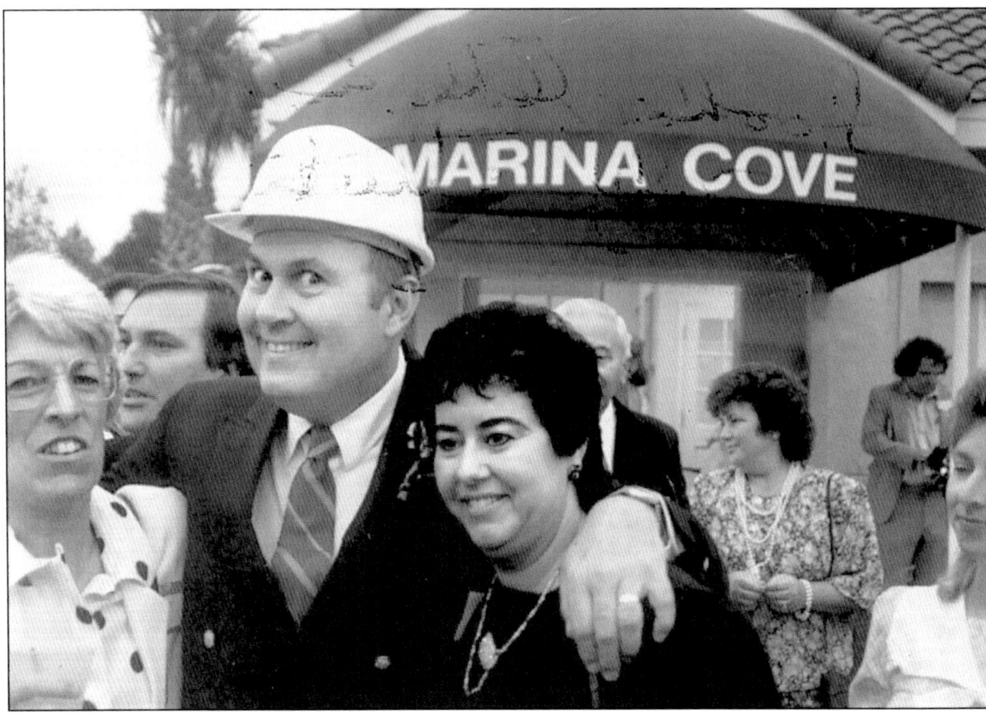

Marina Cove, 1989. At the April 21, 1989 ribbon cutting for this private development by Walter Kehoe, Willard Scott of NBC's *Today* was brought in for the occasion.

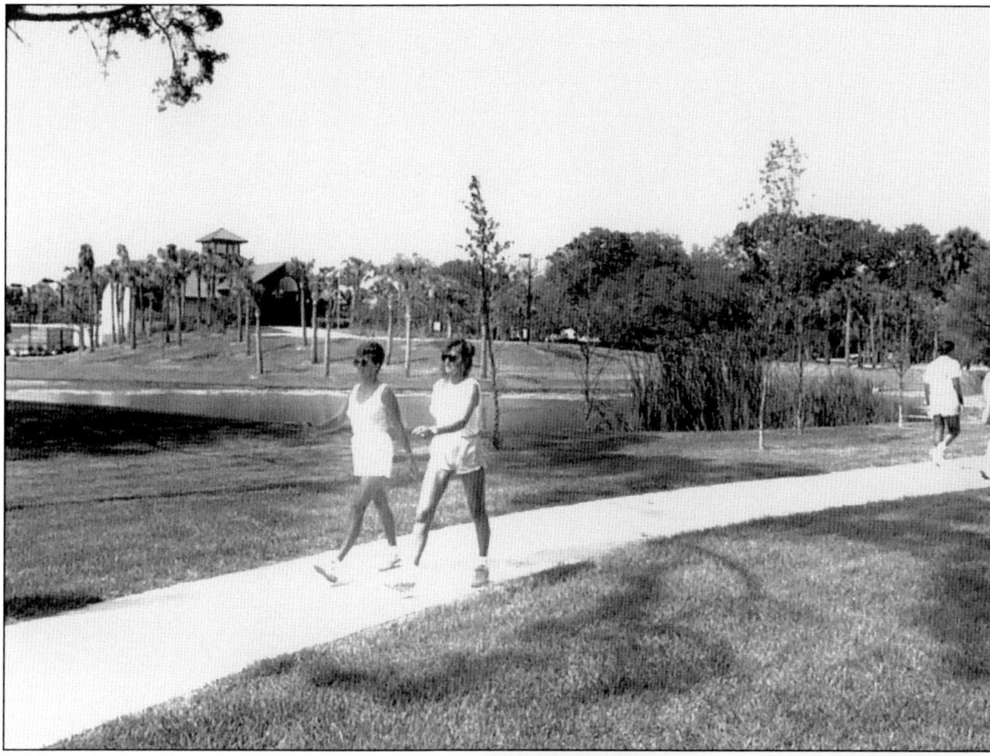

Palm Coast Activities, Walking. The miles of concrete walkways and the level topography of the land makes walking and running in Palm Coast a joy at any level one wishes to pursue it.

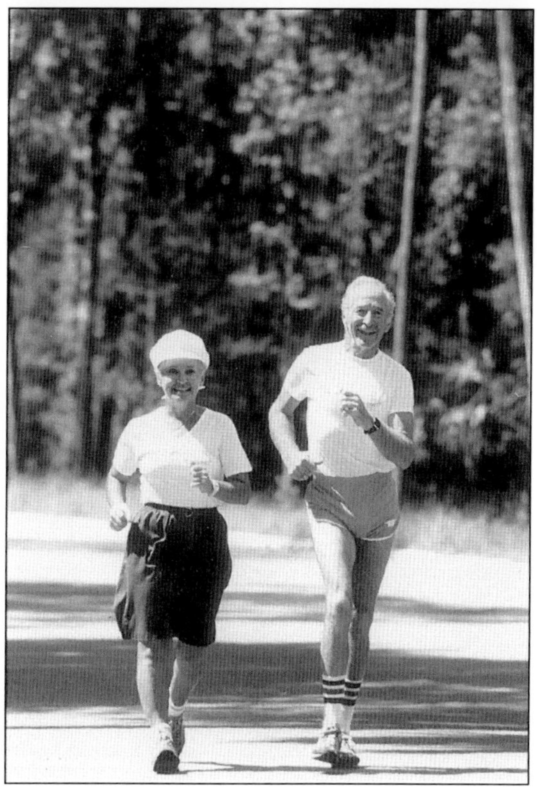

Jogging. Bernie and Jo Tober are physical fitness advocates.

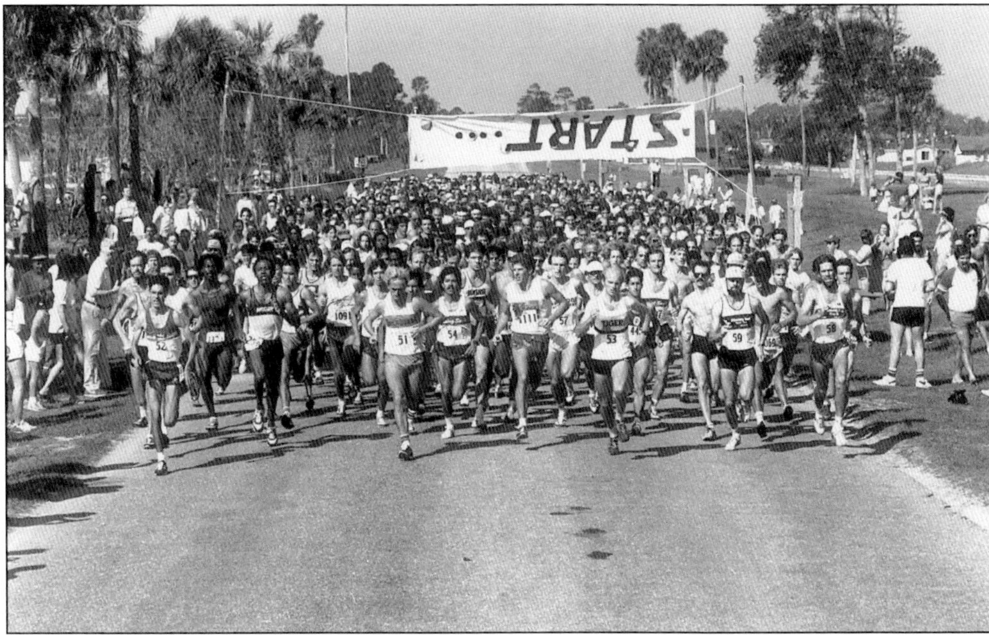

5-K Run. ITT's Jerry Full initiated annual 5-K runs in the early 1980s. This one started on Club House Drive near the Model Center.

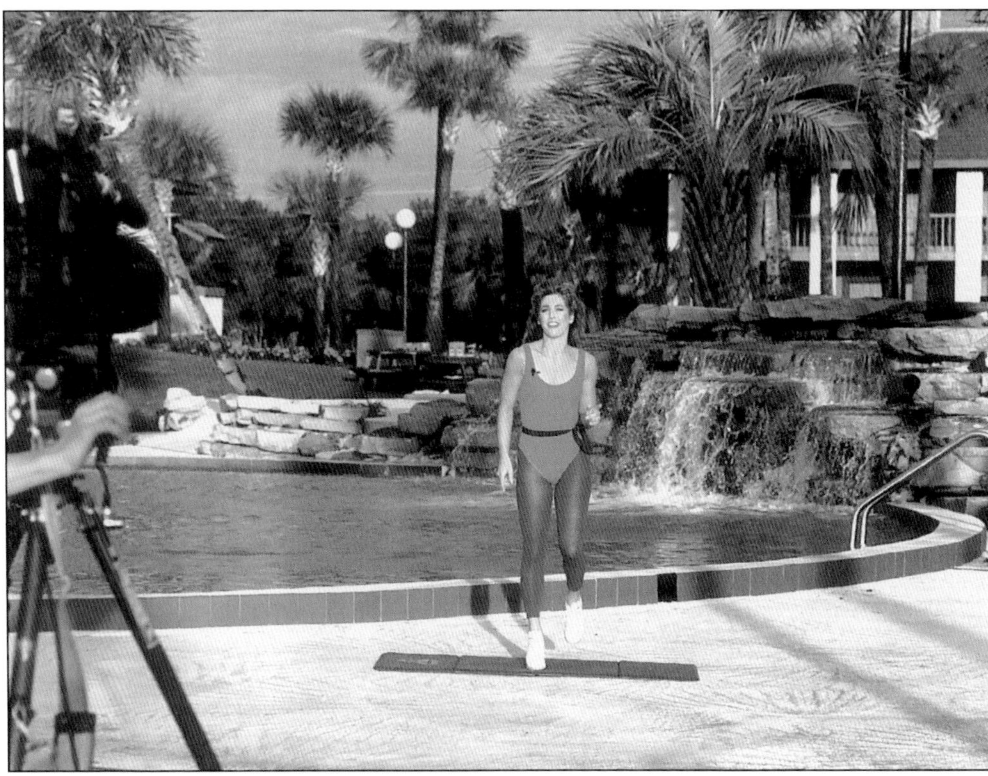

Aerobics. Not everyone can look like ESPN Instructor Denise Austin, pictured at the Harbor Club in 1986.

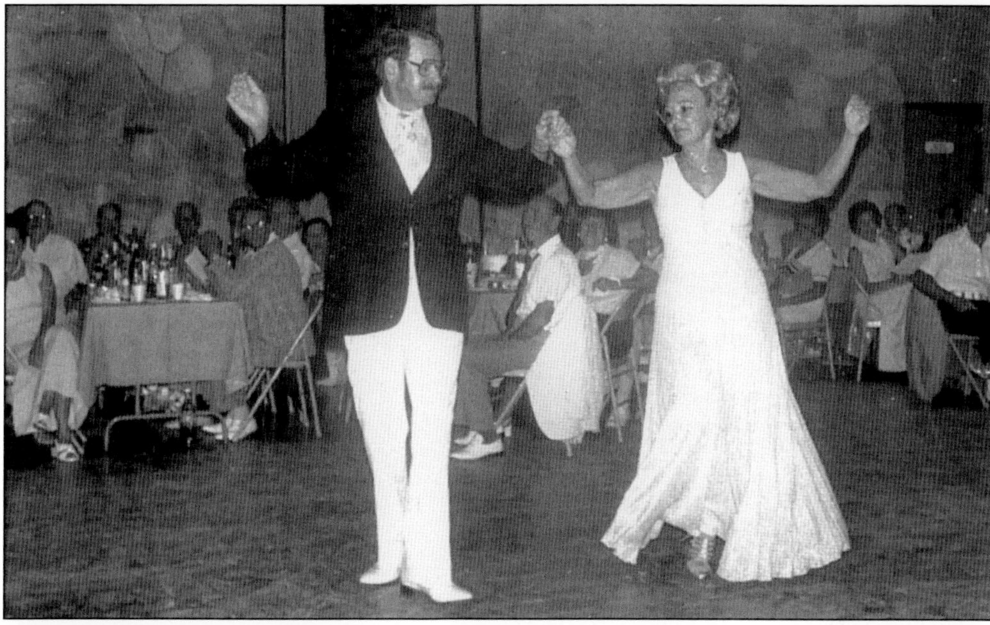

Dancing. The Flagler Ball Room Dancers have been in operation since 1975. Here Frank and Mary Pauly dance in the 1980s. Although he was 98 years old, Frank was still dancing in 2002.

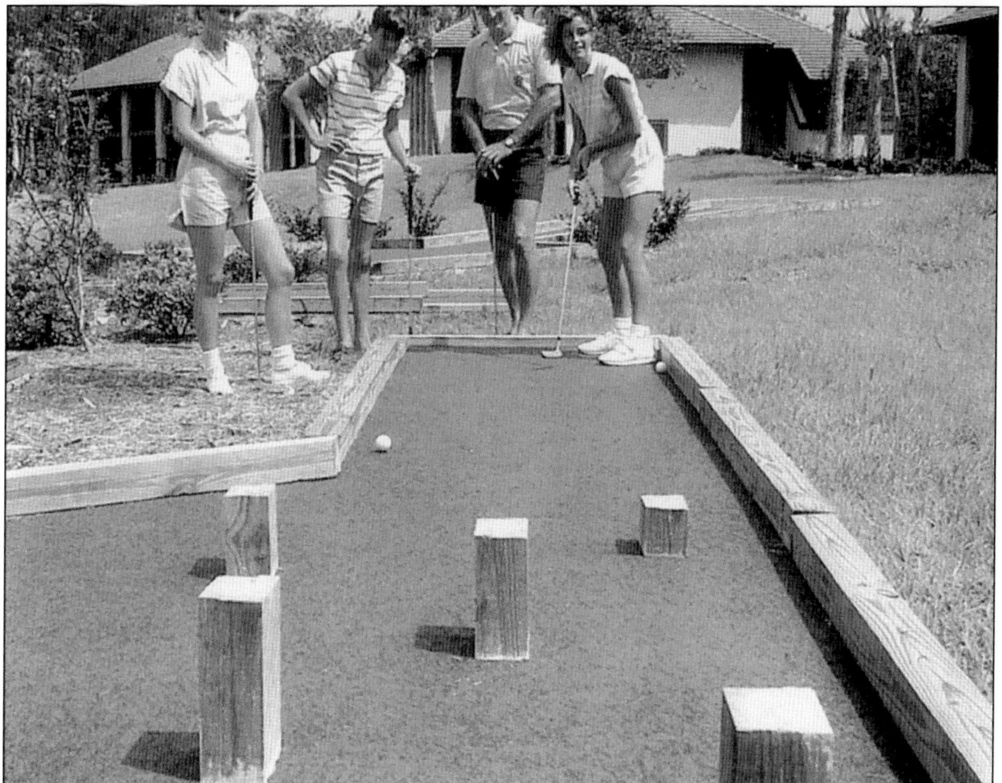

Miniature Golf. For those who don't want to go the long 18 holes in a cart, there is always the abbreviated version.

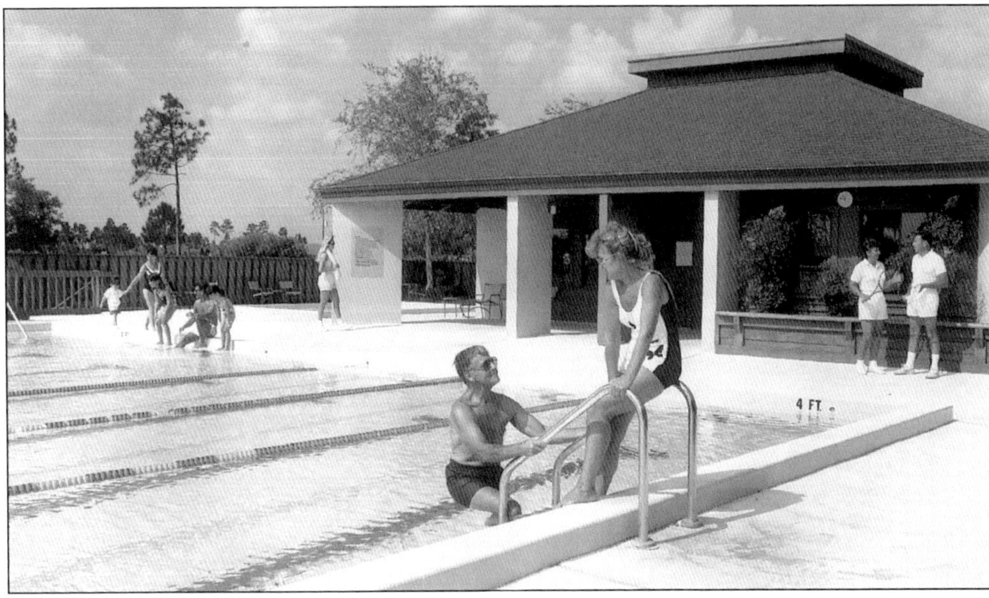

Swimming. Ocean, lake, or private, public, or backyard swimming pool, the water is always inviting in Palm Coast.

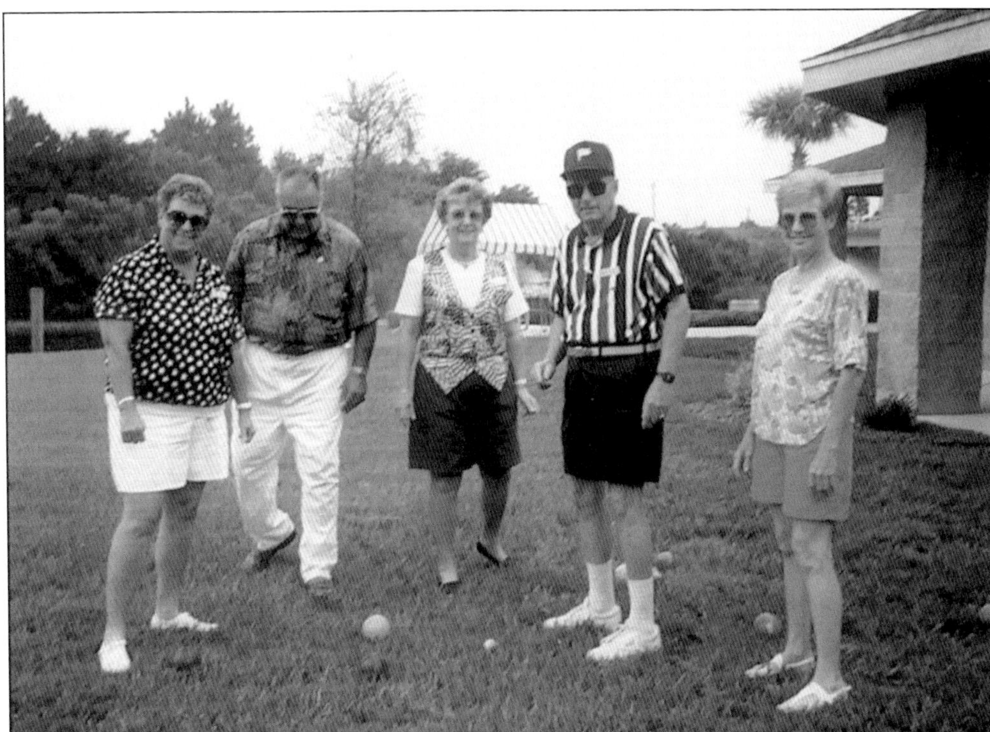

Bocci. Whether on a formal court or on any grass you can find, all you need is a solid ball and the strength to throw it. Clare Houghtaling, Ed Silbernagel, Evelyn Davis Keyes, Ed Squires, and Ida Naglier play on the lawn of the Palm Coast Yacht Club at their Memorial Day picnic.

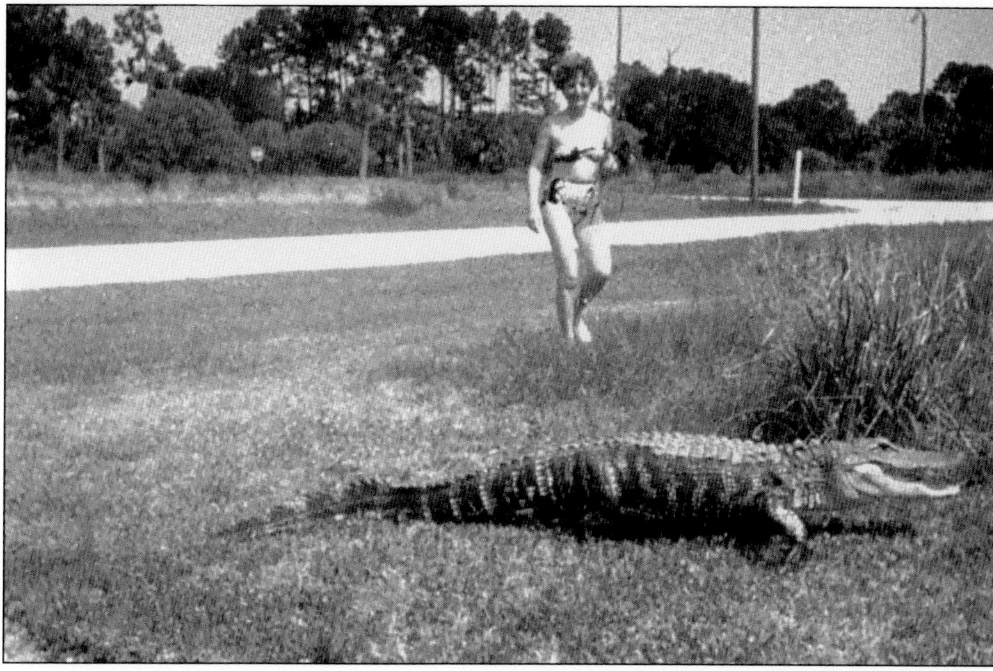

ALLIGATOR CHASING. Terry Neveras is pictured at Coral Reef Court North shooing away this intruding alligator in 1982.

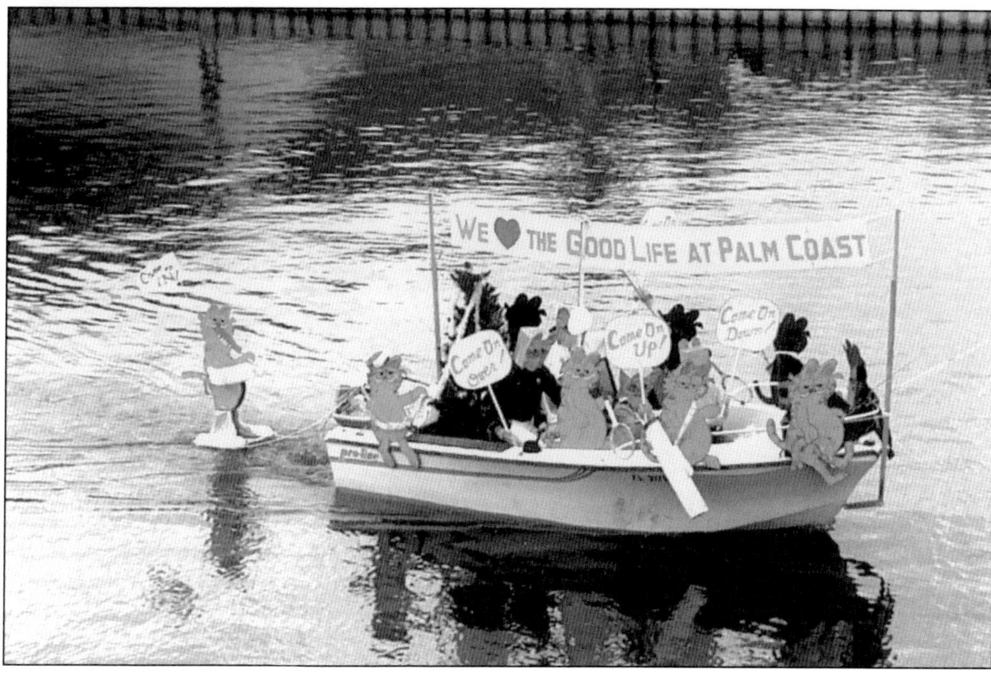

BOAT PARADE. Every year around the first weekend in December, residents gather along the Intracoastal Waterway, Main Canal, or the Palm Coast Golf Resort to view the day and night sections of the annual parade of boats. Here individuals and the area's boat clubs, such as The Palm Coast Cruisers, decorate their boats for the holiday and compete for prizes and bragging rights in their colorful activity.

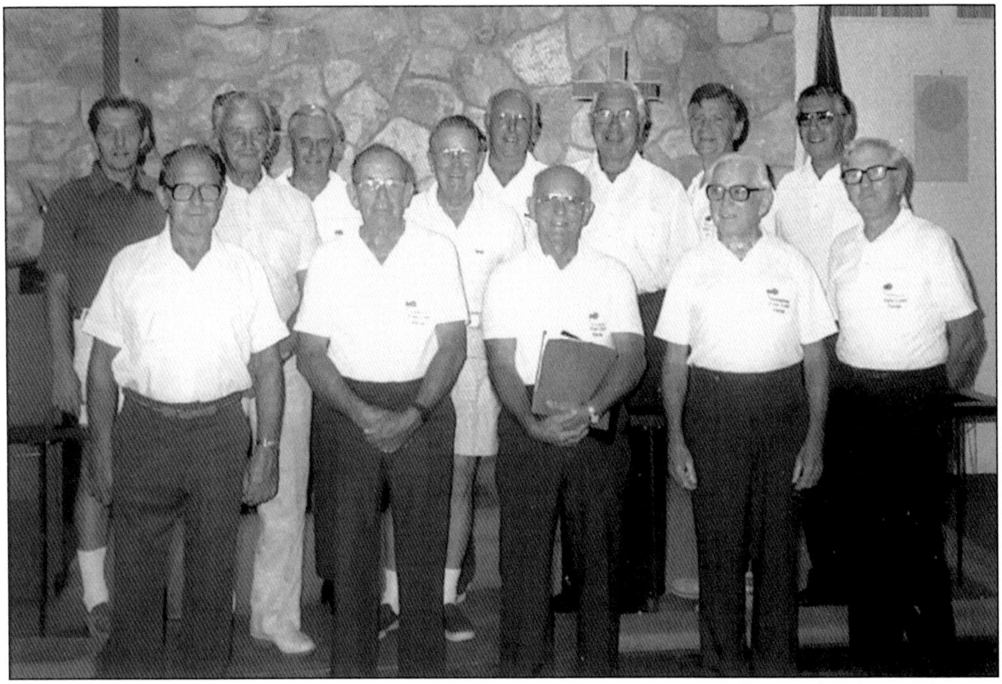

SINGING. The "Palm Coast Toasters" men's chorus is shown at St. Mark By-The-Sea in August 1983. Members, from left to right, are (front row) Art Larson, Dick Wareham, Al Raufarth, George Mott, and Bill Corkery; (back row) Ralph Reel (director), Tom Lenssen (hidden), Ed Statham, Bob Scott, Charlie Morris, Jack Clymer, Alan Tolley, Ted Robbins, Joe Bruno, and accompanist Sid Sackrin.

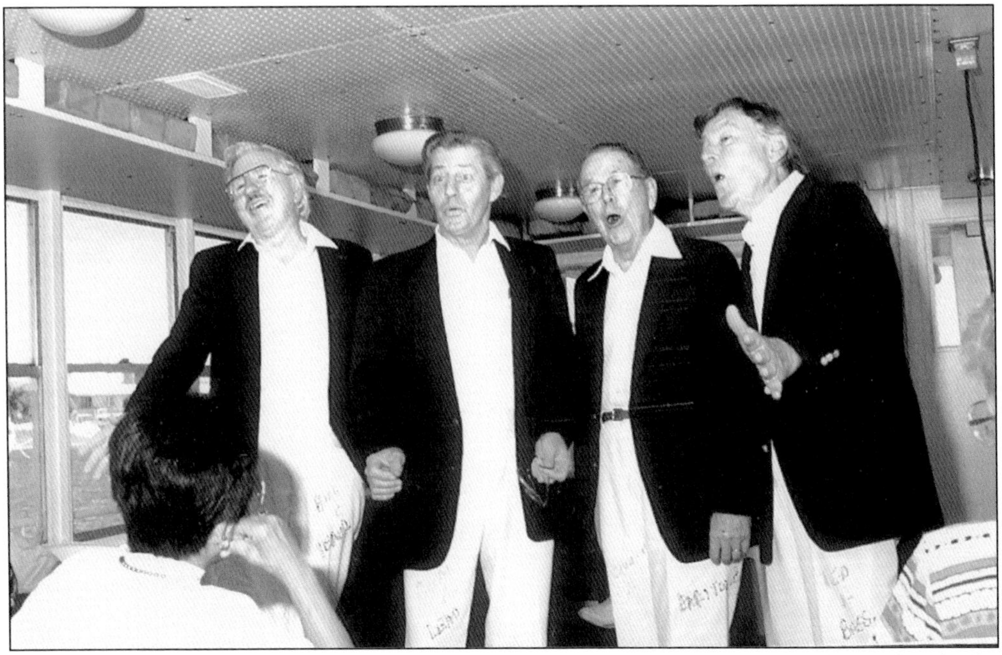

BARBERSHOP QUARTET. Members, from left to right, are Bill Corkery, Ralph Reel, Charlie Morris, and Ted Robbins.

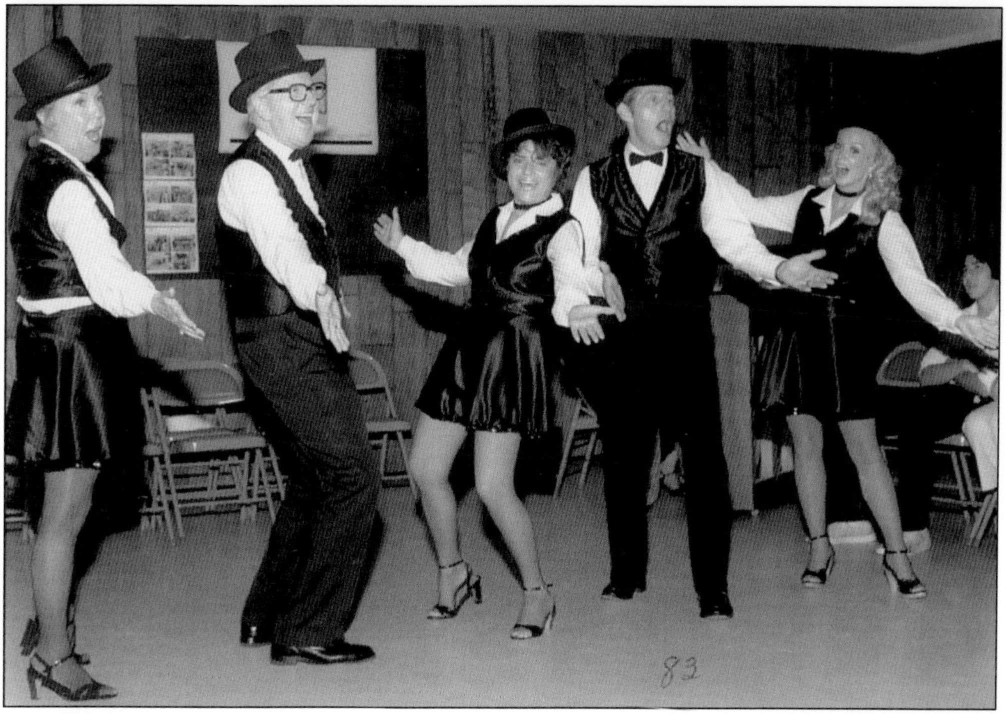

The Palm Coasters. Pictured from left to right are Joyce Bergen, Bill Corkery, Lorna Abjornson, Ralph Reel, and Barbara Davidson.

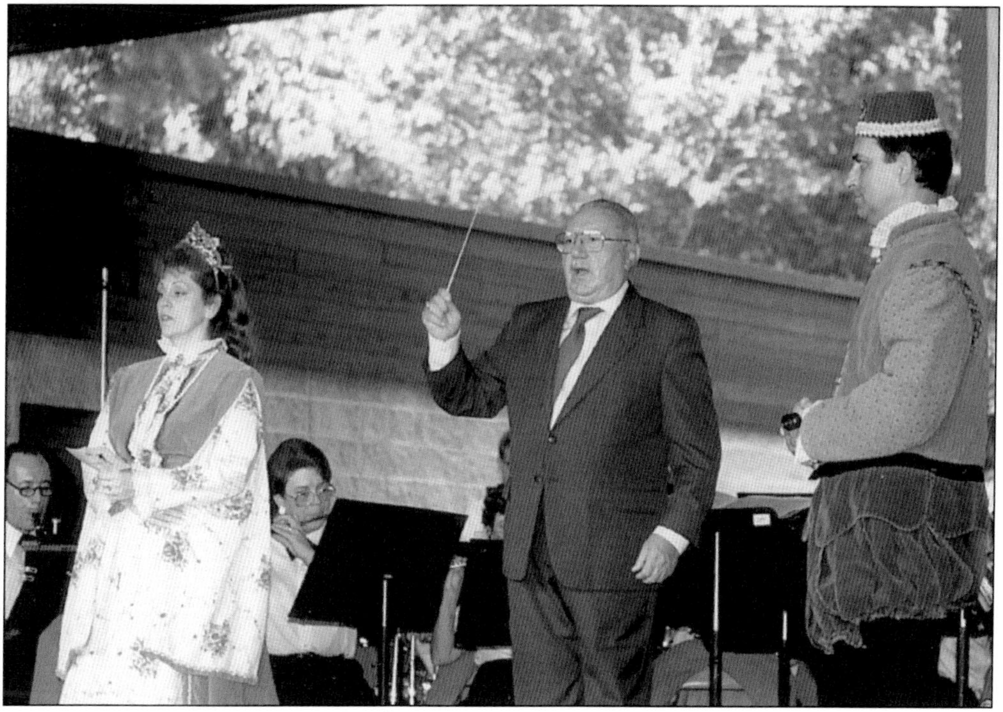

Music. Composer Charles Gabrielle is shown conducting *Christopher Columbus Suite* in October 1989.

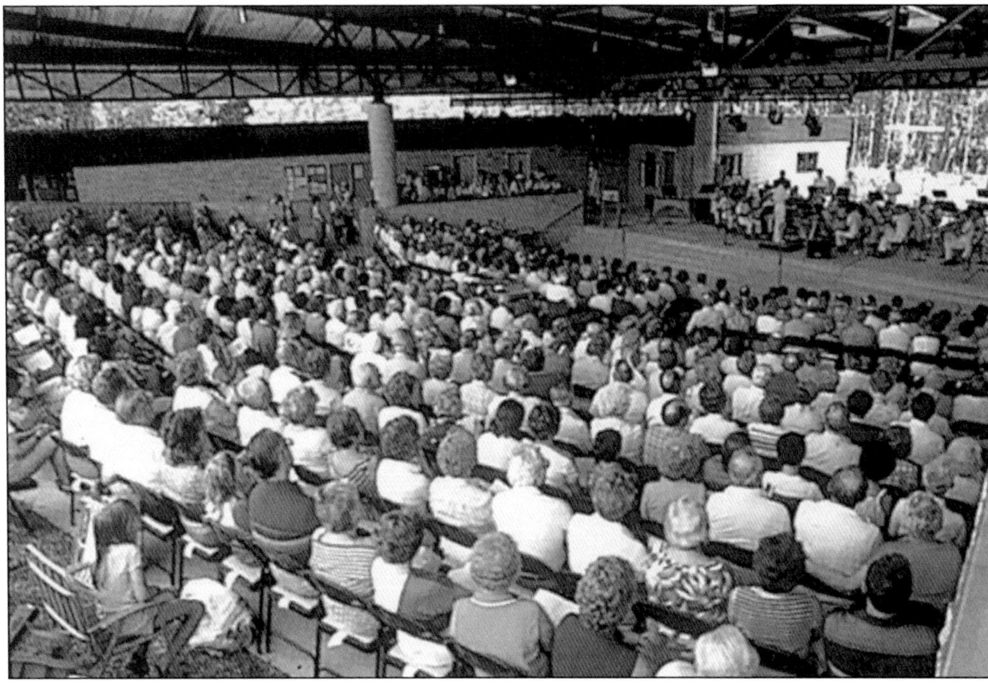

U.S. Navy Band, 1985. Brought to Palm Coast by the American Legion, the U.S. Navy Band from Orlando filled the DBCC Pavilion with inspiring music. The guest conductor was none other than Palm Coast's own Professor Charles Gabriele.

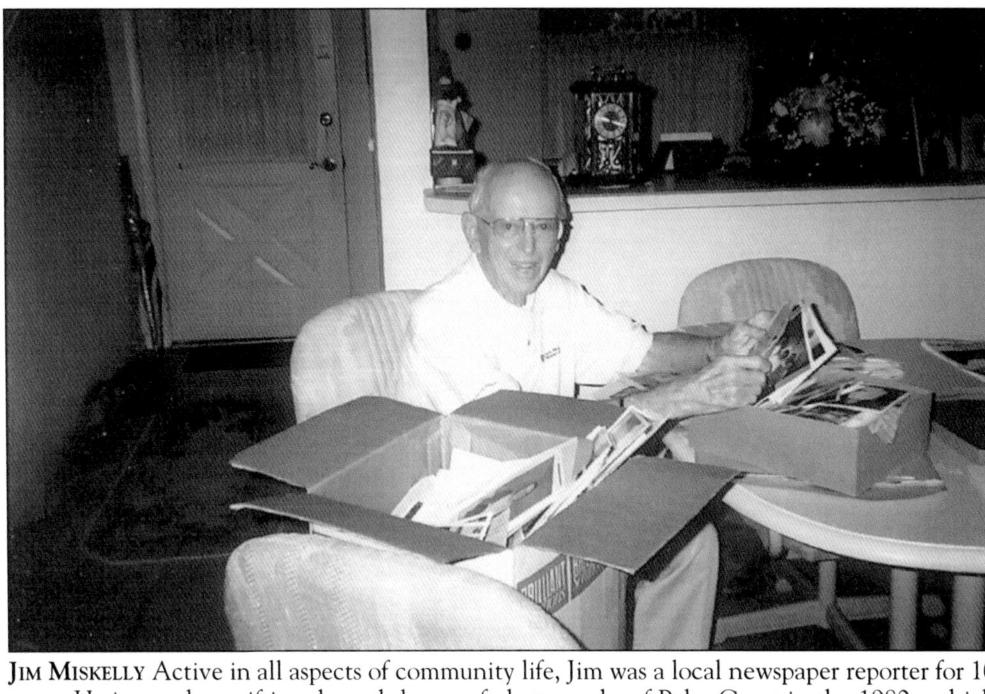

Jim Miskelly Active in all aspects of community life, Jim was a local newspaper reporter for 10 years. He is seen here sifting through boxes of photographs of Palm Coast in the 1980s, which he contributed to this book. Physically and mentally spry at age 89 in 2003, Jim deserves the title, "Mr. Palm Coast."

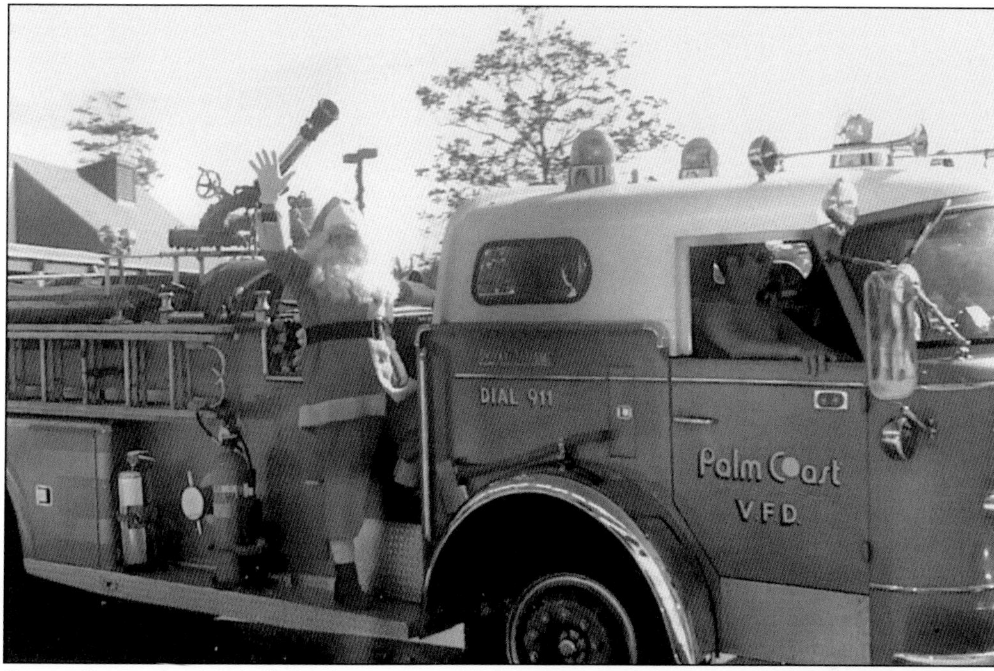

SANTA CLAUS. Jim Miskelly has been in costume in many communities for 63 years. Pictured here arriving on a fire truck, he was ITT's official Santa and one year even arrived in a helicopter.

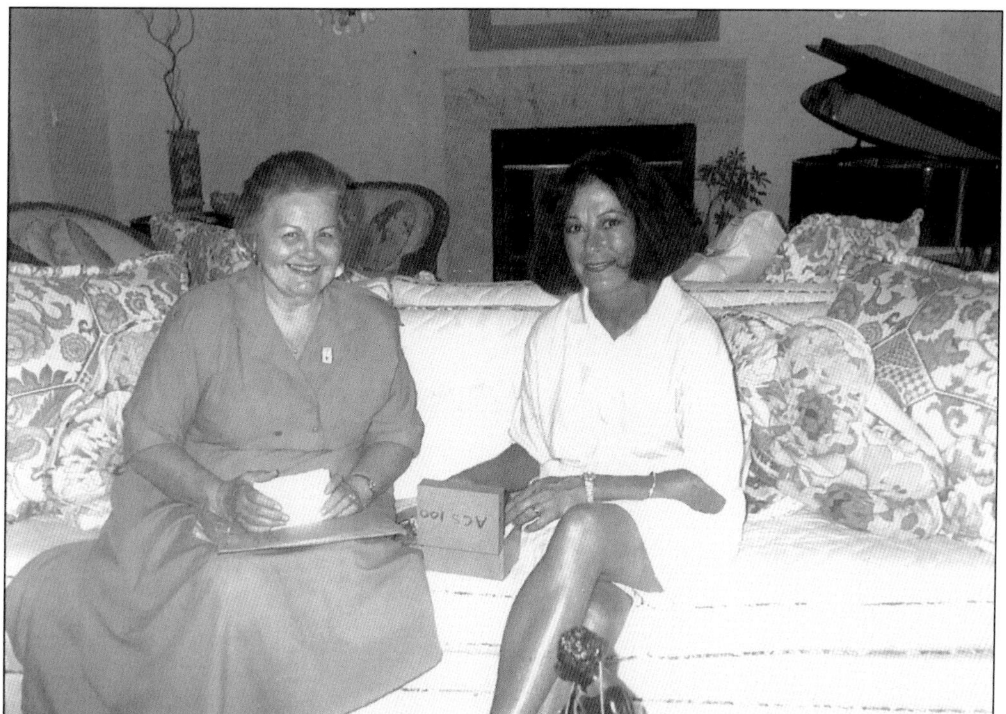

PLANNING. Jan Gardner is pictured here making plans for a buffet in her home to benefit the American Cancer Society with program chair, Ruth Niederstrasse, in October 1990.

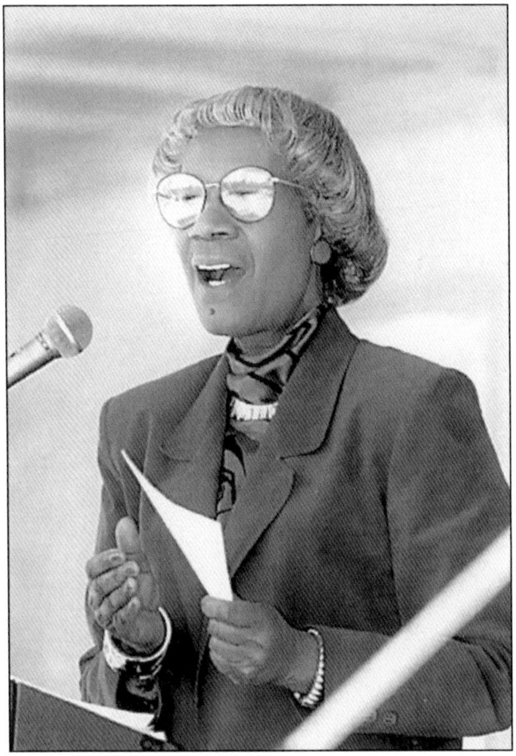

SHIRLEY CHISHOLM. The first black woman in the U.S. House of Representatives, Shirly Chisholm was a Palm Coast resident for years after retirement from her Brooklyn Congressional District.

THE TOMATO MAN. John Johnson set up a card table and tent in front of the former K-Mart in 1993. Today he has two locations, one at St. Joe's and one at Palm Harbor Shopping Center, and at each one, the permanent tent is a familiar sight. When Palm Coast became a city and "tent" sales were no longer permitted, John's business was grandfathered to allow his established and popular business to continue. Each year he renews his permit to conduct business.

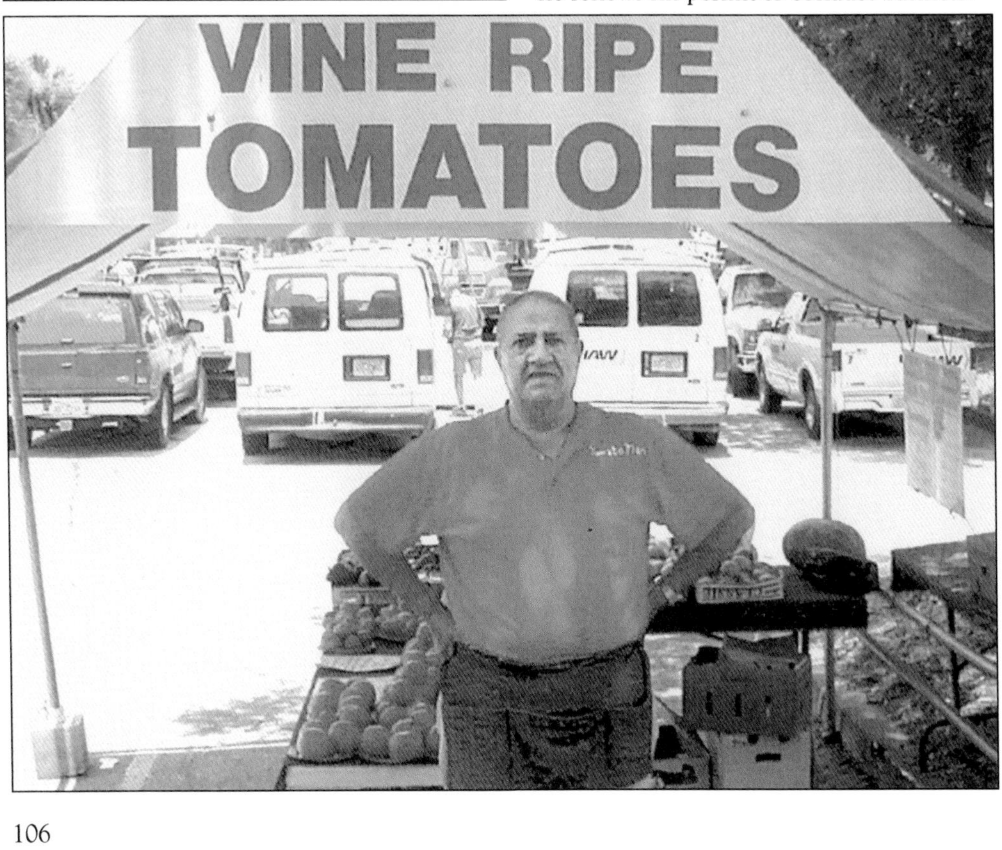

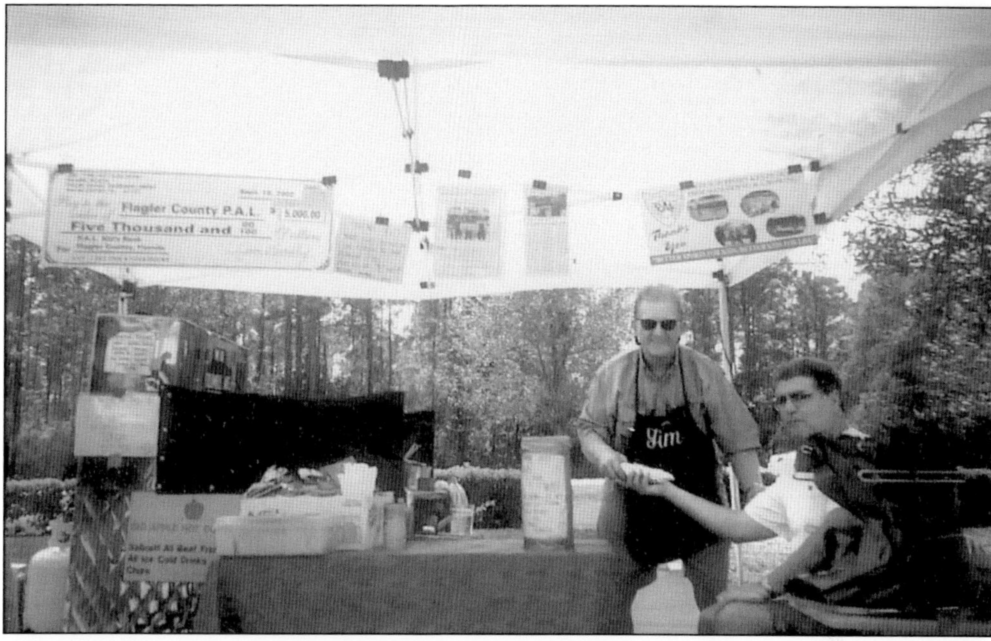

"The Hot Dog Man." Jim Bradley serves Gene Cook. Jim sells lunchtime snacks on weekdays from his tent in the parking lot opposite the Sears store on Palm Coast Parkway West. He is known for making generous contributions to community charities from his proceeds.

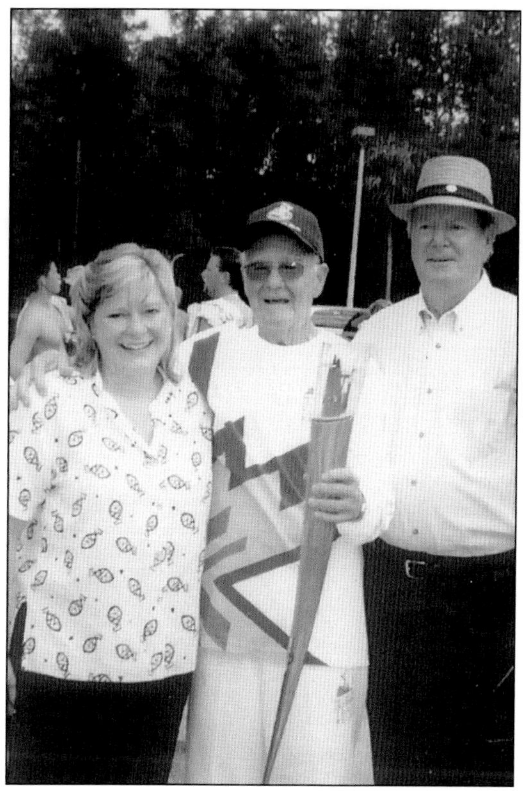

Clarence P. Custer. The Palm Coaster who carried the Olympic Torch for our area for the 2002 Winter Olympics in Salt Lake City was Clarence P. Custer. He is shown here with Cornelia Manfre and Mayor Jim Canfield.

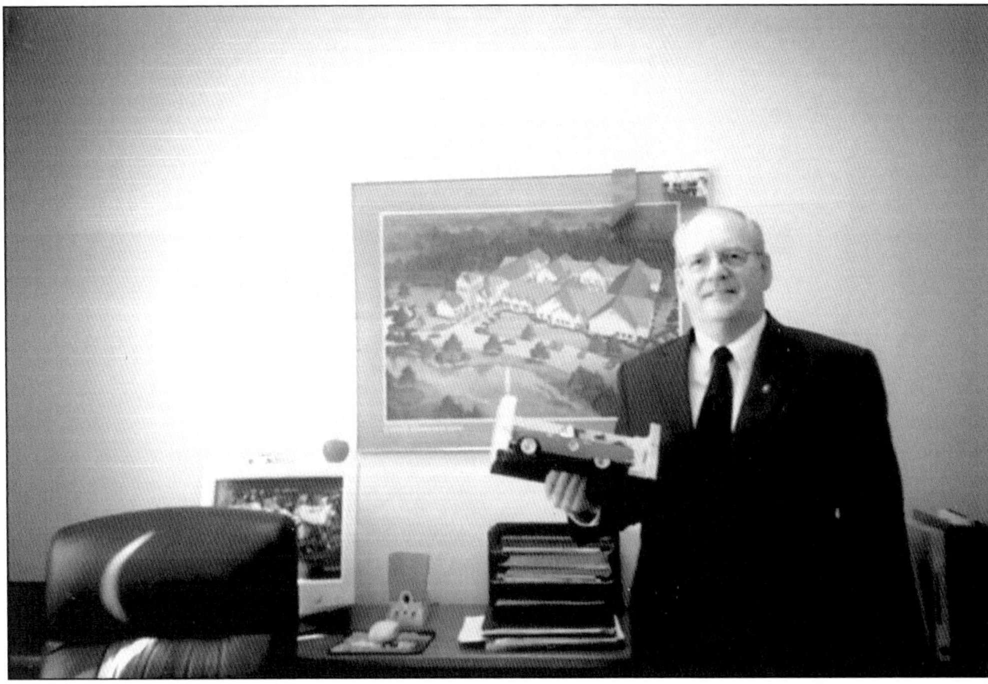

Dr. Howard Turner. The provost of the Flagler/Palm Coast campus of Daytona Beach Community College is shown here holding a present given to him at the end of his term as president of the Flagler Chamber of Commerce. The second phase completion of the campus appears in the picture behind him

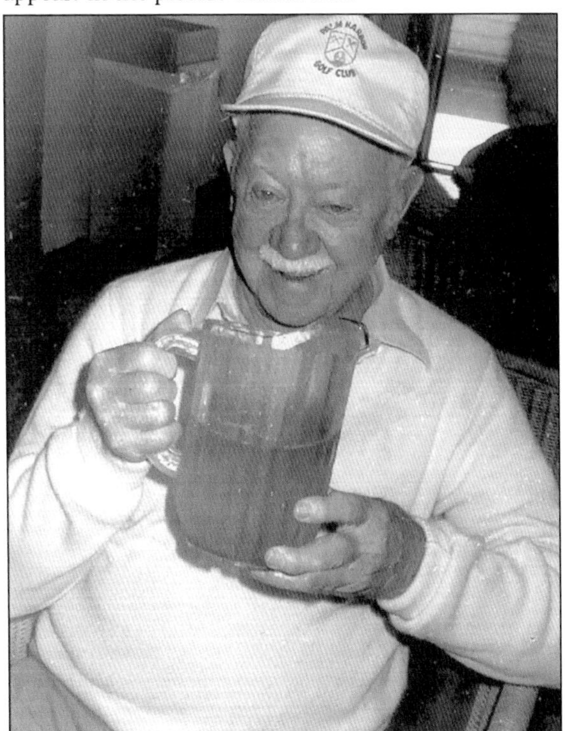

Barney Gates. Barney is pictured cooling himself with a pitcher of suds following 18 holes at Palm Harbor.

Five

Palm Coast Becomes a City

On December 31, 1999, the largest portion of the original ITT Palm Coast area was incorporated to become the Millennium City of Palm Coast. The majority of the residents felt that the new city structure would best preserve and continue expanding the quality of life they enjoyed here. Can the new city government continue the expansion of the good life in Palm Coast?

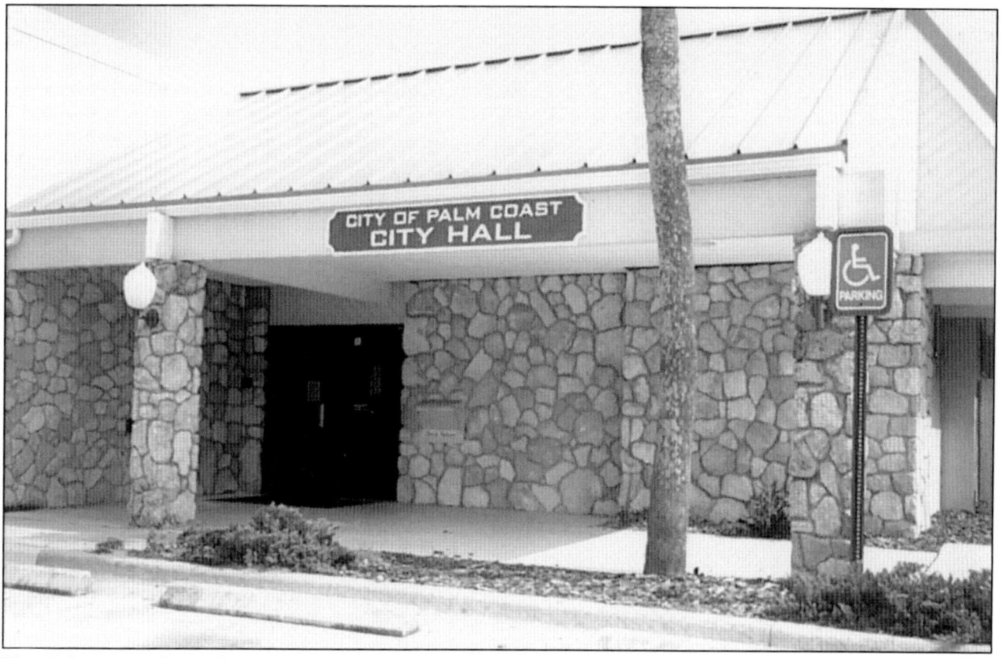

The Home of City Government, 2000. The pictured building in the Palm Harbor Shopping Center was originally donated by ITT for use as a branch campus for Daytona Beach Community College. Dedicated as Palm Coast's library in 1984, it became available when a new library was opened in January 2000. It was renovated to be used as the new City Hall, immediately occupied, and opened for public viewing on October 26, 2000. The space seemed more than adequate compared to the two rooms with one large closet in the Community Center that originally served as the office. The tremendous growth of the community is illustrated by the enormous increase in the number of building permits being requested in 2003. This has the government searching for even more space to properly service the community.

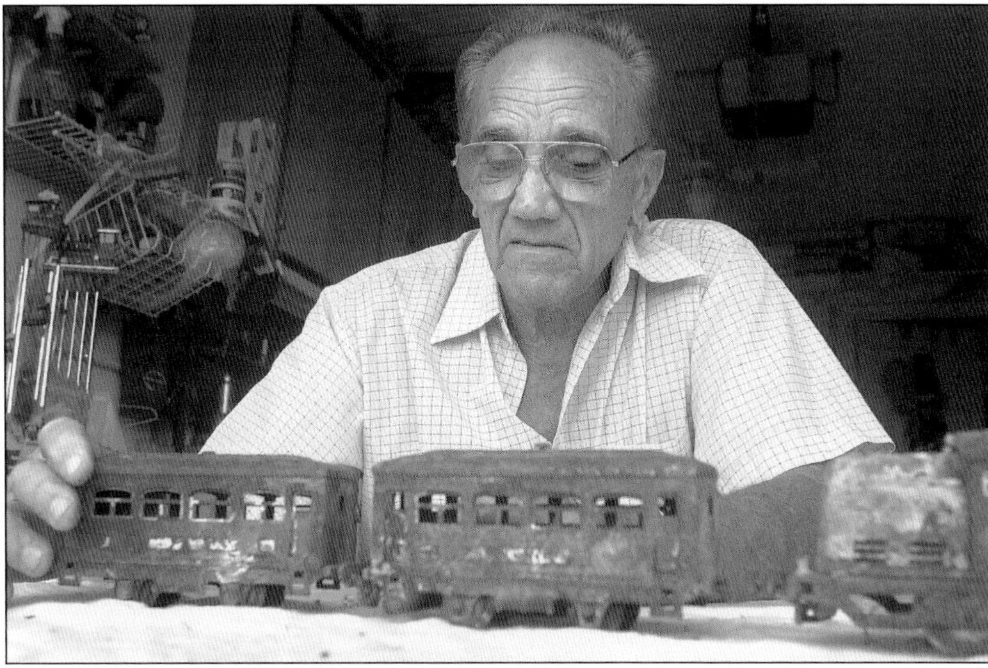

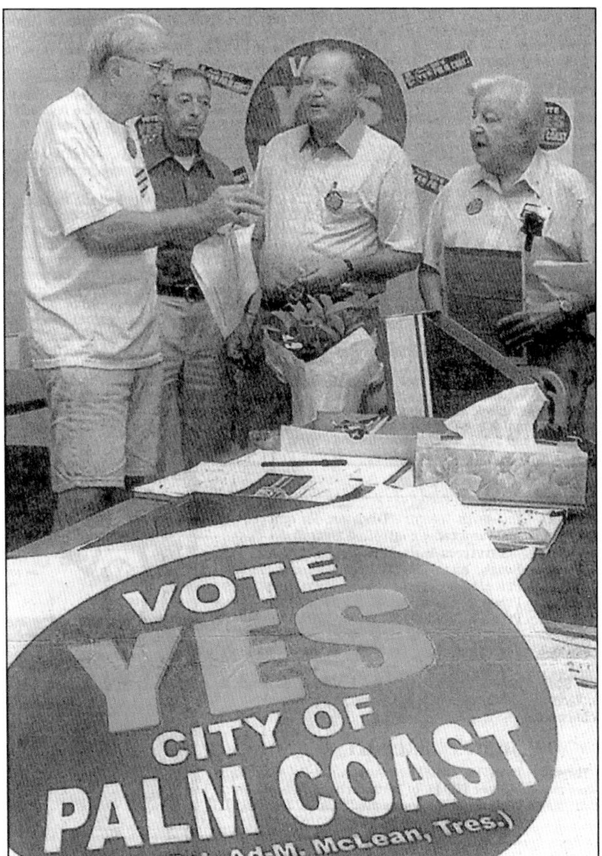

FIRE, 1998. Fire again visited Palm Coast in 1998, causing havoc; evacuation; the loss of 71 homes; heroic prolonged efforts by local, state and national firefighters; and a visit from President Clinton and Vice President Gore. Retired railroad worker Paul Sammartano sits with a toy train set damaged in a fire that destroyed his Palm Coast home. The train set, which Sammartano had since 1936, was one of the few items he simply could not part with after the fire.

PALM COAST HOME RULE COALITION (PCHRC), 1999. PCHRC was the organization that lead the campaign to incorporate Palm Coast. Pictured at headquarters in September 1999 are John Scripp III, Manny Rivera, Jim Canfield, and Bob Crocetta.

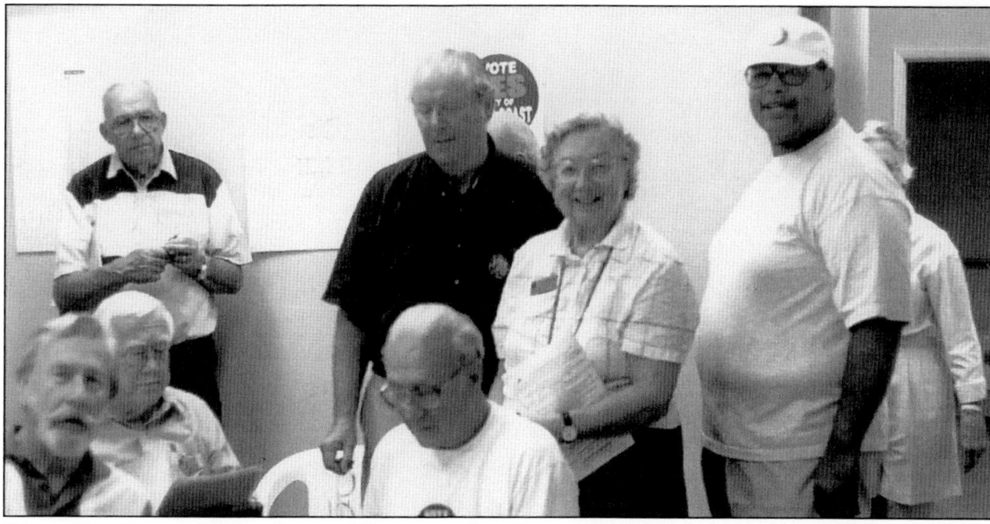

VOTE YES, CITY OF PALM COAST. The sign is barely visible on the back wall. PCHRC supporters are the following: Skip Sedlak, John Eustace, Bill Wagner, John Scripp III, Jim Canfield, Margaret Davie, and Raleigh Stockton.

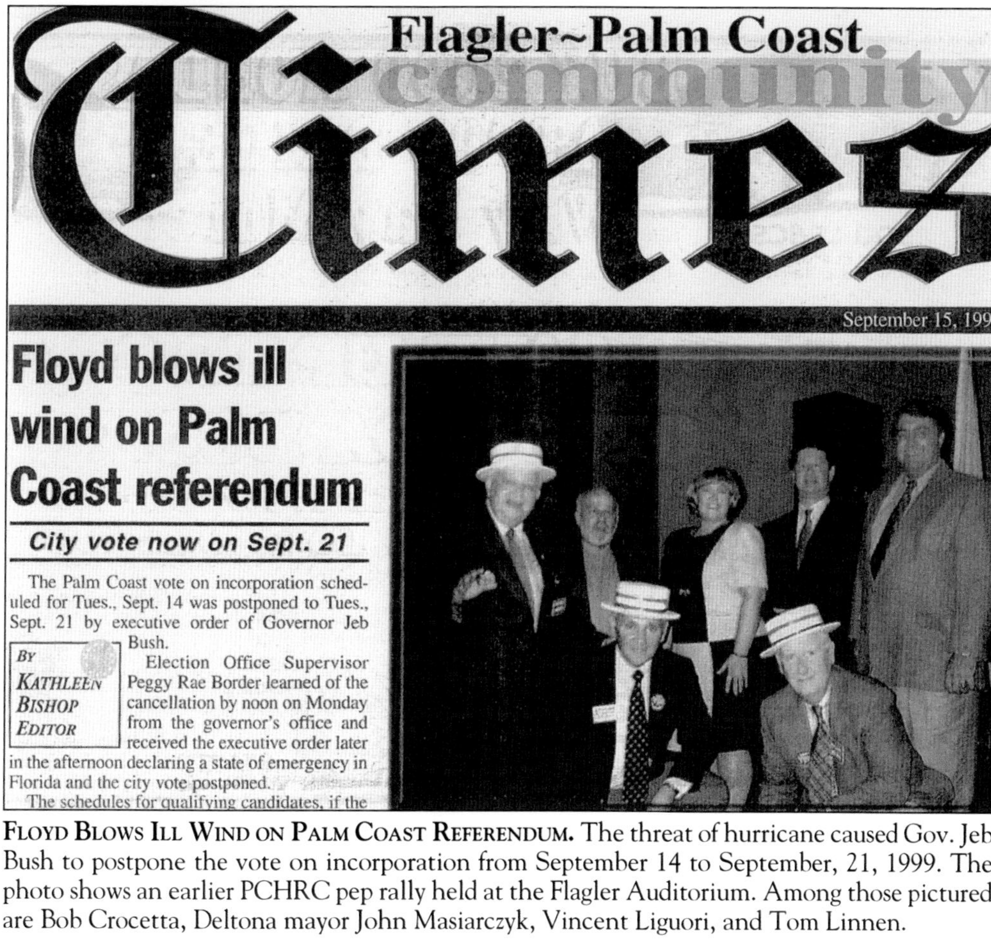

Flagler~Palm Coast community Times

September 15, 199

Floyd blows ill wind on Palm Coast referendum

City vote now on Sept. 21

The Palm Coast vote on incorporation scheduled for Tues., Sept. 14 was postponed to Tues., Sept. 21 by executive order of Governor Jeb Bush.

By Kathleen Bishop Editor

Election Office Supervisor Peggy Rae Border learned of the cancellation by noon on Monday from the governor's office and received the executive order later in the afternoon declaring a state of emergency in Florida and the city vote postponed.

The schedules for qualifying candidates, if the

FLOYD BLOWS ILL WIND ON PALM COAST REFERENDUM. The threat of hurricane caused Gov. Jeb Bush to postpone the vote on incorporation from September 14 to September, 21, 1999. The photo shows an earlier PCHRC pep rally held at the Flagler Auditorium. Among those pictured are Bob Crocetta, Deltona mayor John Masiarczyk, Vincent Liguori, and Tom Linnen.

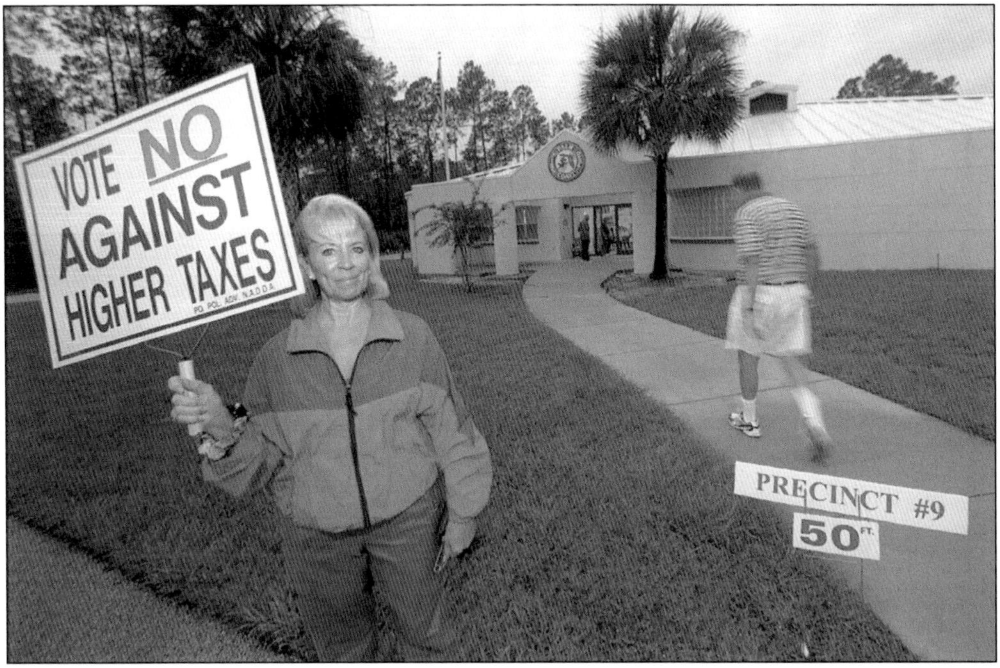

Palm Coast Votes—Finally. Not all Palm Coast residents were as enthusiastic for the incorporation as the PCHRC was. Pictured here, Susan Bereda expresses her opinion. Election officials reported heavy voting reminiscent of presidential elections.

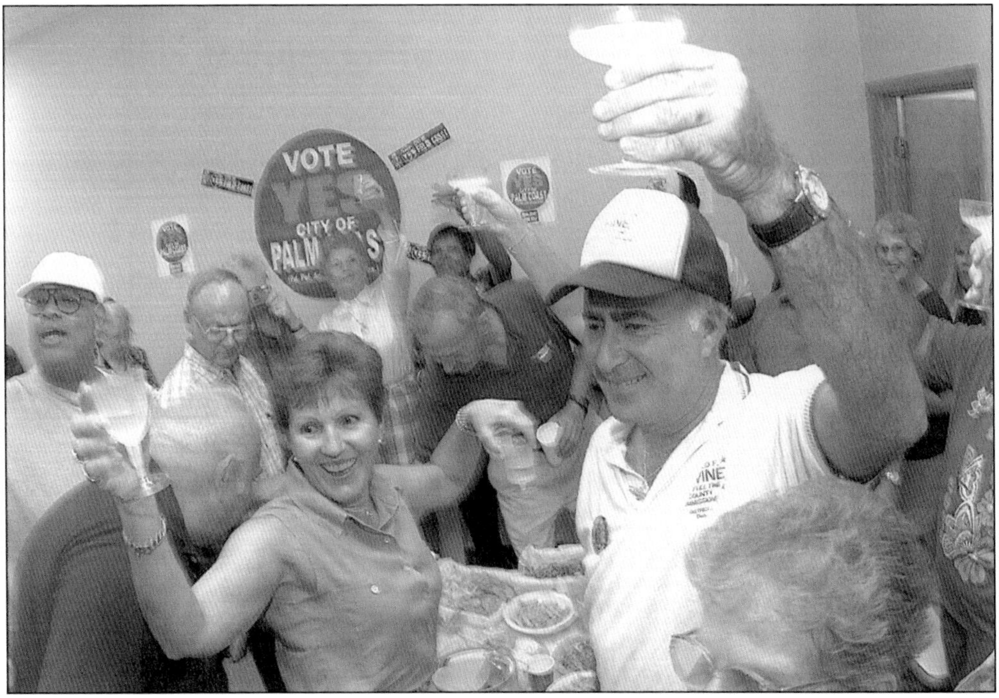

Yes! Palm Coast Votes for Incorporation. With a little over 60% of the people and all but 1 of the 14 election districts voting in favor, the incorporation of Palm Coast won the vote easily on Tuesday, September 21, 1999. Ann-Marie Pitman and Arnold Levine celebrated.

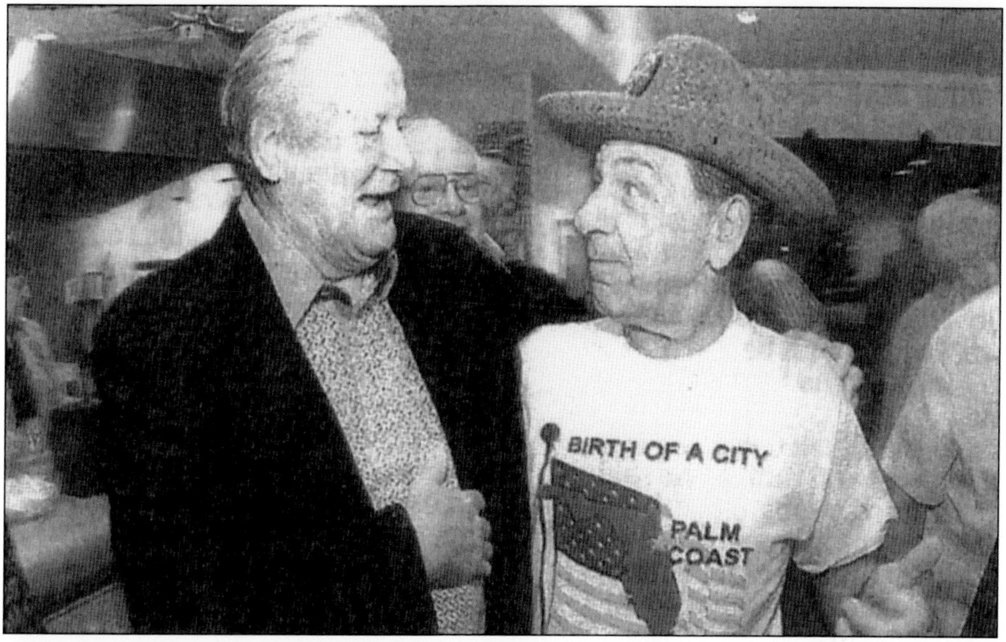

CONGRATULATIONS, MR. MAYOR. Supporter Rudy Pinzone greets Jim Canfield at his election night victory party. There had originally been 28 candidates running for the five positions of mayor and four councilmen.

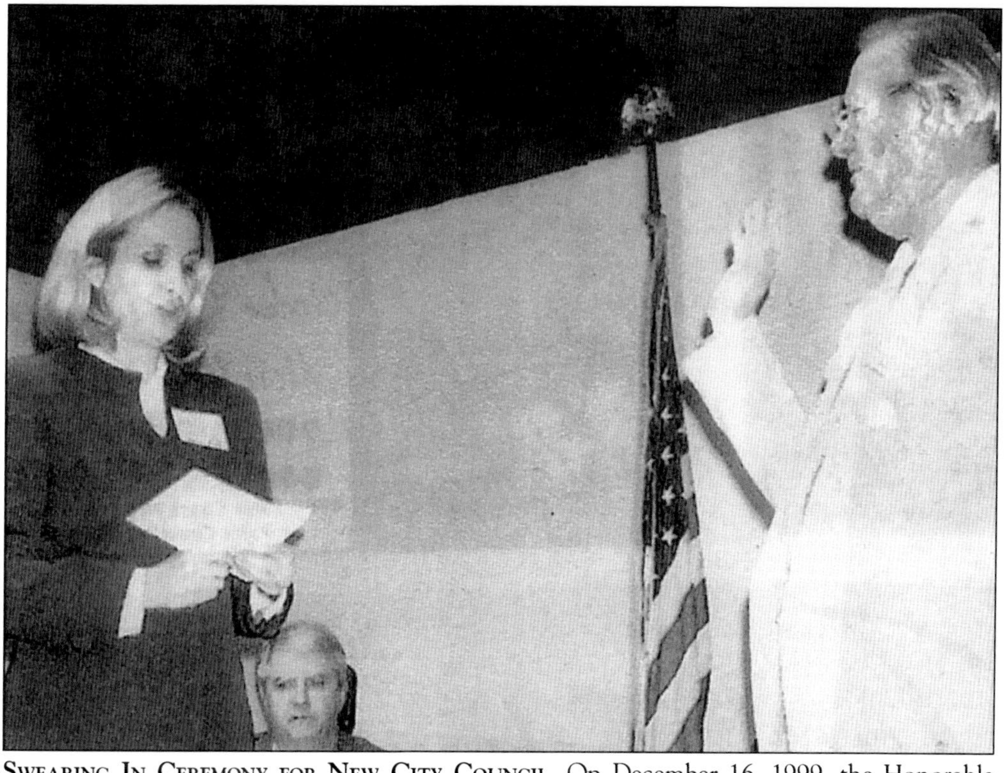

SWEARING IN CEREMONY FOR NEW CITY COUNCIL. On December 16, 1999, the Honorable Sharon Atack delivered the oaths of office to Mayor Jim Canfield and district councilmen.

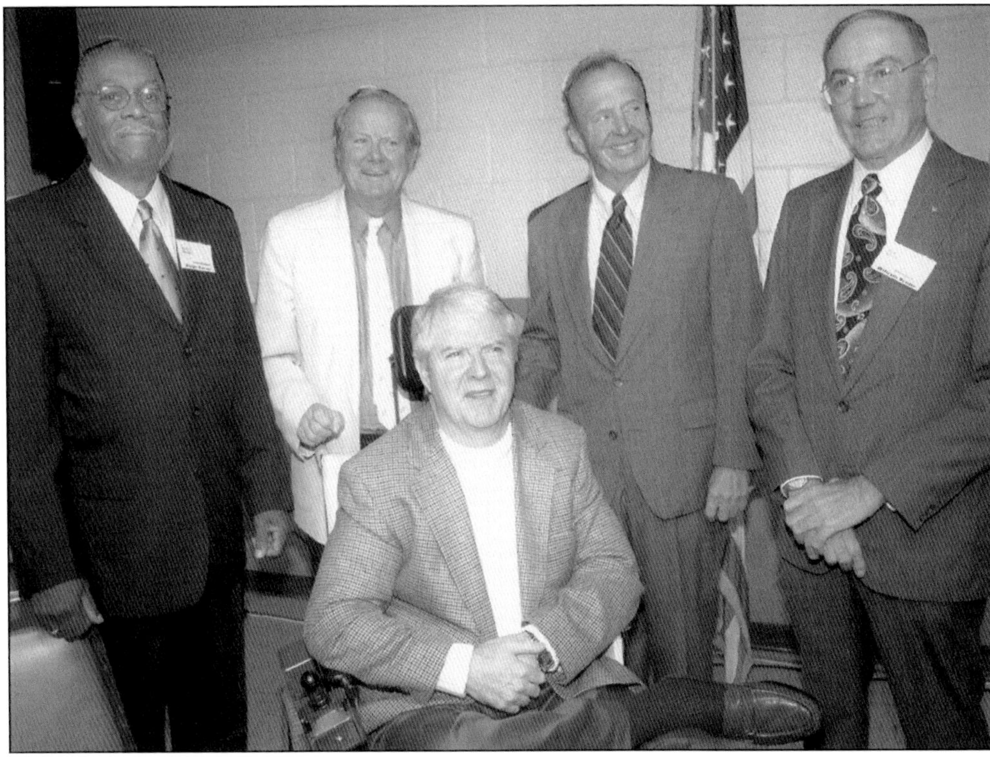

Palm Coast First City Council. Members from left to right are the following: Ralph Carter, Mayor Jim Canfield (seated), James Holland, Jerome Full, and William Venne.

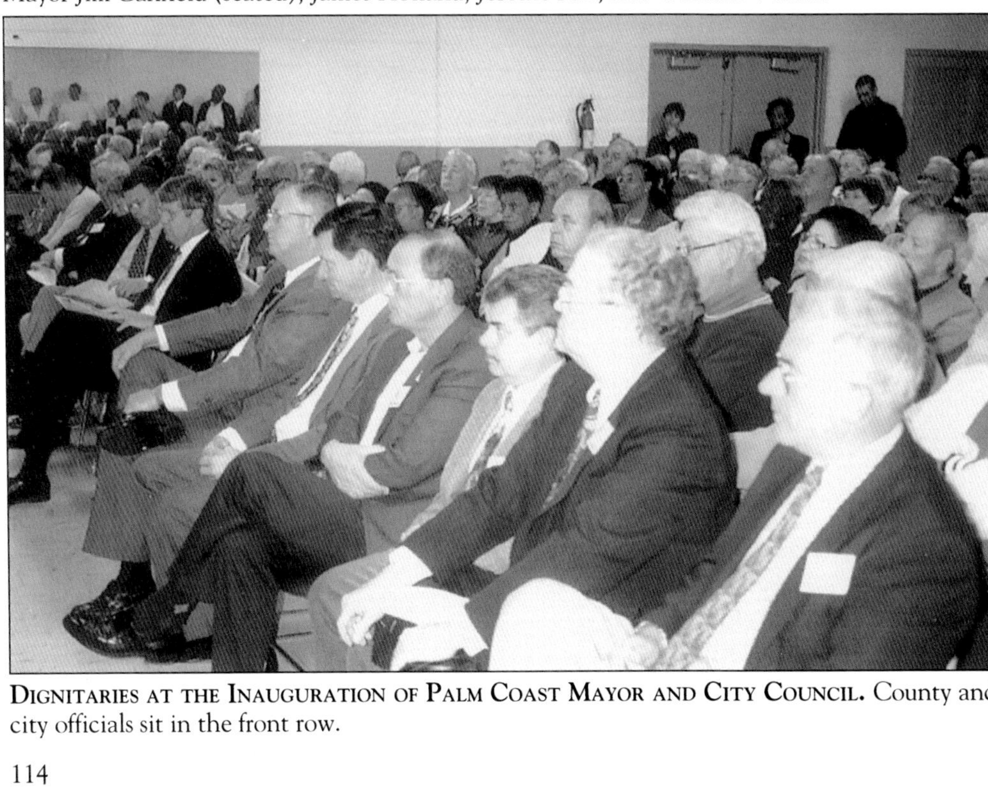

Dignitaries at the Inauguration of Palm Coast Mayor and City Council. County and city officials sit in the front row.

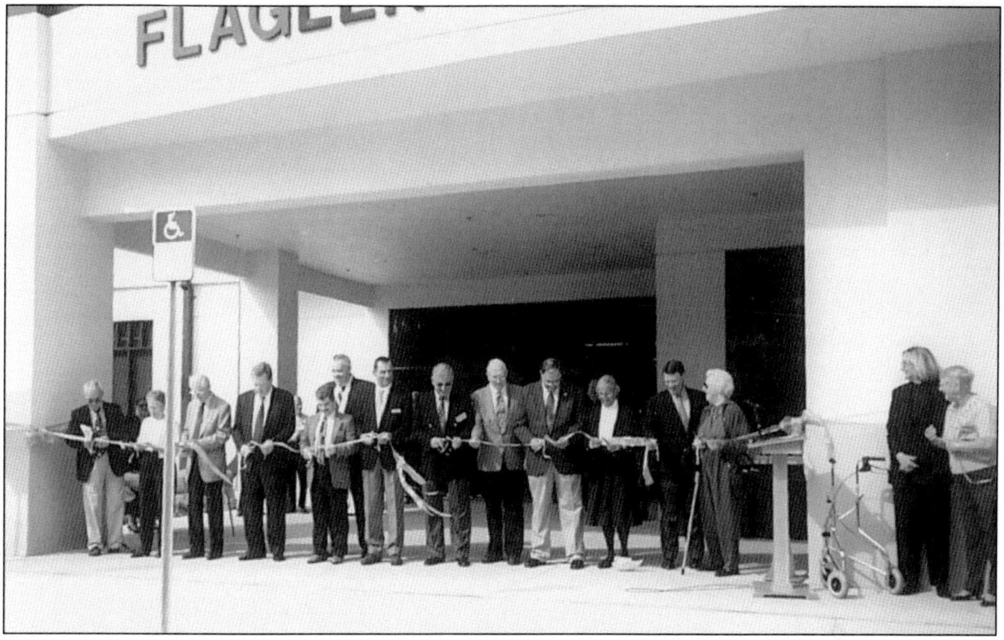

Library Ribbon Cutting, January 23, 2000. Those in attendance, from left to right, are Doug Cisney, Mary Ann Clark, Alan Smolen, John Seay, George Hanns, Syd Crosby, Jim Darby, Blair Kanbar, Al Jones, Pat Paterson, Sandra Rose Friedman, Doug Wiles, Emily Shoemaker, Sharon Atack, and Helen Blanks. The library is located at the northwest corner of Belle Terre and Palm Coast Parkways.

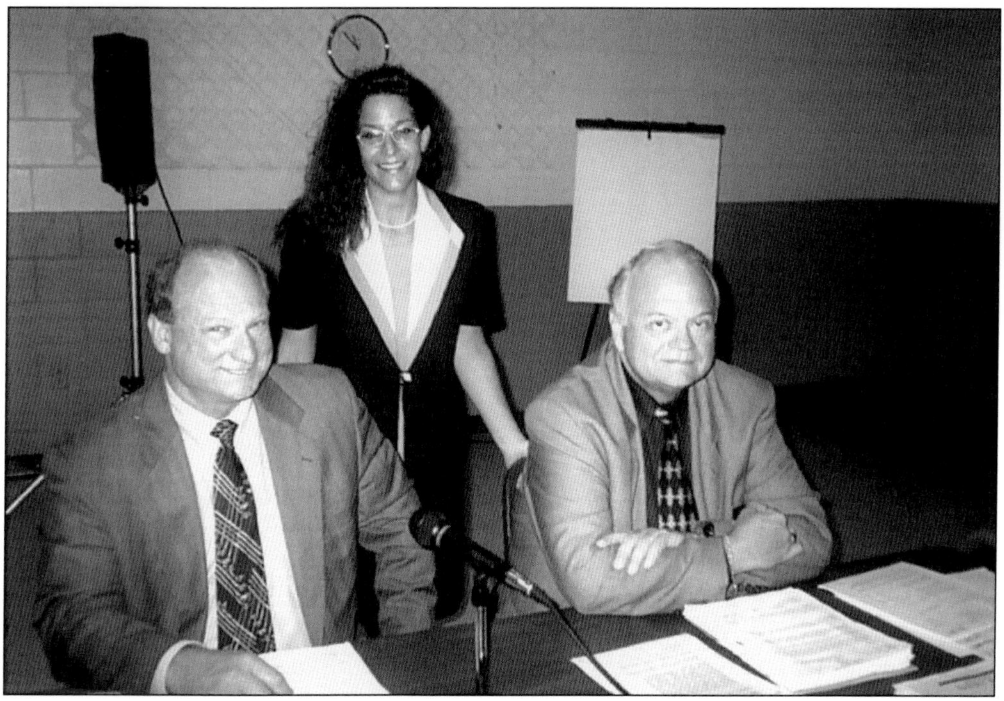

City Manager. Richard Kelton, appointed in April 2000, is pictured (sitting on the left) with deputy city clerk Theresa Wolff and city counsel member Bill Colbert..

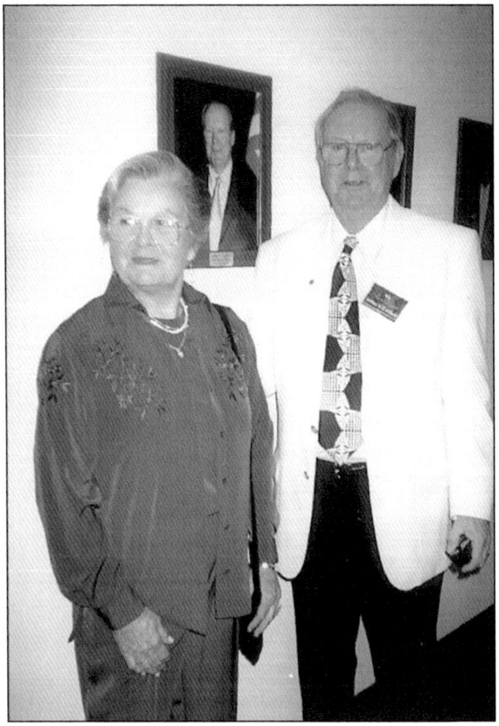

JIM AND MARY ANN CANFIELD. The mayor and his wife are pictured at the opening of the new City Hall on October 26, 2000.

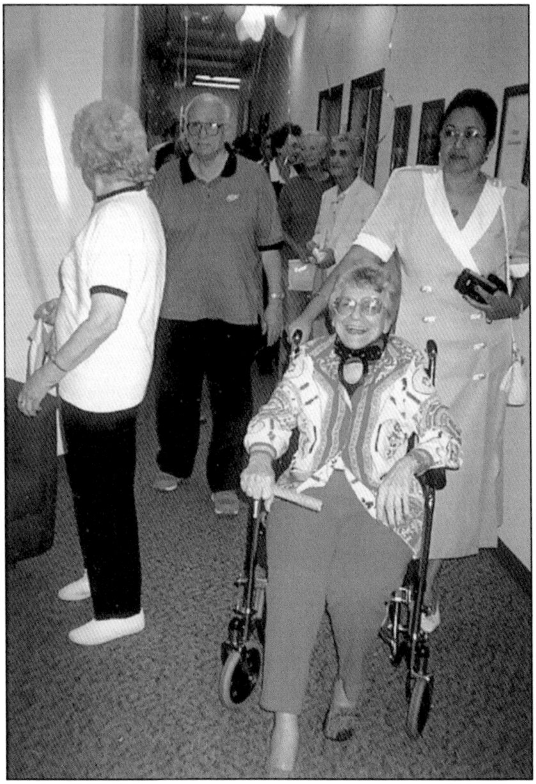

MARTY MCLEAN. Recovering from an automobile accident, Marty is being pushed by Lorna Da Costa-Jones, past president of the Pine Lakes Association, at the opening of the new City Hall.

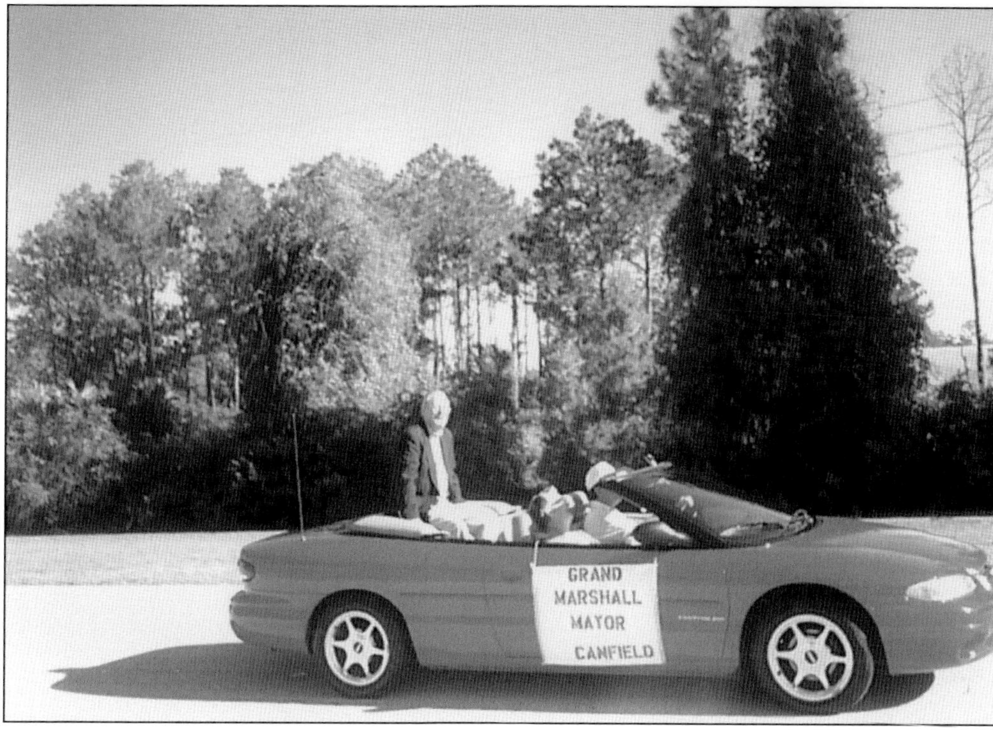

First Parade for the New City. Appropriately, Mayor Canfield served as grand marshal of the parade on December 21, 2000.

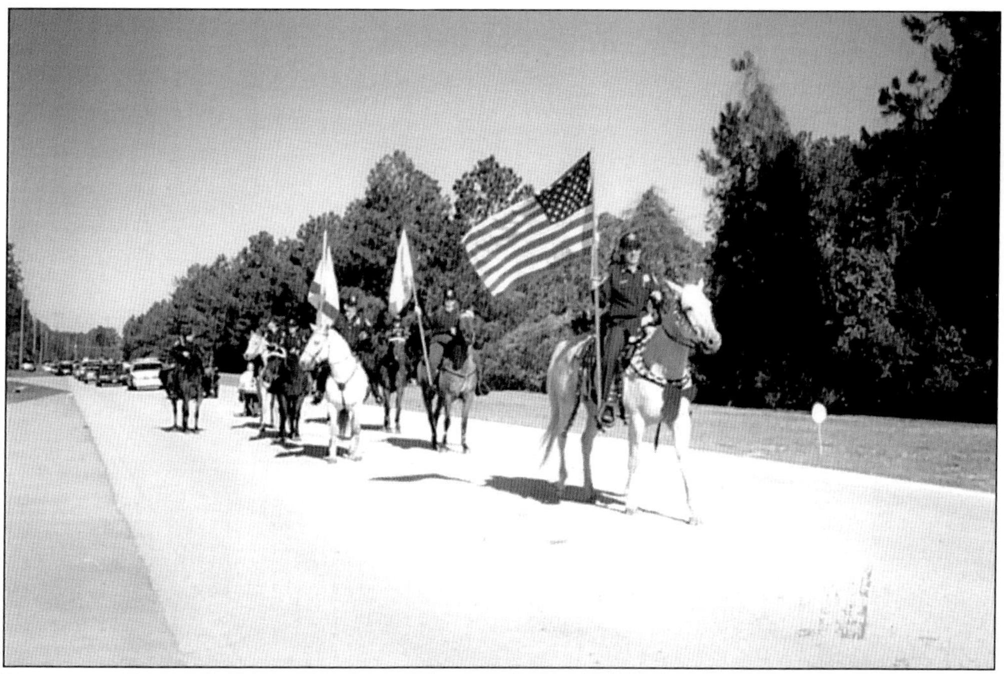

Flags and Riders Lead the Parade. The parade was led by the sheriff's department.

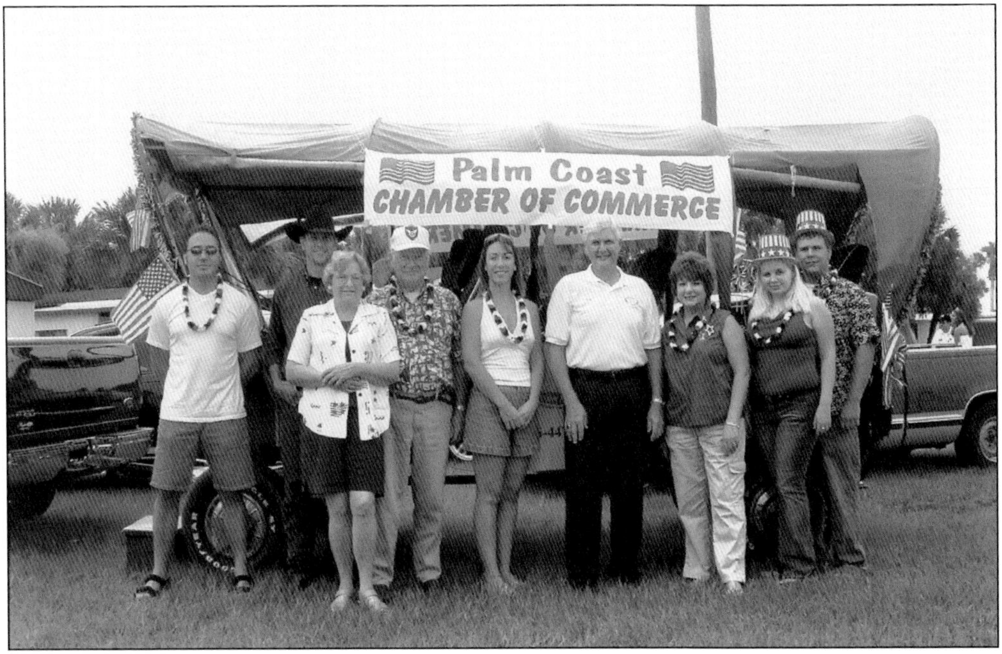

Chamber of Commerce. From left to right are Randal Shane, David Karner, Julie Karner, Max Karner (president of the Palm Coast Chamber branch), Melissa Shane (board member of the Palm Coast Chamber branch), Tom Lawrence, Debi Peterson (vice chairman, Palm Coast Chamber branch,) unidentified, and Tim Graves, at a Fourth of July picnic, 2003.

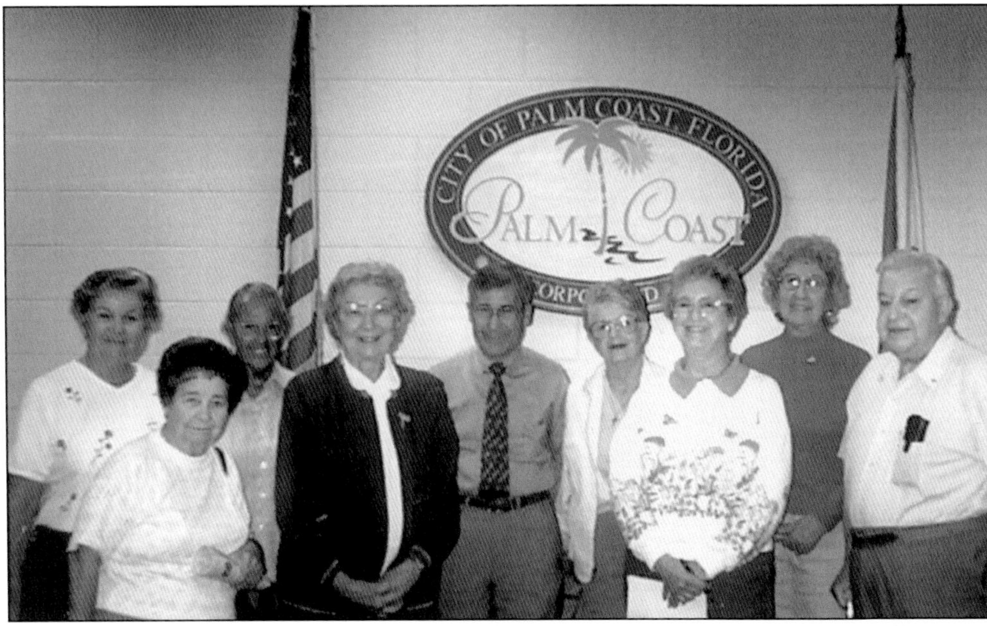

City of Palm Coast Historical Society (COPCHS), 2001. Historical society officers and members meet at the Community Center to see Art Dycke's Powerpoint slide presentation on November 14. Pictured members, from left to right, are Mary Ann Canfield, Connie Horvath, Sandra Rose Friedman, Margaret Davie, Art Dycke, Kay Stafford, Debby Geyer, Jean Sedlak, and Bob Crocetta.

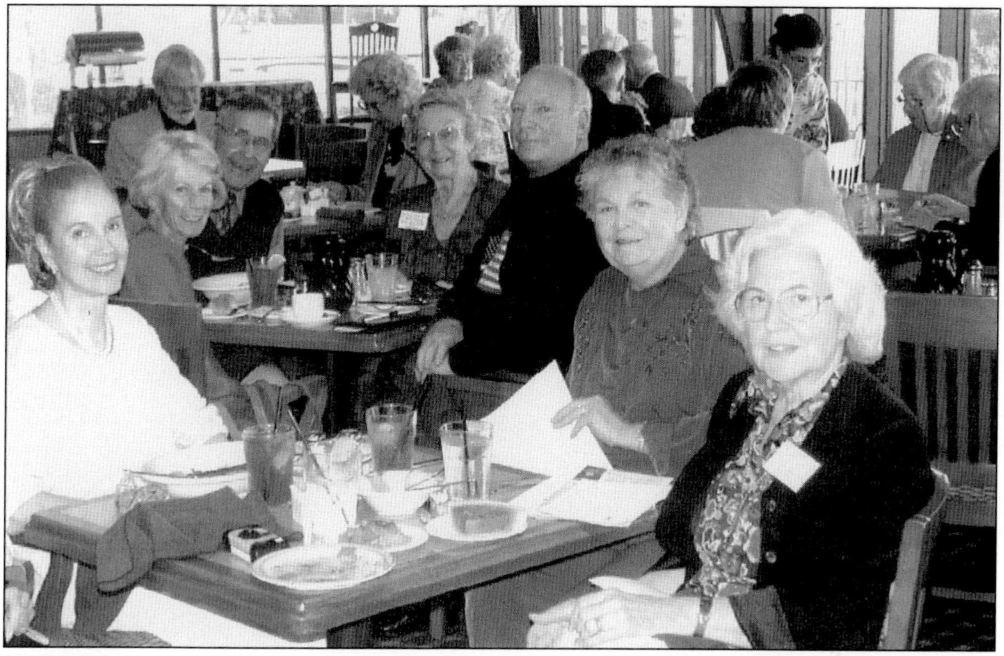

COPCHS DINNER MEETING, 2002. Pictured attendees, from left to right, are Pat McGovern, Louise Dycke, Art Dycke, Skip Sedlak, Jean Sedlak, Margaret Davie, Jon Netts, Mary Ann Canfield, and Jane Culpepper.

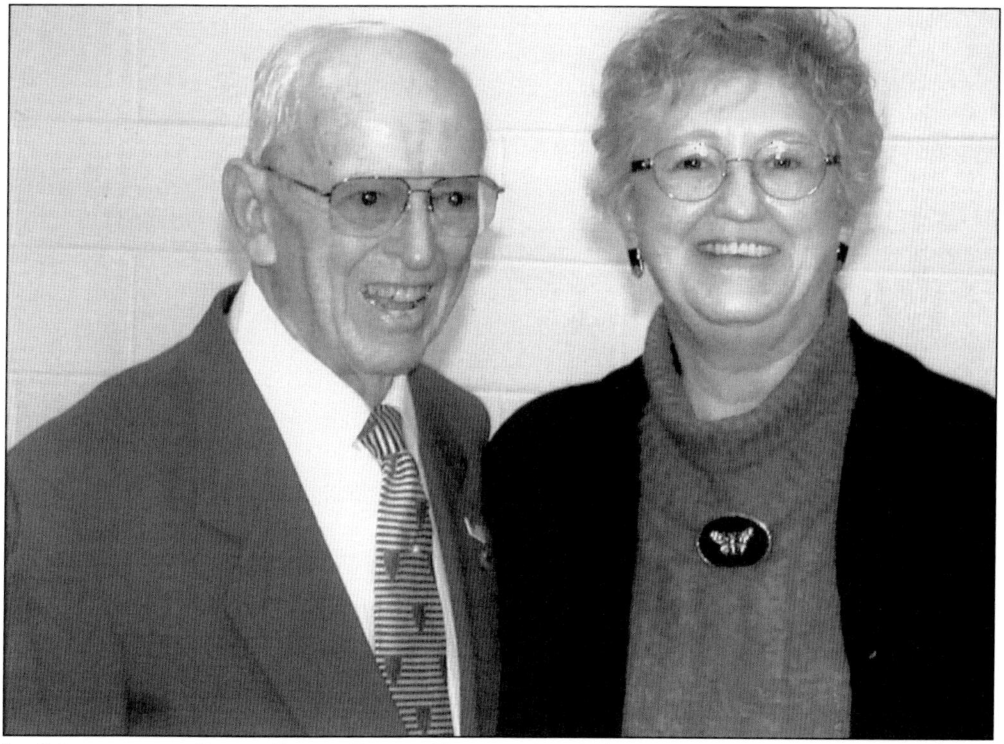

JIM MISKELLY AND DEBBY GEYER. Pictured here are Mr. Palm Coast and the COPCHS President for 2002–2003.

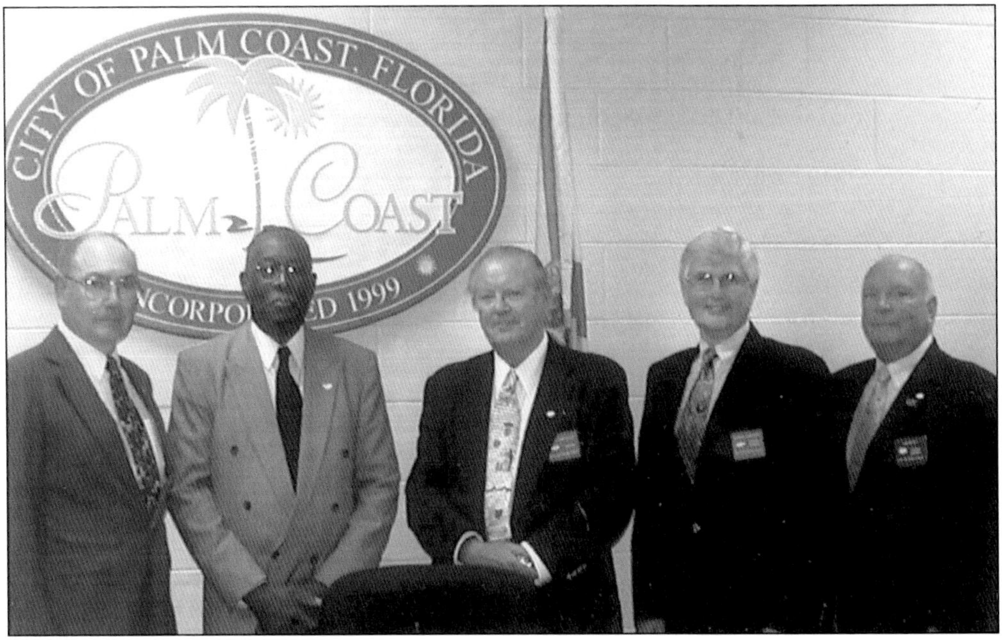

Present City Council. Pictured members, from left to right, are William Venne, Ralph Carter, Mayor Jim Canfield, Thomas Lawrence, and Vice Mayor Jon Netts.

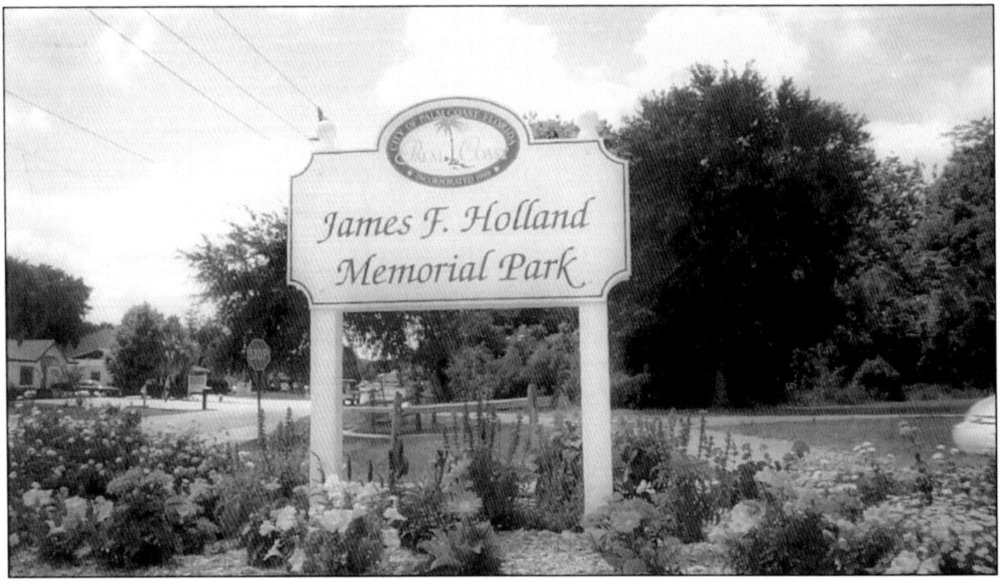

James F. Holland Memorial Park. This park preserves the memory and serves to honor a truly remarkable public servant.

Six

Palm Coast Future and Epilogue

"Palm Coast has become one of the nation's most successful planned communities" said retired ICDC president Jim Gardner. If this is "the perfect place to live," is there anything else still to be done in the future?

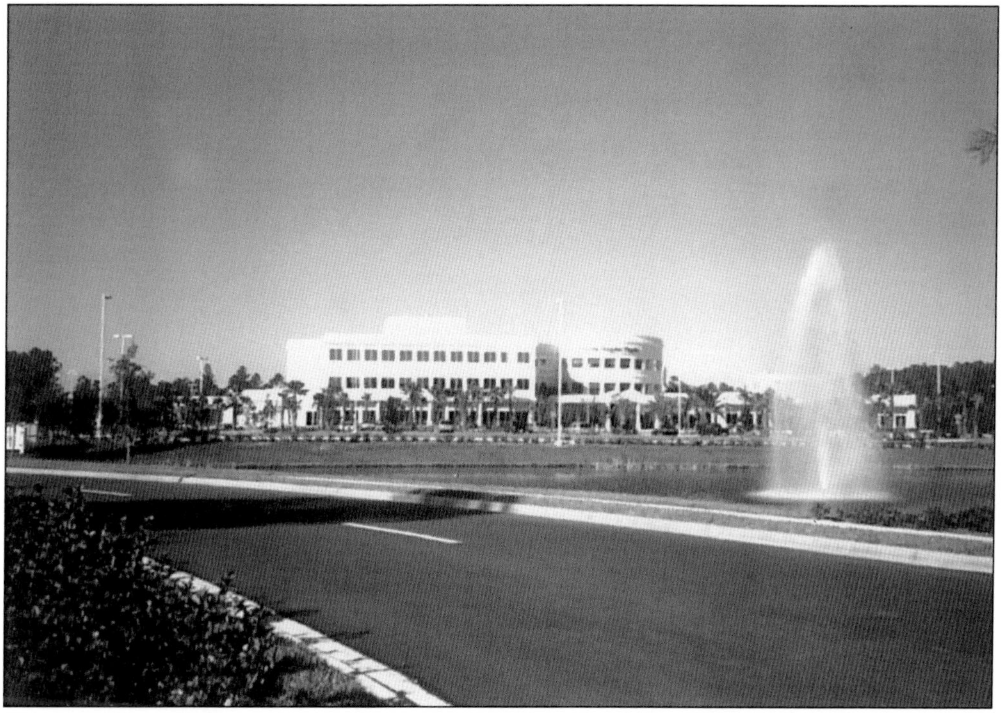

The New Flagler/Palm Coast Hospital, 2002. This building serves as a symbol of hope for Palm Coast's bright future.

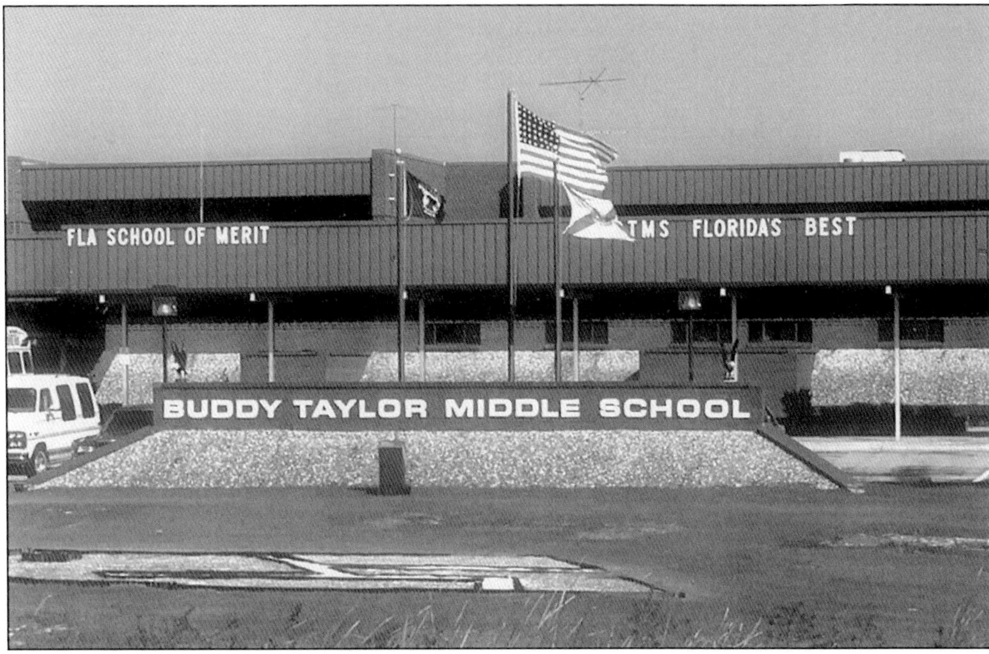

FLAGLER PALM COAST SCHOOLS. These schools are highly rated statewide. Large campuses with excellent sports and technical facilities serve the needs of an ever growing school population. A new high school is already being planned.

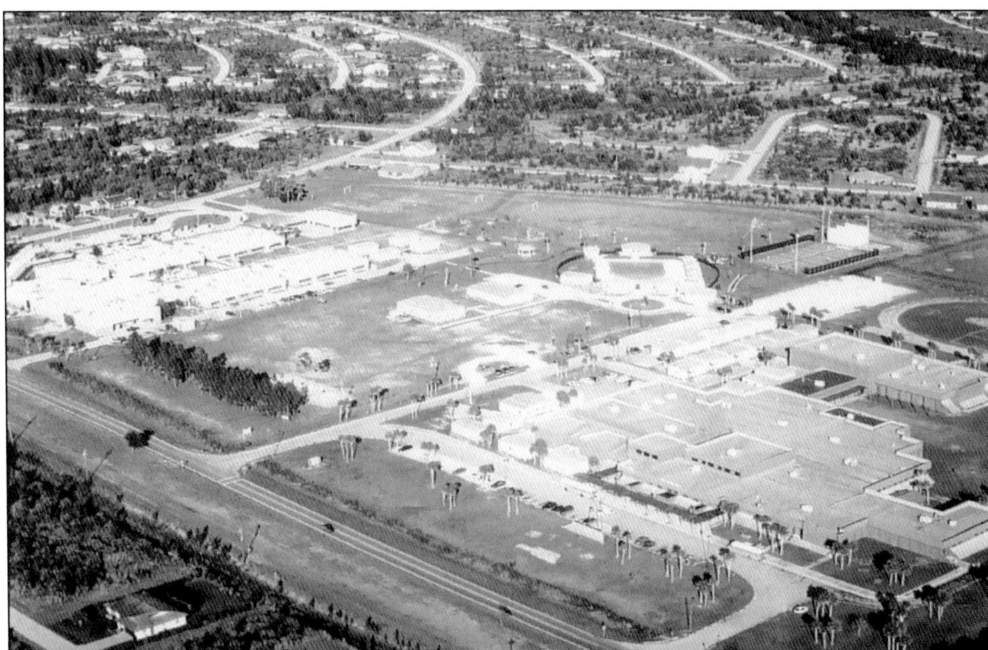

SCHOOL FACILITIES. Wadsworth Elementary, Frieda Zamba Pool, and Buddy Taylor Middle School are all in Palm Coast.

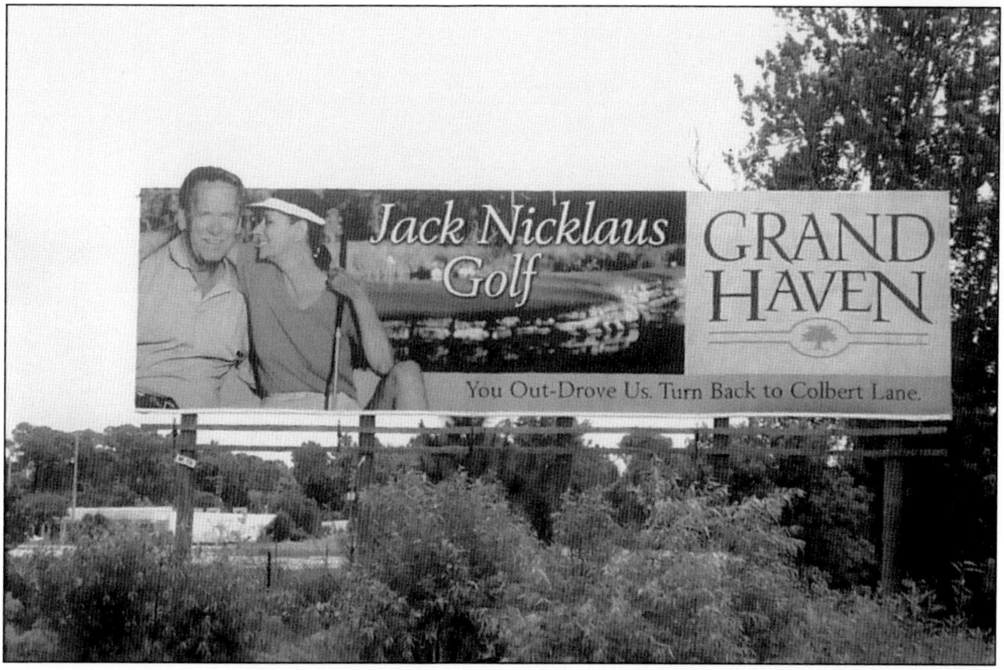

Sixth Golf Course, 1998. Jack Nicklaus attended the opening of the Grand Haven Golf course, playing with Pro Gary Freemans at the grand opening on May 4, 1998. There is a new golf course at Ocean Hammock and others that have recently opened.

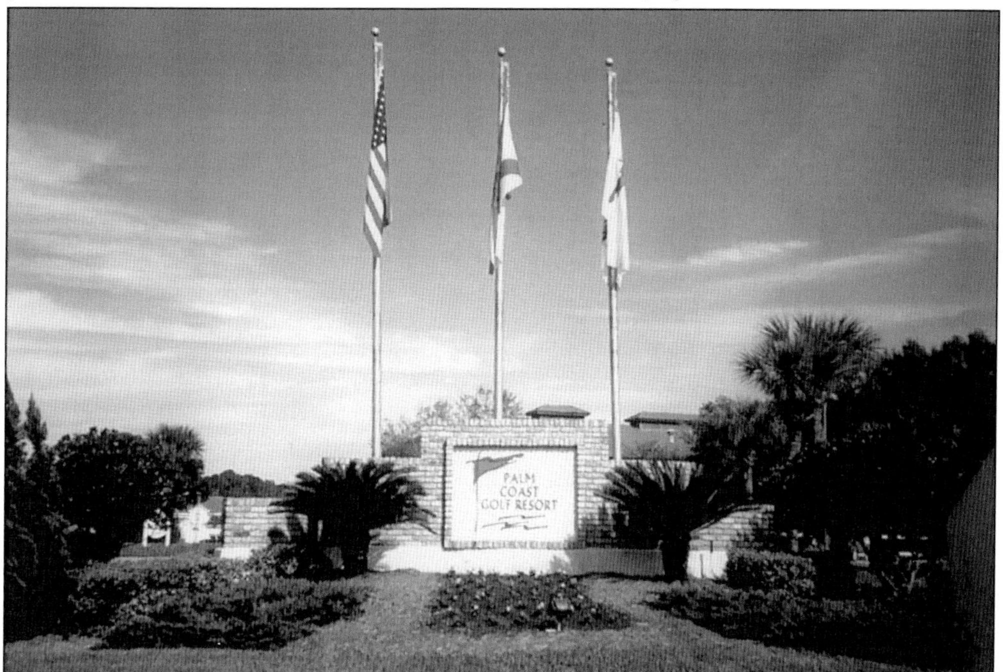

Palm Coast Golf Resort. This was originally the Palm Coast Yacht Club, then the Sheraton, and then the Harborside Inn. The same great location on the ICW invites guests to enjoy all the indoor/outdoor amenities of a four-season resort.

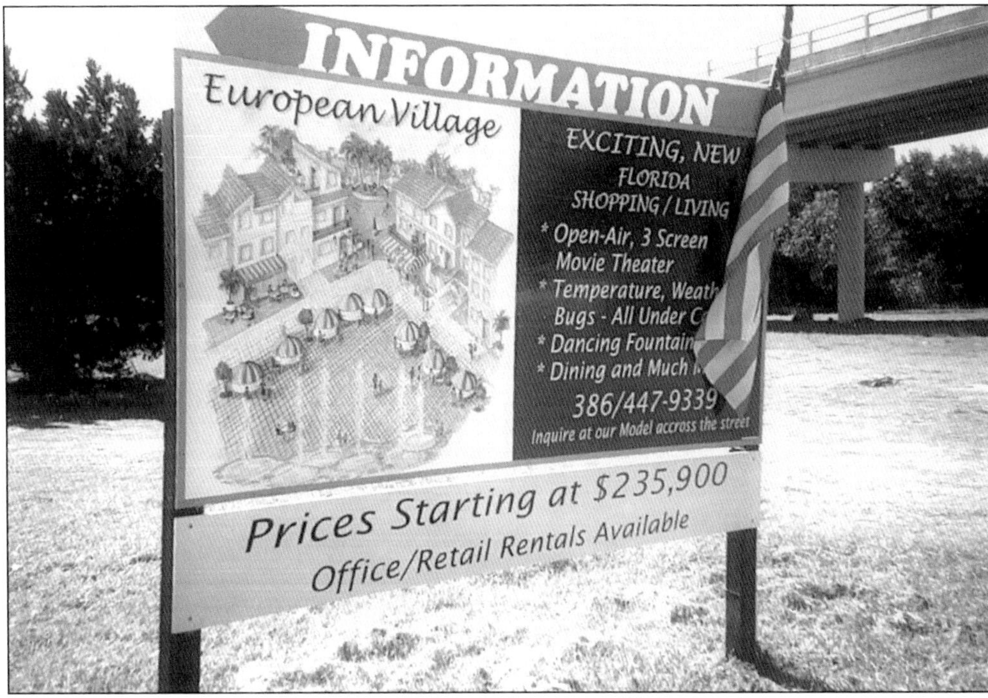

Palm Coast is Expanding. The growth in all aspects of life in Palm Coast continues at a phenomenal pace. Ocean condominiums, gated communities, new real estate and re-sales, businesses, corporate and industrial parks, and a theater are all in the area. There are for sale or lease signs all over. There is just not enough space to document the signs of growth so two must suffice. They range from the European Village above to the Fast Food below.

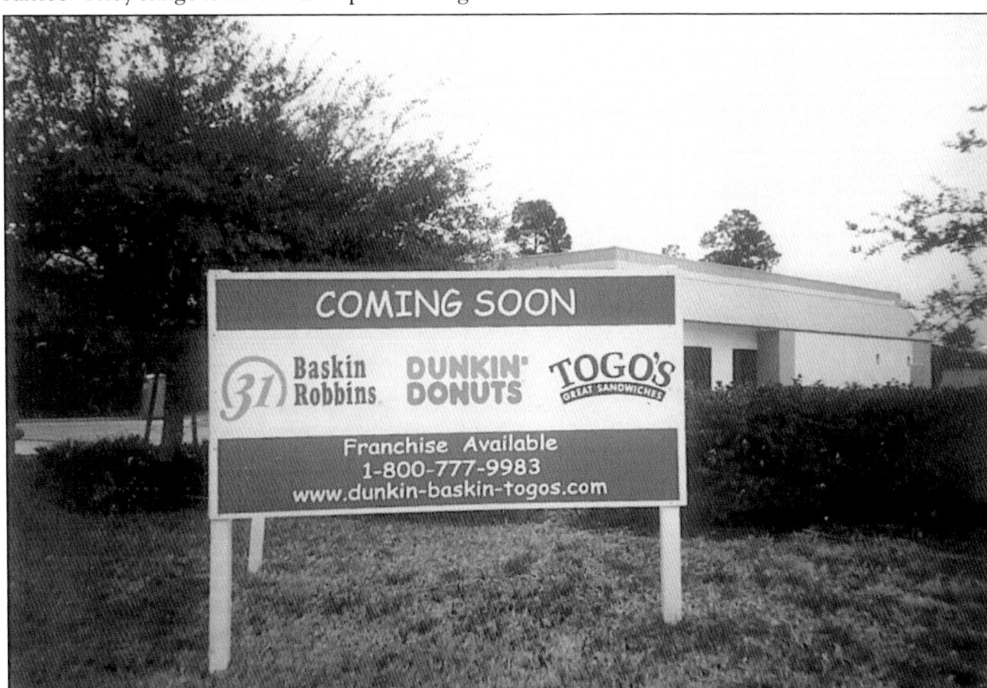

FUTURE

The City of Palm Coast has approximately two-thirds of the population and represents most of the growth of Flagler County, which is presently the fastest growing county in Florida. A few years ago, it was the fastest growing county in the nation, and in 2003 it was the fifth fastest growing. Obviously, the growth of ITT's "Big Pine Covered Swamp" continues today at a phenomenal pace with newcomers attracted here from all over the world.

A newly constructed state-of-the-art hospital opened in Palm Coast in 2002. Home Depot and other national franchises are building in 2003. According to *Discover Flagler 2002–2003*, a partial list of area expansion includes: 7 condominium projects with 385 dwelling units (DU), 2 single-family home developments with 805 DU, more than 25 new commercial projects, 8 new industrial parks/plazas, and 3 new houses of worship. Planning for the town center of Palm Coast, a 1,557-acre development of regional impact, is moving along and six major oceanfront or Intracoastal Waterway developments with approximately 5,000 dwelling units are presently under construction. Later editions of this book will name the newer developments, golf courses, and business that have not been included thus far.

Palm Coast has grown from approximately 100 inhabitants in 1972 to about 42,000 in 2003. It may not live up to Dr. Young's 1970's prediction of a "city the size of Detroit" but it is projected to grow to over 100,000 people by the year 2019. In 2003, the City of Palm Coast was even seeking to purchase its own water utility.

Palm Coast is the last large coastal area to be developed in Florida. Everywhere people look, they see the signs of continuing burgeoning growth. We know that the natural elements of land, ocean, and climate will continue in their beauty. We hope that the pioneer spirit, community pride, and cooperation of the past will continue also.

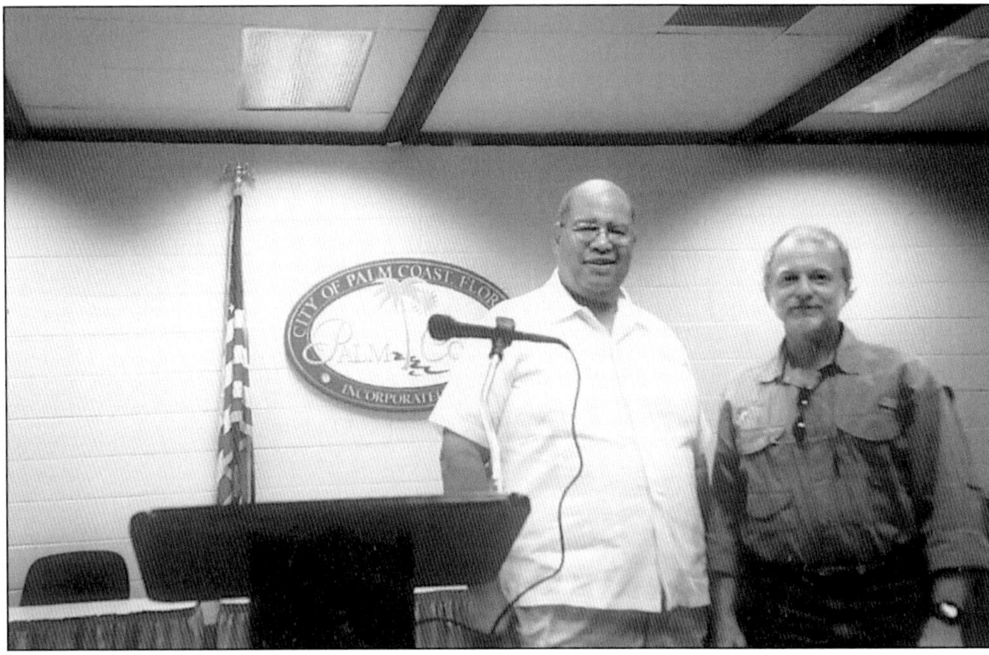

Civic Association, 2003. The Palm Coast Civic Association was the first organization formed by the pioneer settlers. It was their intent to meet to be informed and discuss actions they could take to enhance the quality of their individual and community life. The civic association still meets today with the same purpose. Pictured here are President Raleigh Stockton and Charles Faulkner, V.P. of Palm Coast Holdings, who had just made a presentation about Town Center, a vast regional impact project that will vitally affect the community.

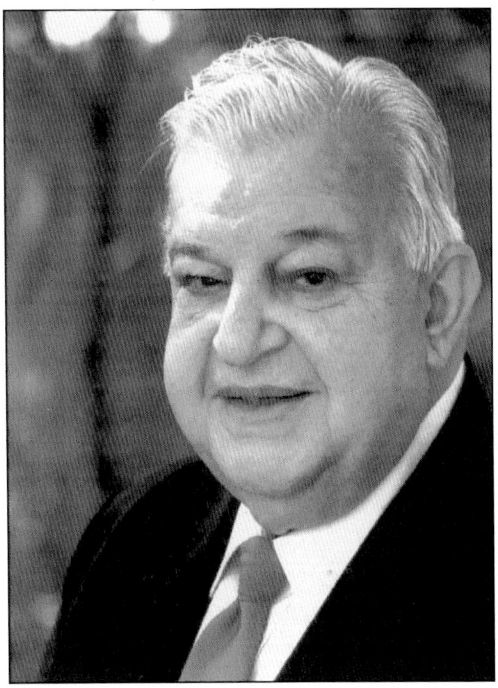

Civic Participation. A major reason Palm Coasters incorporated their city was to maintain a greater control over their destinies. At meetings of the city council citizens have the opportunity to voice their opinions regarding the issues that will shape their future. Pictured here is Bob Crocetta who has attended every meeting held since Palm Coast became a city.

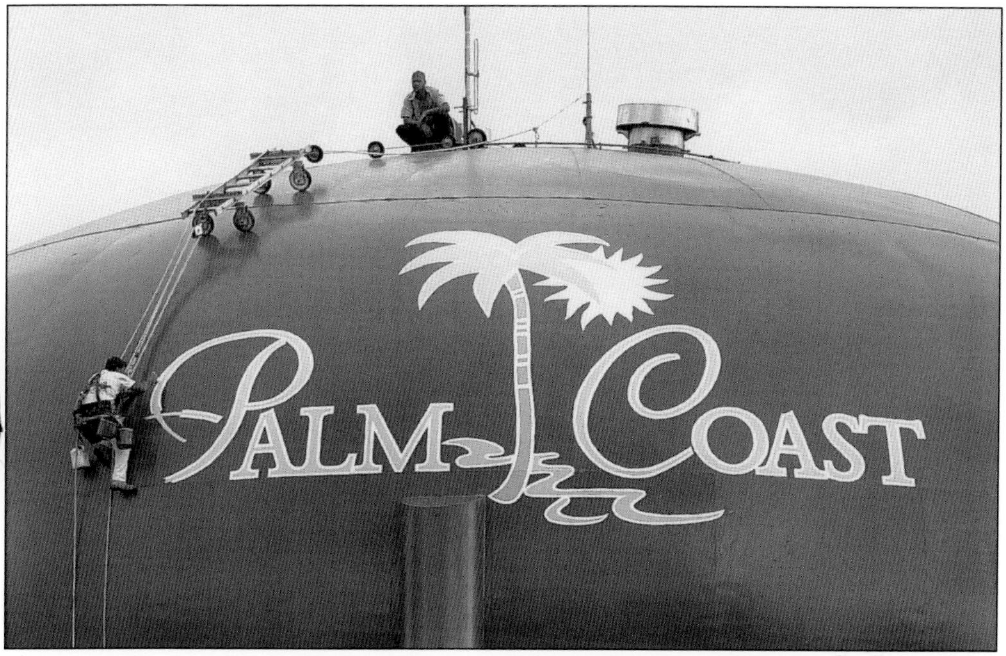

REPAINTED WATER TOWER. The book began with this landmark for the location of Palm Coast. It is repeated at the end because in June of 2003 the tower was repainted to show the official government logo of the City of Palm Coast.

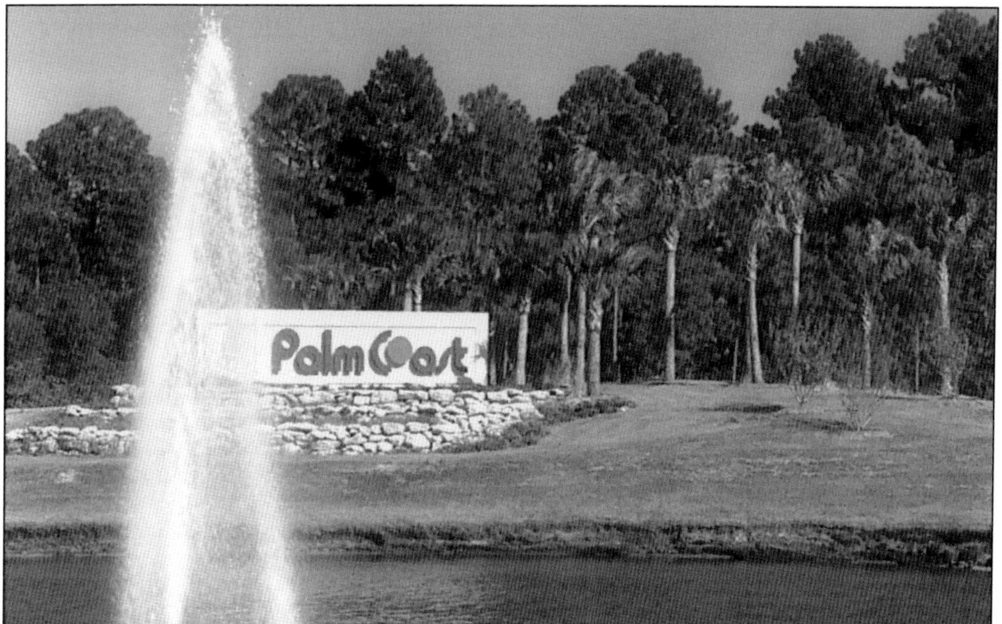

THE FOUNTAIN OF YOUTH. Visitors to Palm Coast are inevitably impressed with the areas landscaping, architecture, and natural beauty. With a complete range of year-round activities available to residents in a stimulating, healthy environmental setting, the author believes that a modern day Ponce de Leon would find the fountain he was looking for at the I-95 entrance to Palm Coast.

EPILOGUE

This book represents the author's continuing love affair with the Palm Coast Community. The people who pioneered Palm Coast formed a partnership with the developer ITT, together overcoming frontier obstacles in a spirit of mutual respect, active participation, and community cooperation. Each contributed to some phase of a rich, full life in a beautiful environmental setting. The author believes that ITT was successful in its 25 years of building and managing a planned growth community. The Palm Coast water tower has just been repainted with the logo of ITT being replaced with the logo of the City of Palm Coast. Residents' awareness of events and participation in their government will shape their future. It is the author's hope that Palm Coast's present, remarkable growth can be sustained, and that its people will continue their cooperative, community spirit channeled toward an even richer, fuller life in pursuit of "the perfect place to live."

BIBLIOGRAPHY

Bishop, Kathleen, Ed. *Discover Flagler*, 2002–03.
Clegg, Jack. *A History of Flagler County*.
Daytona Beach News-Journal including *The News-Tribune* and *The Palm Coaster*.
Florida New Homes and Condominiums Guide.
ITT Community Development Corporation (ICDC). *The Palm Coaster and Palm Coaster*.*
Martin, Jim. *Palm Coast*.
Sampson, Anthony. *The Sovereign State of ITT*.
The Flagler Times.
The Flagler Tribune.
The Random House College Dictionary, 1984.

*Sent by ICDC to Palm Coast community residents sporadically from 1970 to 1993.